"The Damned Red Flags of the Rebellion"

Confederate Standard Bearer
Don Troiani
(Courtesy of Historical Art Prints)

"The Damned Red Flags of the Rebellion"

The Confederate Battle Flag at Gettysburg

by Richard Rollins

Rank and File Publications
1997

Copyright 1997
Rank and File Publications
1926 South Pacific Coast Highway Suite 228
Redondo Beach, California 90277

ISBN Number 0-9638993-3-3

Library of Congress Number 96-067594

First Edition

Printed on acid-free recycled paper

Front Cover Art: "High Water Mark" by Don Troiani, courtesy of Historical
Art Prints. Back Cover Art: 28th Virginia flag, and photograph of Marshall
Sherman with the 28th Virginia flag, both courtesy of the Minnesota Histori-
cal Society.

Jacket Design by Ken Hammond

Printed In Hong Kong

Receive from your mothers and sisters, from those whose affections greet you, these colors woven by our feeble but reliant hands; and when this bright flag shall float before you on the battlefield, let it not only inspire you with the patriotic ambition of a soldier aspiring to his own and his country's honor and glory, but also may it be a sign that cherished ones appeal to you to save them from a fanatical and heartless foe.
—Presentation of a flag to the Desoto Rifles, New Orleans, 1861

The waving battle flags seemed to be the special mark as soon as we came in range of the small arms.
—Robert Mockbee, 14th Tennessee, on July 3rd

No such sight in all the history of battles had ever been seen. On they came regardless of the carnage among them, nearer and nearer until horse and rider, officer and private, standards and banners waving in the lead were plainly seen, and almost within musket range. . . .
—Private R.O. Sturtevant, 13th Vermont, on July 3rd

He fell among the bravest, sealed his devotion to his country by his warm young blood, in the flush of early vigorous manhood when his life was full of hope and promise. He gave up home which was particularly dear and sweet to him, when he knew that hereafter his only home would be under the flag of his regiment, where it might lead, whether on the march, in the camp or on the battlefield.
—Eulogy for Lt. John Jenkins, 14th Virginia
killed in Pickett's Charge

Here is something material, something I can see, feel, and understand. This means victory. This *is* Victory.
—Abraham Lincoln
(Receiving a captured Confederate battle flag)

[The colorguard] did all that mortal man could do in the defense of the flag, as they all lost their lives in the defense of their country.
—Colorbearer William Murphy,
2nd Mississippi, on July 1st

The damned red flags of the rebellion . . . thicken and flaunt . . . and one is already waving over one of the guns of the dead Cushing.
—Lt. Frank Haskell, describing the scene at the Angle

Table of Contents

For
Ann Featherstone Rollins

Footnote Abbreviations

Bachelder Papers David L. and Audrey J. Ladd, eds. *The Bachelder Papers: Gettysburg in their Own Words* (Dayton, OH: Morningside House, 1994-1995).

Clark, Histories Walter Clark, ed., *Histories of the Several Regiments and Battalions from North Carolina in the Great War, 1861-1865* 5 Vols. (Raleigh: State of North Carolina, 1901).

CV *Confederate Veteran* (Nashville, 1893-1932).

Deeds of Valor W. F. Beyer and O. F. Keydel, eds., *Deeds of Valor from the Records of the United States Government* (Detroit: The Perrier-Keydel Co., 1907).

GB *Gettysburg Magazine* (Dayton, OH: Morningside House, 1989 to present).

GNMP Gettysburg National Military Park Library and Archives.

OR Department of War, *The War of the Rebellion: A Compilation of the Official Records of the Union and Confederate Armies* (Washington: Government Printing Office, 1880-1901) 128 volumes. All citations from Series I, Vol. 27, Parts I - III, (given as *OR*, part #, page #) unless otherwise, then cited in full.

"Record" Adjutant General of the United States, "Record of Rebel Flags Captured by Union Troops Since April 19, 1861," National Archives. Published in Richard Rollins, ed., *The Returned Battle Flags* (Redondo Beach, CA: Rank and File Publications, 1995).

Rollins, ed., Pickett's Charge Richard Rollins, ed., *Pickett's Charge: Eyewitness Accounts* (Redondo Beach, CA: Rank and File Publications, 1996).

SHSP   *Southern Historical Society Papers* (Nashville:
                              Southern Historical Society, 1876-1930).

Supreme Court   *Supreme Court of Pennsylvania. Middle
                              District. May Term, 1891, Nos. 20 and 30.
                              Appeal of the Gettysburg Battlefield
                              Memorial Association from the Decree of the
                              Court of Common Pleas of Adams County.*

USAMHI   United States Army Military History
                              Institute, Carlisle Barracks, Pennsylvania.

WD#   War Department number. The number as-
                              signed to each flag when it was accepted by
                              the Adjutant General's office. It was usually
                              stenciled on the edge of the flag.

Introduction

"This means victory. This *is* victory":
—Abraham Lincoln

Riding his horse on Cemetery Ridge, Lieutenant Frank Haskell watched the long gray line of men emerge from the woods across the valley. "More than half a mile their front extends . . . man touching man, rank pressing rank, and line supporting line. Their red flags wave; their horsemen gallop up and down . . . right on they move, as with one soul, in perfect order." Each time he glanced at the Confederate lines, "treason's flaunting rag" caught his eye, floating above the gray ranks. On came the Rebels, making no noise amid the thunder of the Northern guns, "but the courage of these silent men amid our shot, seems not to need the stimulus of other noise."

Now they were at the wall and over it, as "the damned red flags of the rebellion . . . thicken and flaunt . . . and one is already waving over one of the guns of the dead Cushing." As hand-to-hand combat of the most desperate kind raged, little could be seen of the enemy through the smoke, "except the flash of his muskets, and his waving flags." The red in them "maddens us as the same color does the bull." The men of Brigadier General Alexander Webb's brigade, defending the stone wall near the Angle, were nearly overpowered, "with more than a dozen flags to Webb's three." With men dying all around him, Haskell rode, then walked along the line, urging the troops forward into battle. In the middle of all this he saw "Webb's line blaze red with [Confederate] battle flags."

Chaos reigned like thunder and fire, boiling and flashing. This was the emotional peak of the battle and some would say of the entire war. The men in gray broke through and crossed the stone wall near the Angle and planted their flags among Lieutenant Alonzo Cushing's guns. One more push and they would be in the Union rear and on the road to victory. Confederate reinforcements did not appear, but fresh Federal troops soon arrived. The storm receded, the tension was broken. Haskell was exultant: *"The crest is safe."*

Gray prisoners were rounded up, and with them were taken the "red cloths that our men toss about in derision, the 'fiery red crosses,' thrice ardent, the battle flags of the rebellion, that waved defiance at the wall." These proud, colorful banners, inscribed with the names of previous battles such as First Manassas, South Mountain, Sharpsburg, Fredericksburg, Chancellorsville, and many more, "our men have, and are showing about, *over thirty of them.*"[1]

Amidst the euphoria of victory a Federal officer grabbed a captured flag not far from where Haskell stood, mounted a horse and rode out in front of his troops, triumphantly dragging the flag in the dust behind him.

* * *

The importance of the Confederate battle flag is a significant aspect of the life of the "common soldier" of both sides during the Civil War, but one that has been essentially forgotten. The primary objective of this study is to reexamine the Confederate battle flag as it was in 1863, and to better comprehend its significance on the field of battle and in the life of the Civil War soldier.

To do so requires knowledge of the world in which it appeared. Three chapters are offered as context for the narrative of events. We must develop an insight into the mental and emotional world of the civilians who became Civil War soldiers, to understand their cultural background and how it shaped their feelings and ideas about themselves, the war, and the flag that they followed. The struggle over the Confederate battle flag cannot be comprehended without first knowing what the flag meant to the men who fought over it. Thus the first chapter is devoted to outlining as simply as possible the soldiers' perception of what the flag meant, with emphasis on the Southern soldier. Second, since all flags were not alike, a basic knowledge of the evolution of the Confederate battle flag is necessary. While we are principally concerned with the pattern commonly known as the Army of Northern Virginia flag, much of what we have to say also applies to other patterns, as will be discussed later. Since some troops at Gettysburg carried the First National flag, it is included in the term "Confederate battle flag" as used in this study. Finally, we must also understand the role the battle flag played in the Napoleonic tactical concepts that governed Civil War combat. The central focus of *The Damned Red Flags of the Rebellion*" is on those moments when, in the extreme stress of mortal combat, all these factors came together.

* * *

In combat the battle flag served two purposes. First, it provided a crucial means of what modern armies call "command and control," of identifying and maneuvering large bodies of troops. Second, it served as a source of motivation; it inspired men to acts of military excellence, of bravery and gallantry "above and beyond the call of duty."

The Confederate battle flag became the most powerful symbolic object produced during the war. In all its forms, and most especially the First National and Army of Northern Virginia patterns, Confederate battle flags appropriated the myths and symbols of the American past. They incorporated the symbolic language of color, shape, design and inscription, weaving them into a new icon that offered a material and highly visible representation of the differences between North and South. In doing so they merged myth and fact: the traditions and influence of the past, the reality of the present, and hopes and dreams of the future.

By the summer of 1863, all the arguments between the sections dating back to the era of the American Revolution, and all the emotions of the individual soldiers serving in the army and facing combat had become bound up in Confederate battle flags. They had in fact *become an inseparable part of them.* The Confederate battle flag gave physical presence to all the subjective values that the soldiers had in their hearts and minds. Men carried it, followed it, tried to capture it, fought over it and willingly gave their lives for it, but in combat they *always* concentrated their attention on it. The struggle over the Confederate battle flag at Gettysburg brought all of the disparate issues of the war down to a personal level. It transformed abstract concepts into immediate physical reality.

* * *

We rarely see the real thing, the original flags that served as the emotional focal point of an extraordinarily traumatic time. Authentic Civil War battle flags, Confederate and Federal, are among the most treasured and fragile of artifacts, and are by and large locked away from public view except in a few museums in the Northeast and deep South. Most are faded, torn or in pieces, while others have already crumbled to dust. Few living Americans have ever seen an authentic Confederate battle flag.

Yet many survive. Each and every one has a story of its own, about its creation and the people who carried it. Hundreds of local flags sewn by Southern women for militia groups and carried into battle early in the war still exist in museums and archives across the South. The First National flag torn down from atop a hotel in Alexandria, Virginia, by the North's first martyr, Elmer Ellsworth, just before he was killed, is in the New York State Archives in Albany. The First National that served as Robert E. Lee's headquarters flag, and the Second National that flew over Jeb Stuart's headquarters, are hidden away in the Museum of the Confederacy in Richmond. The 26th North Carolina's Army of Northern Virginia flag, carried by 15 men on July 1st (of whom 14 were killed or wounded), lies quietly in storage in the Lee Chapel in Lexington, Virginia. An unidentified Army of Northern Virginia flag carried home from Richmond by Tad Lincoln and held up on the balcony of the White House as Abraham Lincoln spoke to a crowd about the end of the war in April, 1865, resides in the Museum of the Confederacy. A Third National, apparently the flag carried at the head of the march to the surrender ceremonies at Appomattox, rests in the

Alabama State Archives.

The very notion of what a battle flag is has dramatically changed since 1863. No troops go into battle today flying one, for stealth and surprise have replaced *elan* as the essential value in modern military operations. Today's flag, shorn of its emotional power, is used only for ceremony. We mindlessly salute it or pledge allegiance to it at sporting events. Flags rarely provoke the kind of emotions they did in the 1860s, and when they do, the emotions are often negative, not positive.

Yet in 1863 the Confederate battle flag provided a crucial focal point in combat. Note the key place played by one in a Federal soldier's memory of the struggle along Cemetery Ridge:

> Advancing boldly to the battery on our left, the enemy took possession, planting a battle-flag upon one of [the guns]. Their triumph, however, was short. A deadly volley was poured upon them at not more than 30 yards distance. Their color-bearer fell, pierced by a dozen bullets. Many others were killed or wounded, and they were forced to fall back to their cover, and the battery was saved.[2]

This is a typical account of combat written by a participant, representative of reports and reminiscences written frequently during and after the war. It highlights the importance of the flag to both sides. The Confederates had their flag in the forefront of the charge, guiding the men. When they gained control of the gun, they placed the flag in a conspicuous place, marking their possession and achievement. The Federal soldier focused on it in his description, and it obviously drew the attention of his comrades, for they aimed their fire at it, hitting the standard-bearer with a dozen bullets. When the flag fell, the Confederates retreated and the Federals rejoiced.

Captain John Cook of the 76th New York described another scene on July 1st. "Here we shot down their colors (having done so twice in the first engagement), and a portion of our regiment charged . . ," he said, "and took a large body of the enemy and a stand of colors."[3] Note that the Confederate battle flag was always a target in combat; that when its bearer was shot another man picked it up, knowing that he would be in the sights of the same men who had shot his predecessor. Note also that the capture of the flag was important enough to merit a key place in the narration of events.

Another incident involving a Federal observer took place on the same day. The 7th Wisconsin was on the firing line, and could barely see the enemy through the dense smoke. A courier from the division commander rode up to the officer in charge. "I asked could he tell what troops those were firing in the ravine," the regimental commander later reported. "He pointed a little farther to the left up the ravine (where I saw the rebel battle flag), and said it was the enemy, and that the general directed that we should drive them out. I moved the line forward to the crest of the ridge, delivered a volley, and gave the order to charge." In this incident the flag was the primary determinant of the identity of troops in the distance, and the recognition of the flag prompted specific action.[4]

In all three of these examples, the Confederate battle flag played a central role in combat. Lt. Frank Haskell and the other observers quoted here wrote with no special or unusual awareness of the Confederate flag. They did not set out to write about it; the Confederate battle flag intruded into their consciousness and dominated their thoughts and memory because of its key importance in the events they witnessed and described. Their views were essentially unselfconscious, reflecting accurately the deeply-held assumptions most Federal soldiers had about the Confederate flag and its role in their experience.

A reminiscence by a Confederate soldier, Private W. E. Berry of the 4th Texas, in General John Bell Hood's Texas Brigade, gives us some insight into the emotion that Confederate soldiers had for their flags. He was captured on September 17, 1862, at Antietam in the Cornfield, having survived some of the war's most bitter fighting. While he was waiting to be sent to the rear an incident occurred that revealed the depth of his attachment to the flag, *even though it was not the flag of his regiment:*

> While standing there I saw coming up the road from the battlefield some colors, with an escort. When they arrived the Major asked the Yankee with the colors where they got them. He said in the cornfield. He turned to me and inquired if I knew the colors. I told him they belonged to the First Texas Regiment, remarking at the time that where he got the flag there was many a dead Texan there. He said there were thirteen dead men lying on or around it when he found it. I asked him to hand it to me a moment, which he did. I took it in my hand, kissed it, and handed it back to him, tears blinding my eyes.[5]

The men who captured the 1st Texas flag were so proud of it that they made a major demonstration of their triumph. They hauled it up on a "music wagon," raised the Stars and Stripes over it, then drove through camp playing "Yankee Doodle." To make their victory especially noticeable they carried the captured Rebel banner to the headquarters of their commander, Major General George McClellan, where they "delivered themselves of spread eagle speeches" about their glorious deed.[6]

When a flag was lost it was a source of deep embarrassment and even shame to the men of that regiment. The officer in charge of the 1st Texas flag at Antietam, Lieutenant Colonel Phillip Work, recorded the seriousness with which he considered its loss. He took care in his official post-battle report to his superior to absolve his regiment of the criticism he expected from others at all ranks:

> It is a source of mortification to state that, upon retiring from the engagement, our colors were not brought off. I can but feel that some degree of odium must attach under the most favorable circumstances, and although such are the circumstances surrounding the conduct of this regiment, the loss of our flag will always remain a matter of sore and deep regrets. . . No blame, I feel, should attach to the men or officers, all of whom fought heroically and well. There was no such conduct upon their part as abandoning or deserting their colors. They fought bravely, and unflinchingly faced a terrible hail of bullets and artillery until ordered by me to retire. The colors started back with them, and when they were lost no man knew save him who had fallen with them.[7]

* * *

On the ride into Pennsylvania, Colonel Arthur Fremantle, an English military observer traveling with Lee's army, noted the color and design of their flags, and that the battle flag had become part of the new national flag that had been recently approved by the Congress. He watched as Major General William Dorsey Pender's division rode past. "The colors of the regiments differ from the blue battle flags I saw with Bragg's army [the principle Confederate force in the west]," he wrote:

> they are generally red with a blue St. Andrew's Cross showing the stars. This pattern is said to have been invented by General Joseph Johnston, as not so liable to be mistaken for the Yankee flag. The new Confederate flag had evidently been adopted from this battle flag, as it is called. Most of the colors in this division bear the names Manassas, Fredericksburg, Seven Pines, Harper's Ferry, Chancellorsville, &.[8]

Yet after the war, as the veterans grew older, emotions receded and memories of war grew dim. By the end of the century, many had forgotten how important the flag had been to them. Thus the United Confederate Veterans chose as their official symbol not the Army of Northern Virginia pattern, described by Fremantle and probably the most famous Confederate flag, nor the First National flag, the pattern that had been carried most widely and was most easily recognized, probably the most famous Confederate flag. Instead they decided to honor the relatively obscure, rectangular-shaped, 13-star battle flag first introduced in late 1863 and early 1864 in the Army of Tennessee. By the end of World War II, the Confederate battle flag was largely forgotten, only to be revived for football games in Southern colleges, and by those who opposed the Civil Rights movement of the 1950s and 1960s.

Today battle flags are not something we spend much time thinking about, even those of us who are ardent students of the American Civil War. To some the Confederate battle flag is still a powerful symbol, though the meaning commonly projected onto it is far different than that which it carried during the war. Many of us are aware that the NAACP has decided to lobby for a removal of "the Confederate battle flag" from public buildings, and their efforts have sparked others to call for a ban on its display in virtually all areas. People in Georgia and Mississippi are trying to change their state flags by removing the St. Andrew's Cross, an integral part of the designs. For them as well as numerous social activists and politicians, knowledge of American history is limited to current race relations and to the events of the last three or four decades. They know little if anything about the Civil War, the men who fought it, and the flags they carried. From their perspective, Confederate flags are linked not to the Civil War but to memories of the Ku Klux Klan and other right-wing, segregationist and extremist groups, and especially to those who opposed the Civil Rights movement of the 1950s and 1960s. When they do think of the Confederate flag in terms of the Civil War, they think only of slavery, as if Confederate and Federal soldiers had no other reason for fighting.

This view, which has become the conventional one held by most contemporary Americans, is shaped in part by the mass media's sensationalistic coverage of current events. As seen through television and the press, the Confederate flag is the banner of hate, a convenient and colorful symbol of racism and oppression. Whenever social conflict occurs, one will usually find a Confederate battle flag, and all cameras will turn toward it. On one level this limited but conventional perspective is reasonable and understandable. Throughout the last half of the Twentieth Century Confederate battle flags have indeed been widely used by extremist groups and for their own purposes.[9] And for most Americans recent events have far more emotional power than those of more than a century ago. Our perceptions are shaped by the present, not the past.

But to the student of the Civil War, and especially to a student of the rank and file soldiers, the conventional perspective seems distorted. Virtually no one living in 1863, North or South, black or white, would have thought of the flag in those terms, or agreed with that interpretation. The conventional view ignores the history and development of Confederate flags and their significance to the civilians and soldiers, on either side, during the Civil War. Professional historians used to call similar portraits of the past "ahistorical" or "presentist," an analysis of a past event that is essentially a projection of personal opinion onto the past, with little regard for the subtleties of the actual historical events or period.

The American Civil War, like most wars, was begun by politicians for their own reasons, but fought by ordinary citizens. Most historians, concerned with the workings of political, economic or social forces on the national level, have shown little interest in the lives of common people, and especially not the men who marched into battle. In their efforts to explain the "big picture" and reveal the shaping influences of particular belief systems, economic interests or social groups and movements, they have portrayed slavery as the overwhelming influence in Southern life; the sole, or the most important, cause of the war. This has been especially so for the last three or four decades.

While historians have often added to our understanding of broad themes in society, politics and culture, they have generally done so without pointing out that the vast majority of Southerners and Confederate soldiers were not slaveowners and had many other reasons for following the flag in 1861 or 1863. Likewise few Northerners were committed abolitionists and fewer still marched off to war to end slavery. To imply that all Civil War soldiers were primarily motivated by a concern for the institution of slavery is, at best, an exaggeration and oversimplification.

Southerners, white or black, were not all alike. They did not all think the same thoughts and embrace the same values with one monolithic mind. Each and every Southerner did not automatically base every important decision in his or her life on their relationship to the institution of slavery, to slavery's existence, or to debates among politicians at the national level. To indicate so, directly or by omission, is to indulge in the very kind of simplistic economic or racial determinism and stereotypical thinking that historians usually try to avoid. The lives of individuals, North or South, black or white, were much more complicated than the stick-figures marching in lock-step, that we have come to envision.

Even more narrowly focused military historians, concentrating on generals and their strategy and tactics, have little to say about the life of the common soldier. While the literature on the Civil War is massive, all the books written specifically about the common soldier can be listed in a single paragraph. The significance of the battle flag and its role in combat have rarely received scholarly attention.

Thus the physical reality of the flags' history, and the subjective emotions they symbolized during the war, are now largely forgotten. The curtain of time has been drawn across our historical vision making it difficult to see what a Confederate battle flag looked like in 1863. Its image is refracted through the lens of 130 years of social conflict, of volatile political, economic and racial relations. Between the citizens of 1863 and of the late 20th century stands a host of events that have altered the United States almost beyond recognition. Among them are the defeat of the Confederacy, the tumultuous years of Reconstruction in the Southern states, the rise of the KKK and racial segregation, two world wars against totalitarianism, the threat of nuclear destruction, the Civil Rights movement and the rise of black nationalism, the New Deal, Great Society and the growth of the welfare state, and massive immigration. America at the close of the Twentieth Century is not the America of 1863.

In short, the Confederate flag has become obscured by the lengthening shadows of our own beliefs about ourselves, our assumptions (often incorrect) about our collective past, what we think the symbols carried by Southern soldiers during the war stood for (or *should have* stood for) and events that since the end of the war.

Yet the reality of the past has not disappeared. It waits for us to rediscover it, to reclaim the past from the dustbin of contemporary social concerns and political beliefs. If we are to understand what the Civil War soldiers themselves actually saw and felt, what the Confederate battle flag actually meant to Americans living in 1863, we must put aside our own notions of what the flag was all about and listen to what they said with their words and actions. We must try to understand Civil War soldiers on their own terms, not on ours.[10]

* * *

The dual nature of the Confederate battle flag as a physical means of communication and as an emotional symbol gave it a crucial, transcendent place in the life of the Civil War soldier. In his eyes and in his heart (and thus in his experience), the Confederate battle flag fused objective reality with subjective values and became a key focal point in his most vulnerable and stressful moments.

Northerners found several meanings in the Confederate battle flag. It primarily symbolized the South's illegal rebellion against the Union, one that threatened to undermine freedom and democracy, the principles they believed were embodied in their government. The rebellion was treason, and the flag flaunted it in their faces. In addition, a captured Confederate flag was a trophy, a symbol of personal or unit bravery and of their superiority in combat. Its capture was a way of keeping score, much like the Great Plains Indian tribes' custom of "counting coup."

Immediately after the repulse of Pickett's Charge, Brigadier General Alexander Hays and two of his aides symbolically illustrated their feelings for the Confederate battle flag when they rode horses along the crest of Cemetery Ridge, each man trailing a captured flag in the dust behind them. In 1865, President Abraham Lincoln summed up this perspective when he held a captured flag. "Here is something material, something I can see, feel, and understand," he said. "This means victory. This *is* victory."[11] Twenty-three Federal soldiers were awarded the Congressional Medal of Honor for capturing Confederate flags at Gettysburg.[12]

Many, many more Confederates were wounded or killed carrying or defending the flag. General Robert E. Lee, like the other officers in the Army of Northern Virginia, watched the flags in battle to see how the conflict was going. At the battle of Second Manassas in 1862, Brigadier General John Bell Hood found Lee and gave him an ecstatic report of victory, replete with the details of the retreat of Federal battle flags over Bull Run, with the Confederate banners in hot pursuit. Lee replied, "God forbid that I should ever live to see our colors moving in the opposite direction."[13]

Southerners found many meanings in their flag. They used it as a means of marking their superiority by placing it in the forefront of a charge and upon captured works or artillery pieces. To the majority of Southern soldiers it represented their defense of family, home and community. It stood for their belief in the rights of an individual, community and state to make important decisions governing their lives. It represented their state and new nation's struggle against an aggressive and oppressive United States government. It symbolized God's will that they succeed, and the political concepts and traditions of self-government, liberty and freedom tracing back to the American Revolution, to which they believed their movement was dedicated. Perhaps most of all, in the stressful moments of combat, the Confederate battle flag reminded Southern soldiers of the men who served with them: men who were their friends, family and neighbors and who fought and marched beside them, many of whom had been wounded or killed at places like Manassas, the Seven Days, Sharpsburg and Chancellorsville. To a few—those who owned slaves or profited directly from slavery—it represented a perpetuation of that institution.

The Confederate battle flag, like any flag, did not have a singular, dominant meaning but a constellation of many meanings, and allowed individual interpretations. What people saw in it varied across space and time and among individuals. It allowed each person to feel part of the Southern community without compromising their individuality. To one person it might represent the cause of state's rights, while another saw in it the defense of home and family. The relative meaning that people bestowed upon a flag was a matter of feeling, a matter which resided in the mind of the individual. The intensity of the emotions imbued in it came from the cultural solidarity of the group it represented, and the passion of the struggle against those who opposed it. In addition, a flag also served as a sort of boundary for the community that it represented. For someone outside of that community, it could, and did, mean something entirely different.

Despite the massing of men in regiments, brigades and divisions, marching shoulder-to-shoulder, Civil War combat was an intensely personal experience. British military historian John Keegan has found that "all infantry actions, even those fought in the closest of close order, are not, in the last resort, combats of mass against mass, but the sum of many combats of individuals—one against one, one against two, three against five."[14] An examination of the actions surrounding Confederate battle flags certainly underscores the truth of Keegan's insight when applied to the American Civil War.

But we cannot recreate history; we can never fully comprehend what each individual felt or thought at a specific point in time. Thus most historians feel more at ease dealing with amorphous groups, which they usually portray as monolithic. In our own time it often seems axiomatic that people are shaped by, and thus act in concert with others of, their sex, ethnicity or socioeconomic class. But human beings are now and have always been individuals first, and only thereafter members of any group. Human behavior, especially in the extreme stress of deadly combat, is not uniform. Individuals act and react in different ways according to their individual character. Some Northerners fought for the South, and some Southerners fought for the North. Even black Southerners did not always act as a simplistically deterministic interpretation based on class, race or ethnicity might suppose they would.

Civil War soldiers were called upon to do something that few people in modern life ever do: put their strongest beliefs into action, and lay their lives on the line for the ideals (and unacknowledged assumptions) in which they believed. Occasionally they addressed those points directly, and stated in speech or in writing what they felt and thought. More often, their actions spoke for them. Modern readers can separate physical and emotional reality; Civil War soldiers could not, for belief and action were fused together in the searing experience of war. I have tried to identify as many direct statements of motivation and meaning, of values and beliefs, as possible, and to interpret actions within the context of those statements.

* * *

The incidents surrounding the battle flag cited above, including Lt. Frank Haskell's essay, (perhaps the single best account of the battle of Gettysburg written by a participant and almost certainly the most quoted), raise several additional questions. What exactly did the battle flags carried by Confederate soldiers at Gettysburg look like? The flag we now think of as the "Confederate battle flag," is rectangular in shape, with 13 white five-pointed stars evenly spaced on a blue cross, edged

in white, on a red field. That flag, which was in fact a pattern introduced by General Joseph E. Johnston, did not appear on any Civil War
battlefield until early in 1864, when Johnston imposed it upon the Army
of Tennessee. It flew in the western theater only, and *did not appear at
Gettysburg*.

In his study of the Army of Tennessee Howard Madaus noted
that the Western army carried at least eight different designs of flags,
excluding state and local flags, into battle in 1863. Most of them bore
no resemblance to the "Southern Cross," as the primary banner carried by the Army of Northern Virginia at Gettysburg was called.[15]

Did the Army of Northern Virginia carry numerous designs at
Gettysburg, or just one? Some participants left accounts of seeing the
"Lone Star" Texas flag and the "Stars and Bars" as the Confederate
First National flag is often called. George Stewart, in the best narrative history of Pickett's Charge, said Virginians carried blue state flags,
while the regiments under Pettigrew and Trimble carried the red,
square Army of Northern Virginia flag.[16] Unfortunately this was not
an important question for Stewart, so he did not examine the flags
themselves nor the scattered evidence concerning their design or capture. He based his judgment on three quotes, none of which were made
by notable authorities.[17] Many historians have made the mistake of
taking Stewart's word and repeating the error, including Glenn Tucker
in *High Tide at Gettysburg*.[18]

How many were captured? How many were carried to the stone
wall during Pickett's Charge? How many got inside the Angle? The
record is unclear, and a detailed analysis of the sources and the possible answers to those questions will be undertaken.

An examination of the historical record and the captured battle
flags still in existence reveals that almost certainly no blue Virginia
flags were carried in battle in Pickett's Charge.[19] *No* state flags of any
kind were reliably recorded as captured in the Gettysburg campaign.
While some regiments had state flags with them, they were only for
ceremonial use and were kept in wagons behind the lines during battle.

The Army of Northern Virginia took 269 units into battle at Gettysburg.[20] I have been able to locate documentation indicating that
probably only three, the 1st Texas and 8th South Carolina infantry
regiments, and the 1st Maryland infantry battalion, carried state flags
into battle. In those cases the state flag was carried as a second flag,
in addition to the battle flag, and carried against orders that only one
flag, the battle flag, be carried by each unit.

The "battle flag" was just that: a symbol to be carried in battle.
An order issued in the summer or fall of 1862 directed that only the
square battle flag be carried in the Army of Northern Virginia.[21] The
earlier flags were returned to the states, and many still survive. For
example, when the 3rd North Carolina sent their state flag home in
October, 1862, it was accompanied by a letter from Major S. D. Thruston,

to Governor Zebulon Vance:

> I beg leave, sir, to return to you the colors intrusted(sic) to us by the State of North Carolina at the commencement of this contest. When the regiment was first attached to the army before Richmond the Confederate battle-flag was issued to it and all other colors ordered to be discarded. Previous to the battles in Maryland, however, our colonel, at the request of both officers and men, once more unfurled our North Carolina colors, a special guard was detailed for its defense, and, in addition to our battle-flag, carried this into the engagement at Sharpsburg. This is the only one in which it has ever been, and it bears evidence in its folds that it was in the very thickest [fighting]. . . .[22]

The documentary record of the capture of Confederate battle flags at Gettysburg is sketchy. Our knowledge of this subject will never be complete, but we can use what we have to develop an understanding of what happened and why it occurred. In 1863 no mandatory or systematic reporting procedure existed for either side, so many captured Confederate flags were not preserved or sent to the War Department. Some of those that were sent to Washington had no documentation with them.[23]

A formal order governing the handling of captured Confederate battle flags did not go out until long after the battle of Gettysburg. In October of 1864 Assistant Adjutant-General E. D. Townsend firmly told one officer that he could not keep a captured flag or give it away. Townsend had read a newspaper account that the man had given one to the city of Philadelphia. "All flags, munitions of war, and public property taken from the enemy belong to the United States, and such flags when captured should be forwarded to the Adjutant-General," wrote Townsend. "Please report for the information of the Secretary of War whether the statement in the papers is correct; and if it is, cause the flag to be obtained and forwarded to this office, to be deposited in the archives of the War Department."[24] Sometime between Townsend's letter and the spring of 1865 orders were finally issued detailing what to do with captured flags.

If the correspondence of Major General Horatio Wright, commanding the VI Corps, is indicative of the situation throughout the army, it is clear that many captured flags were valued quite highly as trophies of war and had been kept by their captors. The government had responded by formulating a policy that not only governed the ownership of captured flags, but also awarded recognition to those who captured them. On April 16, 1865, Wright wrote to the Chief of Staff of the Army of the Potomac:

I have the honor to inclose(sic) herewith a list of rebel
flags captured by troops in this corps during the recent
campaign, with the names of the captors, and it is
proposed to forward them to your head-quarters
tomorrow, the captors carrying them with an escort of
honor of one regiment from each division of the corps;
the flags to be delivered by a staff officer from these
headquarters at or about 11 a.m. I have also the honor
to request that the captors be permitted, as is
customary, to accompany these flags to Washington, and
that, after they are received and registered there they
be returned to their captors, the latter to receive such
other testimonials as are usually granted. As showing
the value attached to the flags by the men it may be
stated that there are many other flags known to have
been captured by the corps, which have been secreted
and which it has been found impossible to obtain, the
men much preferring to retain them to receiving
furloughs and medals of honor.[25]

Apparently even a furlough, a highly treasured pass that would
allow a soldier to get away from the danger of combat and go home for
a period of time, was not enough to convince some men who had captured Confederate battle flags to give them up.

Other factors add to the difficulty of tracking captured flags.
Many Confederate regiments did not file a post-battle report simply
because they had no field officer left to write one. Those who did file
reports rarely mentioned the loss of a flag. It is perhaps a measure-
ment of the importance of the flag in the minds of Southerners, as well
as of their state of shock, embarrassment, and depression after the
battle, that not a single regimental report mentioned the loss of a flag.
Only three brigade-level reports accounted for the loss of flags.[26] Therefore only seven of the losses were recorded in Confederate official reports.

Mistakes, conflicting accounts and contradictions appear frequently in the official reports, as well as in personal letters, diaries etc.
For example, a soldier in the 8th Ohio captured two flags, but was
apparently called by three different first names. He turned out to be
two different men, one of whom is called by two different names. The
flag of the 15th Georgia was reported as captured on July 1st, 2nd and
3rd. The capture of the 4th Virginia's banner was claimed by three
different Federal regiments, at three separate locations and times. Two
regiments that were in Tennessee in July 1863 reportedly lost their
flags at Gettysburg. The documentation often cites incorrect regimental numbers: the 26th Alabama was listed as the 16th, the 2nd Missis-

sippi called the 20th, the 55th North Carolina listed as the 54th, and so on. Accounts of flag captures and losses usually are most accurate at the individual or regimental level. The higher up the chain of command, the less detailed and reliable is the information. All citations, quotes, etc., have been checked, compared with other sources and carefully analyzed to the best of my ability.

When a captured Confederate flag was turned in to the War Department in 1863, it was often accompanied by a slip of paper or cloth with the information concerning its capture written upon it. The flags were not numbered and cataloged until December, 1863, and in some cases, much later. Some flags had no information with them. The identifying pieces of paper or cloth were often lost. In still others, the flag was incorrectly identified. During the years between 1863 and 1905, when the Federal government returned the flags to the states, more errors occurred. Over the years numerous scholars, government and museum personnel, have made attempts to correct these errors. The research in this area by Howard Michael Madaus has been most notable and productive, and this study has benefited significantly from his work. Unfortunately, many flags are still missing or unidentified.

A running commentary on these problems will appear in the footnotes. In cases in which a flag has been unidentified or misidentified, and I believe there is a reasonable conclusion that can be drawn from the research done by myself and others, I have given my "best guess" as a tentative conclusion, and marked them in the tables and captions to their photographs with an * asterisk.

* * *

It should be abundantly clear that *"The Damned Red Flags of the Rebellion"* is not "drum and bugle" history, seeking to assign some imagined glory. War is tragedy, and civil war perhaps the most tragic of all. There is no glory in combat, only survival, dismemberment or death. Mortal combat during the American Civil War was perhaps among the most horrendous experiences that mankind has ever endured. The combination of Napoleonic tactics that dictated large masses of men deployed in tightly packed, linear formations, with the technology of rifled muskets and cannon firing soft lead projectiles that crushed bone and horribly mangled human tissue, produced gruesome conditions and horrifying scenes. Battlefields after actions such as the Federal attack on Marye's Heights in 1862 or Pickett's Charge at Gettysburg, are essentially incomprehensible to most modern minds.[27]

This study is in the tradition of a handful of historians who have examined the lives of the common soldiers: Larry Daniel, John Keegan, Gerald Linderman, James McPherson, Reid Mitchell, James Robertson and Bell Wiley. It is an effort to understand the hearts and minds of Civil War soldiers, to decipher what the experience of war meant for them, and how and why they lived, fought and died.[28]

We must also look at the flags themselves, to ascertain just what the Confederate battle flags fluttering over Cemetery Ridge, Culp's Hill, and Little Round Top looked like. Color photographs are included of all 41 flags captured during the Gettysburg campaign that have survived 130 years of neglect and obscurity. Most have not been published previously, and several are identified here for the first time. We have also included information about the current location and condition of the flags as a means of encouraging support for their preservation and restoration.

* * *

Gettysburg provides the focus for this study because, in research as in the Civil War, all roads seem to lead there. The battle took place near the village where no less than 10 roads met in 1863. Gettysburg served as the crossroads for the war; nothing was the same thereafter. Never again would the Army of Northern Virginia be as confident in itself and its future, as sure of its military prowess, as determined to win independence as it was in July of 1863.

Gettysburg occurred at a crucial point in the war. The society that produced the Confederate battle flag, and the one that despised it, were not monolithic nor static. Their concerns and values were evolving before the war, and continued to change during the war. Confederate confidence and hopes were at their highest ebb. Many Northerners and Southerners believed that the life of the Confederate States of America depended upon the results of the Pennsylvania campaign.

For some, the experience of combat at Gettysburg was forever etched in memory. Their thoughts and writings often turned to allegorical, apocalyptic and religious themes in an effort to explain the larger significance of what they had seen and done. Thus a relatively large amount of documentation is available; indeed at times it seems that every soldier who survived the battle wrote an account of what he had witnessed.

Finally, this is not a narrative history of the battle of Gettysburg. It is not a complete analysis of Southern culture, nor the full story of the Confederate battle flag. The focus here is on the actions of individual soldiers, the rank and file, in the summer of 1863. Yet enough of the larger battle must be included to furnish a meaningful context for the struggle over the flags. Thus a basic narrative ties the events together. I have deliberately included lengthy quotations with the intention of letting the men speak for themselves as often and as fully as possible, to allow the reader to read their words rather than mine. Chapter Nine is my effort to make sense of the mass of conflicting evidence of flag captures. Appendix A is a table listing all the Confederate battle flags captured during the campaign, arranged in alphabetical order by state, intended to be used by the reader for reference. Appendix B offers a listing of the variations of the Army of Northern Virginia flags carried during the campaign. Appendix C is a database of the materials and dimensions of each flag that was captured at Gettysburg and is still is existence. A special section inserted in the middle of the book includes color photographs of all the flags captured during the campaign, in chronological order of their capture.

Notes

[1] Frank Haskell, "Gettysburg," in Richard Rollins, ed., *Pickett's Charge: Eyewitness Accounts* (Redondo Beach, CA.: Rank and File Publications, 1996), 40-43, 71-75, 117-124, 328-336, 369-373. Hereafter cited as "Haskell."

[2] Report of Maj. Sylvanus Curtis, 7th Michigan, July 16, 1863, Department of War, *The War of the Rebellion: A Compilation of the Official Records of the Union and Confederate Armies* (Washington: Government Printing Office, 1880-1901) 128 Volumes, Series I, Volume 27, Part I, page 447. Hereafter this will be cited as *OR*. All citations (unless otherwise noted) are from Series I, Volume 27, only the Part number (I, II or III) and the page number will be given. Those citations not in Vol. 27 will be given in full.

[3] Report of Capt. John Cook, 76th New York, July 11th, 1863, *Ibid.*, 286.

[4] Report of Col. William Robinson, 7th Wisconsin, November 18, 1863, *Ibid.*, 279.

[5] W. E. Berry, "Dauntless Courage and Heroic Deeds," *Official Minutes of Hood's Texas Brigade Monument Dedication and 39th Annual Re-Union* (Houston: Privately Printed, 1911), 108.

[6] *Ibid.*, 16.

[7] Report of Lt. Col. Phillip Work, 1st Texas, *OR*, Series I, Vol. 19, Part I, 933.

[8] Arthur Fremantle, *Three Months in the Southern States: April-June 1863*, (New York: John Bradburn, 1864), June 22, 1863.

[9] For a summary of the controversy, and a study of the actual development of the Georgia flag, see Kelly Barrow, "Attacks on the Colors," *Confederate Veteran* [Hereafter cited as *CV*] (Sept.-Oct. 1992), 4-5.

[10] This paragraph is a huge oversimplification of a large and complicated subject that has been debated by scholars and philosophers for nearly two hundred years. This is a subject far beyond the boundaries of this study, but it is also an important one, and certainly shapes what is written here. For an introduction to recent debates on postmodernism and the study of history see Gertrude Himmelfarb, *On Looking into the Abyss: Untimely Thoughts on Culture and Society* (New York: Knopf, 1994) and Joyce Oldham Appleby, et. al., *Telling the*

Truth About History (New York: Norton, 1994).

[11] Quoted in Sylvanus Cadwallader, *Three Years With Grant. . . , Benjamin P. Thomas, ed. (New York: Knopf, 1956), 307. For the context of this quote see Ronald Rietveld, "Lincoln Triumphant: From Crisis to Victory, 1864 to 1865," in Richard Rollins, ed., *A Day With Mr. Lincoln: Essays Commemorating the Lincoln Exhibition at the Huntington Library* (Redondo Beach, CA: Rank and File Publications, 1994), 66.

[12] *Medal of Honor Recipients, 1863-1973* (Washington: U.S. Government Printing Office, 1973).

[13] Quoted in Burke Davis, *Gray Fox: Robert E. Lee and the Civil War* (New York: Holt, Rinehart and Winston, 1956), 127.

[14] Keegan, *The Face of Battle* (New York: Penguin Books, 1974), 100. Keegan's quote comes from his study of the battle between French and English forces at Agincourt in 1415, but his insight is no less valid for Gettysburg.

[15] Howard Michael Madaus and Robert D. Needham, *The Battleflags of the Army of Tennessee* (Milwaukee: Milwaukee Public Museum, 1976). See also Joseph H. Crute, Jr., *Emblems of Southern Valor: The Battle Flags of the Confederacy* (Louisville: Harmony House, 1990), and Paul Ellingson, ed., *Confederate Flags in the Georgia State Capitol Collection* (Atlanta: Georgia Office of Secretary of State, 1994). Since the publication of *The Battleflags of the Army of Tennessee,* Madaus has been widely acknowledged as the leading expert on Confederate flags. He is currently Curator of Historic Firearms at the Buffalo Bill Museum in Cody, Wyoming.

[16] George R. Stewart, *Pickett's Charge: A Microhistory of the Final Attack at Gettysburg, July 3, 1863* (Boston: Houghton, Mifflin, 1959), 309-310. Numerous historians have taken Stewart's belief as correct and repeated his error.

[17] *Ibid.*

[18] Glenn Tucker, *High Tide at Gettysburg* (Dayton, OH: Morningside House, 1966), 390. See also Phillip Katcher, *The Army of Robert E. Lee* (New York: Arms and Armour, 1994). Katcher accepts Stewart's mistakes as fact.

[19] I hesitate to make this a definite statement only because it is impossible to prove a negative. I have seen no indication that a blue Virginia flag was carried during the charge, and all 15 of Pickett's flags were Army of Northern Virginia flags. Thus if a blue Virginia flag was carried, it was the second flag in a regiment and was carried against orders. The odds weigh heavily against it having happened.

[20] The official records list 170 infantry units, 62 artillery units and 37 cavalry (including horse artillery). See *OR*, II, 252 ff.

[21] Conversation with Howard Madaus, August 30, 1994, and an examination of all records. No order concerning this issue has been located, but several documents accompanying state flags returned in

1862 refer to one. In addition, a similar order was issued in the western theater. See General Orders No. 54, *OR*, Ser. I, Vol. 27, Part III, 801. Don Troiani included a blue Maryland flag in his portrayal of the "Band of Brothers" and based his conclusion of several bits of research including the diary of a member of the battalion, George Marden, a drawing by Alan Redwood, a member of the battalion, and an article in the "Murray Confederate Association."

[22] Major S. D. Thruston to Zebulon Vance, October 5, 1862, *OR*, Series 1, Vol. 51, Part II, 632.

[23] Though no official order has been found governing the reporting procedure, captured Confederate flags were typically sent up the chain of command and then to the War Department. Two inventories of captured Confederate flags were made after the war. William C. Endicott, "Letter From the Secretary of War," House of Representatives, Executive Document No. 153, 50th Congress, First Session, 1888" (hereafter cited as "Letter") prepared one. The second, and more comprehensive, was begun in 1863 and completed in 1905 when the flags were sent to the Governors of the former Confederate states. Unidentified flags were sent to the Confederate Memorial Literary Society, an organization of Virginia women, and ended up in the Museum of the Confederacy in Richmond. The second inventory is known as "Record of Rebel Flags Captured By Union Troops Since April 19, 1861", published in Richard Rollins, ed., *The Returned Battle Flags* (Redondo Beach, CA: Rank and File Publications, 1995). It is hereafter cited as "Record." The original is in the National Archives. Confederates also lacked orders for the processing of Federal flags. See Robert E. Lee to Headquarters, July 20, 1864, *OR*, Series I, Vol. CL, Part III, 785.

[24] E. D. Townsend to Brig. Gen. E. B. Tyler, October 27, 1864, *OR*, Series I, Vol. 28, Part II, 480.

[25] Maj. Gen. H. G. Wright to Maj. Gen. A. S. Webb, April 16, 1865, *OR*, Series I, Vol. 46, Part III, 790.

[26] Report of Brigadier General A. R. Wright, September 28, 1863, *OR*, II, 625, records the loss of the 48th Georgia flag. Report of Lt. Colonel S. G. Shepard, August 10, 1863, *OR*, II, 646-647, records the loss of the 1st and 14th Tennessee, 13th Alabama and 5th Alabama Battalion flags. Report of Colonel David Lang, July 29, 1863, *OR*, II, 632, describes the loss of the 2nd and 8th Florida flags. Report of Captain J. J. Young, 26th North Carolina, *OR*, II, 645, reports their loss on July 3rd.

[27] Warfare in earlier times had been less destructive to human bodies. See John Keegan, *A History of War* (New York: Penguin Books, 1994).

[28] John Keegan, *Face of Battle*; Gerald F. Linderman, *Embattled Courage: The Experience of Combat in the American Civil War* (New York: The Free Press, 1987); James Robertson, *Soldiers Blue and Gray* (Columbia: University of South Carolina Press, 1988); Bell Irvin Wiley,

The Life of Johnny Reb: The Common Soldier of the Confederacy (Baton Rouge: Louisiana State University Press, 1943), and *The Life of Billy Yank: The Common Soldier of the Union* (Baton Rouge: Louisiana State University Press, 1952). See also Larry J. Daniel, *Soldiering in the Army of Tennessee* (Chapel Hill: The University Of North Carolina Press, 1991); Joseph Allan Frank and George A. Reaves, *"Seeing the Elephant": Raw Recruits at the Battle of Shiloh* (New York: Greenwood Press, 1989); Randall C. Jimerson, *The Private Civil War: Popular Thought during the Sectional Conflict* (Baton Rouge: Louisiana State University Press, 1988); James McPherson, *What They Fought For, 1861-1865* (Baton Rouge: Louisiana State University Press, 1994); John Michael Priest, *Antietam: The Soldier's Battle* (Shippensburg, PA: White Mane Publishing, 1989); Reid Mitchell, *Civil War Soldiers: Their Expectations and Experiences* (New York: Simon and Schuster, 1988); and *The Vacant Chair: The Northern Soldier Leaves Home* (Chapel Hill: University of North Carolina Press, 1994), and Joseph Glathaar, *The March to the Sea and Beyond: Sherman's Troops in the Savannah and Carolinas Campaigns* (New York, 1985).

Chapter One

Combat and Culture:
The Battle Flag in the Heart and Mind
of the Confederate Soldier

Combat and Culture

"In war the chief incalculable is the human will," wrote British military historian Liddell Hart.[1] The events surrounding the Confederate battle flag provide a means of understanding, in the life of the Southern soldier, what Hart meant, and what another prominent British military historian, John Keegan, called the "will to combat." The role of the flag in command and control is of vital importance, but it does not explain the Southern soldier's willingness to give up his life for it. To have some understanding of why acts "above and beyond the call of duty" occurred so frequently around the battle flag we must attempt to understand what it meant to him; what it symbolized when he saw it flying above him in battle; what powerful emotions it carried with it.

Southern culture produced the Confederate soldier, the flag and the emotions that linked the two. The emotions he felt, that caused him to fight, came from his location in the society in which he had grown up and lived. That world, now long gone, instilled in him certain expectations about how the world should function. When those beliefs, values and ideals were challenged, Southern men marched off to fight a war to defend and preserve them.[2]

The South in the years before the war was predominately a rural, agricultural society. Its economy, a mix of small subsistence farms and large plantations, was dominated by the production and exportation of cotton. Much of the area west of the Appalachian mountains was still unsettled, or recently settled, the sort of area historians used to call a frontier. Virtually all the cotton was raised and processed by black slaves, descendants of Africans who had been brought to America before the slave trade was outlawed in 1808. Of the ten million people in the South, four million were black. The six million whites were largely from northern and western European stock, with a smattering of others here and there. In politics the South was heavily egalitarian in rhetoric, but oligarchic in both leadership and political structure.[3]

The essential fact that shaped the attitudes of the Confederate soldier, as well as the nature of his life in the army, was that the companies and regiments in which he served were drawn from, and thus were a part of, the local community in which he lived. This fact cannot be overemphasized. Southern civilians who became soldiers were born, by and large, in the South before 1850. They grew up in a particular environment at a specific period of time. They lived in families often extended to include grandparents, aunts and uncles and cousins as well as the core of parents and children. They lived in communities and went to schools, patriotic functions and churches together. As they grew up they learned to see the world from a certain perspective. Part of that perspective included ways of looking at the world and understanding how they should live and interact with their friends, families and neighbors and how they should be governed.

The Confederate soldier went to war not by himself, nor with a group of strangers from different parts of the country, people with whom he had no ties. He went with members of his family, with friends and neighbors, people with whom he assumed he would resume his life after the war. All took with them the essential elements of Southern culture. These beliefs and assumptions were reinforced and solidified by the socialization process of army life and by his wartime experiences. He became even *more* of a Southerner than he had been before the war. The Confederate battle flag came to represent the army and the community from which it sprang, no matter which pattern or place we care to discuss.[4]

When a Confederate soldier saw the flag in the summer of 1863, it symbolized ideals that varied from individual to individual. Among the most powerful were the emotional ties to his family and community. He comprehended the flag, and his participation in the war, within the framework of the heritage of the Revolution and the political concepts of state's rights and individualism as he understood them. He felt he had to display in combat the central tenets of the code of behavior with which he had been brought up: honor and courage. His belief in evangelical Protestantism helped him face death and fight with little fear and a good deal of élan. But perhaps most importantly of all, in the summer of 1863 he fought for his fellow soldiers, the men he lived with and fought alongside: his comrades. A few, mostly slaveholders, also sought to preserve the economic system that provided their daily sustenance.

We must be careful to underscore that what we are trying to describe here are *not the causes of the Civil War*. Instead, we are interested in why typical citizens became soldiers and went off to fight. The two were not identical; frequently they were not even similar. In the broadest sense the Civil War surely was the result of the breakdown of the American two-party political system, where interstate and national disputes are dealt with in our society. That breakdown can be traced to questions of political and/or economic power; to the question of slavery; slavery's extension; the election of a sectionalist president; the unwillingness of that president and the Southern opposition to compromise; the acts of secession; the firing on Fort Sumter; or the calling out of troops to suppress secession. One's choice of focus dictates what

2

one concludes was the "real" cause.[5]

What we are dealing with in this chapter is the life of the Confederate soldier in the summer of 1863. Our subject is the way in which the Confederate soldier perceived the flag, the war and his place in it, not why the war began. An individual soldier had a direct or indirect relationship to the larger political issues on the national level, varying according to the specific circumstances of his life.

Large numbers of individuals have patterns of behavior that can correspond to any number of variables. Individual human beings, however, may or may not feel, think or act in keeping with peer group expectations. We cannot analyze the emotions of each individual soldier, yet we must always recognize that individuals differ according to their own lives. An individual Confederate soldier might experience all of the sources of emotion described here, or just one of them. There may have been additional sources of the "will to combat" for the men of the Army of Northern Virginia in the summer of 1863. With all these factors in mind, what appears here is what seems to be the most influential factors that shaped the Confederate soldier's feelings about himself and the flag for which he fought.

Bruce Catton once remarked on how deeply felt and complex were the emotions of the time and of our need to try to comprehend them:

> The deeper meaning of the American Civil War, for the people who lived through it and for us today, goes beyond the historian's grasp. Here was an event so complex, so deeply based in human emotions, so far-reaching in its final effects, that understanding it is likely to be a matter primarily for the emotions rather than for the cold analysis of facts. It was an experience that was probably felt more deeply than anything else that ever happened to us. We cannot hope to understand it unless we share in that feeling, simply because the depth and intensity of the feeling are among the war's principal legacies.[6]

In order to understand the meaning of the Confederate battle flag to the Southern soldier, we must try to comprehend these emotions. Before we begin, however, it might be wise to take note of the conclusions of an individual who marched and fought with the Army of Northern Virginia at Gettysburg, and who tried to figure out the tangled relationships between the soldier, the war, and the flag. He felt that he failed to do so.

In fact, in his denial of the possibility of understanding these complex issues, Private Carlton McCarthy stated a few of the major themes that we will deal with: emotions engendered by the soldier's feeling for his home, family, God, and sacred honor. McCarthy concluded that the Southern soldier's feelings about his flag, the war and his role in it were essentially irrational, though he did not use that word. They were rooted in his past, in his community and upbringing. "It is not fair to demand a reason for actions above reason," he wrote:

> The heart is greater than the mind. No man can exactly define the cause for which the Confederate soldier fought. He was above human reason and above human law, secure in his own rectitude of purpose, accountable to God only, having assumed for himself a 'nationality,' which he was minded to defend with his life and his property, and thereto pledged his sacred honor.[7]

We may accept McCarthy's belief that the causes for which the Confederate soldier fought are beyond our comprehension, but we can also try our best to understand them, or to develop the best insight that is within our grasp. I have chosen the latter course, fully cognizant of the insecure footing here. A margin for error does exist. This chapter represents an impression at best, but one that I believe is the result of an honest effort to understand Confederate soldiers on their own terms. It is an important topic, and if we do not make this effort, the true character of the Civil War soldier on both sides, and the true meaning of the Confederate battle flag to men on both sides, will remain a mystery to us. If there are errors in this essay, perhaps those who come later can correct them and gain further insight into the experience of the common soldier in the Civil War.

The Army of Northern Virginia in the Summer of 1863

As it marched into Pennsylvania the Army of Northern Virginia was at the apex of its existence. The summer of 1863 was a special moment for these men, perhaps an even more intensely emotional one than numerous others. During the previous ten months, they had decisively defeated their principal adversary at Manassas, Fredericksburg and Chancellorsville. Yet after each defeat the Federal army retreated, reorganized and came back stronger than ever. Now these men in gray would face them again, this time on their adversaries' native soil.

Who were these men marching North? While no historian has yet made an exhaustive analysis of the statistical evidence available, a few generalizations may be made.[8] About 70 to 80% of all white, male Southerners of military age served in Confederate armies: thus in general they were fairly representative of their society.[9]

Captain Henry Owen, a schoolteacher from rural Virginia, marched to Gettysburg with the 18th Virginia. Owen ended up on July 3rd commanding about 50 men, all that was left of his regiment.

was a fierce defender of the army after the war. His view of it was passionate and colored by his experiences during the war and his commitment to the men who had served with him, so it must be considered carefully. Yet he took care to think about who his comrades had been, and after the war he wrote a sketch of the Army of Northern Virginia, with emphasis on Pickett's division. He described them as they made camp in the Pennsylvania woods on June 30th. Owen noted that most of his state's finest families were well represented:

> The three brigades present, in camp near Chambersburg, were composed entirely of Virginians and nearly every family of honorable mention, in the brief but brilliant annals of the commonwealth, had its representatives here, either among the officers or among the privates marching in the ranks of this celebrated body of soldiers. There marched in the line presidents, professors and students from universities of learning, graduates of law and of medicine, editors and divines, men of learning, of reputation[,] of wealth, and refinement; and these men actuated by personal or family pride often displayed upon the field of battle the loftiest heroism in the charge against superior numbers, were held firmly in front of hotly worked batteries, decimating their ranks or fell back slowly and sullenly disputing every inch of ground. . . .

Owen also noted that the army contained men from all walks of life. Indeed, implicit in his account is a recognition of class differences within the army. He was somewhat exclusionary in his view of ethnicity, and today we might point out to him that the ethnic make up of the army included men who had been born in Ireland, Germany, France and a few other European countries as well as the northern Europeans he mentioned, but the point is that the army included elements from every social origin or background:

> There was another class of volunteers present that followed in the wake and influence of these proud cavaliers, no less deserving of mention. The yeomanry of the Old Dominion, the plowman, the mechanic, the laboring men from the town and country, whose stout hearts and brawny arms had sprung from a warlike ancestry, whose individual names and acts in war are unrecorded upon the scroll of fame, but mustered as a mass, worthy scions and worthy sires, as Briton, Dane, Saxon, Norman, English and Virginian, can point to deeds in arms by sea and land, in every clime that have

made the race famous on the historic page for more than a thousand years.[10]

The army also included Southerners of African descent, as had most previous American armies. In the summer of 1863 black and white Southerners marched together, ate together, worked together, as they had in all sections of the South before the war. Of course they did so within the structure of race relations of the day: they were not socially or legally equal citizens.

C. Vann Woodward, perhaps the most prominent Southern historian of our time, concluded that the two races have always been inextricably linked:

> The ironic thing about these two great hyphenate minorities, Southern-Americans and Afro-Americans, confronting each other on their native soil for three and a half centuries, is the degree to which they have shaped each other's destinies, determined each other's isolation, shared and molded a common culture. It is, in fact, impossible to imagine the one without the other, and quite futile to try.[11]

Woodward's insight holds true for the summer of 1863. The Confederacy was a biracial, caste society, and the Army of Northern Virginia reflected that peculiar social reality. It was a product of that social structure and could hardly have not reflected it. Thus with the army came thousands of black servants and a few black soldiers carrying guns.[12]

The enlisted men were young. Again, no thorough statistical analysis has been done, but those few scholars who have made an effort to analyze muster rolls, enlistment documents and the like have found that the average age upon enlistment was less than 24 years. They were by and large young men in their teens and early twenties, largely from rural areas, their officers somewhat older.[13]

Regardless of class or age, these men were veterans, having served most of the previous two years. They had learned the hard lessons of army life through experience: long and difficult marches, tedious camp life, disease and brutal combat. One historian called these Southerners among the simplest people that American society has produced. He meant not that they were of low intelligence, but that they were honest, straightforward, hard-working rural people who wore their attitudes, ambitions and emotions on their sleeves.[14] They adopted a "matter of fact" attitude in their personal relationships and expressed little interest in politics on a national or army level. They were lean and wiry, lightly dressed in gray or home spun "butternut" uniforms, and carried a minimum of equipment. Their exterior simplicity resulted from the inconsistent delivery of goods from home or the Quartermaster department and their experiences on the road, but it also mirrored their inner sense of individualism and self-reliance. Henry Owen recalled their appearance:

> They were footsore and wearied. Their faces were tanned by summers' heat and winters' storms and covered over with unkempt beards. Boys who enlisted in their teens appear changed now into men of middle life. Their tents were burned early in the war and their baggage had been reduced . . . until the men marched for weeks and months together without a change of raiment, climbed mountains, waded rivers, slept upon the bleak, snow-clad hills under a single blanket and the cold bare heavens for a covering, shivered in the chill blasts upon the outpost or tramped barefoot the stony turnpikes and tangled swamps; often the van in battle [and] rear in retreat, they breasted alike the storms of weather and of war and, though thinly clad and poorly fed, fought long and well. . . . The missiles of war had ploughed their ranks and fallen comrades had been left upon every field, whose bleaching bones marked the track of the division and must tell as a monument where the contest raged the fiercest. . . . The bright uniforms and braided caps of earlier days were gone and have given place to the slouched hat, the faded threadbare jacket and patched pantaloons.[15]

A Texan in their midst recalled a similar image of the army just after the battle:

> My shoes were old and so were my clothes. My pants were frazzled and split up to the knees, so I cut them off just below the knees, and though if I looked like I felt, I was a fright. Short sleeves worn to near point of the elbow, no socks or drawers, and knee breeches. It was not long after leaving camp, marching in mud about six inches deep I lost the sole of one shoe. I jerked off the upper and tried walking a short distance with one bare foot. It looked like at nearly every step there was a rock to jam between my toes as my foot slipped down and forward. I soon pulled off the other one, thinking that I could walk with less danger to both. This was a mistake, so I soon got out of the road and made my way as best I could through woods and fields, keeping near the road.[16]

Edwin Forbes, Prisoners of War, July 3rd
(Courtesy of the Library of Congress)

Even a Northern newspaper artist, watching prisoners taken during Pickett's Charge move to the rear, noticed that their strong personal character could not be missed, even when wrapped in shabby clothes. "Most of them were finely-formed fellows, with resolute faces, and evidently good soldiers," wrote Edwin Forbes:

> They seemed to be in a cheerful mood, and chatted pleasantly as they marched along, guarded on each side by Union infantry and cavalry. They were poorly clothed, in a variety of uniforms, a dingy gray color prevailing; some wore jackets, others gray-skirted coats trimmed on collars and sleeves. There were many ragged slouch hats, and caps of various kinds with visors. Some wore boots, others shoes, and many were barefooted.[17]

Sure of their mission, trusting of their leadership, the men in the Army of Northern Virginia were, on June 30, 1863, above all else convinced of their abilities as soldiers. The wild patriotic fervor of the spring of 1861 was gone, but the disillusionment of late 1864 and early 1865 had not yet arrived. In general, their spirits were high. Indeed, as a recent historian has said, "The general condition and attitude of these men in the regiments and batteries . . . was perhaps at its peak."[18] A certain cockiness pervaded the army, a feeling that they knew no others were quite so good, that they faced an enemy they had beaten before and would defeat again. They also held a deep certainty that there was no general anywhere that could match their leader, Robert E. Lee. One soldier in the 3rd Virginia summed up their attitude when he observed that on the march toward Gettysburg there was less straggling "than ever before. Our Division . . . has perfect confidence in the leaders and feel themselves to be almost invincible."[19] A sergeant in the 8th Virginia well remembered the same thing:

> Pickett's division had fewer "stragglers" than ever before, and while all the men realized that they were to have bloody work, none despaired of ultimate triumph. Reports of our successes on the first and second days were rife in the command, it was seen that we had driven the enemy for miles, and captured 5,000 prisoners, and all these things were an unquestioned guarantee of continued success.[20]

Perhaps the best summary of the supreme confidence and overall mood of the Army of Northern Virginia was recorded by South Carolinian J. F. Caldwell, who after the war would become the historian of McGowan's brigade:

> I have little doubt that we had now the finest army ever marshalled on this side of the Atlantic, and one scarcely inferior to any Europe has known. Its numbers were not so imposing, for the effective force of

infantry did not exceed sixty thousand men. But we were veterans—thoroughly experienced in all that relates to the march or the battle-field, sufficiently drilled to perform any maneuver at all likely to be demanded, sufficiently disciplined to obey orders promptly and with energy, yet preserving enough of the proud individuality of Southern men to feel the cause our own, and therefore to be willing to encounter the greatest amount of personal danger and moral responsibility. The world probably never saw all the advantages of the volunteer and the regular systems so admirable combined.

In addition to this, we were in excellent health, and more properly equipped than at any period prior or subsequent. It is undoubtably the moral force which enables a man to engage or to endure peril, but it is equally true that the physical condition has an incalculable influence on the spiritual system.

A last and vastly important element in the army was the confidence of the troops in the valor of their comrades and the skill of their officers. The victories of 1862 and the great battle of Chancellorsville this year had led us to believe scarcely anything impossible to Lee's army; and the management of our generals, which had wrung even from the North the highest encomiums, gave us assurance that every particle of our strength and courage would be most judiciously and powerfully applied. Lee, in himself, was a tower of strength. Not only had the works on the Chickahominy and the lines at Manassas gone down before him, not only had the great wave of battle been beaten back at Sharpsburg, and the sea of men been rolled away at Fredericksburg, not only had the heights of Chancellorsville, frowning with artillery and walled around with thousands of troops, been stormed and carried; but he had ruined every Northern general sent against him, not merely with the South and with Europe, but in the eyes of their own people. McClellan, Pope, Burnside, Hooker, had successively vanished before him, and he now appeared to be invincible, immovable.[21]

These men, so full of passion for life and good humor, were also strongly self-reliant and individualistic in nature. Idealistic, rough-hewn and perhaps even naive by modern standards, the Confederate infantrymen were not accustomed to arbitrary authority and was best led into battle by example, not ordered or forced by military law. They

10

carried with them powerfully negative attitudes toward the intervention of government in any aspect of their lives, preferring to rely on individual effort and relationships.[22] Thoroughly independent on an individual and social level, they would quickly and aggressively defend their word of promise and their sense of personal honor.[23]

The emotions they felt concerning their lives, the war, and the world in which they lived were bound up in their battle flags. Those emotions were multiple, deeply held, interrelated and complex. Today those emotions can be peeled back, examined, and studied in layers in a detached, scholarly manner. These emotions were a product of the ideas, beliefs, and unstated assumptions that had come to them from their families and the culture and communities in which they had been raised and continued to live. In 1863 they were frequently assumed and acted upon rather than consciously articulated. As historians we cannot define these emotions with precision. Each man was different, and each had his own personal story. Yet as a group they had certain characteristics, and while they might differ as individuals in their degree of intensity of belief and commitment to a specific principle, most shared common experiences and a common outlook on life.

To concentrate on the struggle over the Confederate battle flag is to look at peak moments in their lives, when their deepest-felt emotions, values and beliefs came to the surface and dominated their immediate present. It offers us an opportunity to see them at perhaps the most crucial moments of their lives, as they put their beliefs into action. Their behavior directly expressed their strongest-held ideals, those for which they were willing to fight and die. The Confederate battle flag is a window into the heart and mind of the Confederate soldier.

Family and Community

The Confederate soldier's relationship to his family and his community played the most significant role in shaping his feelings about the flag. Raising units by locality meant that when a man marched off to war, and experienced combat, he was often surrounded by members of his family and community: brothers, sons and fathers, cousins, friends and neighbors; men he had likely known all his life. Company-level officers were elected by the men, so the leaders might be community leaders: a local sheriff, politician or landowner. Those who acted courageously in battle might become heroes at home; deserters would be shunned. When these companies joined regiments, they were with men from the same state. In the summer of 1863 most brigades in the Army of Northern Virginia were made up of regiments from the same state, and even an entire division, such as Pickett's Virginians, were men from the same state.[24]

Local organization and recruitment of the army was not an accident. It was an extension of the values and ideals of the small communities and rural areas throughout the South. Indeed, American society throughout the second half of the eighteenth and first half of the nineteenth century worked essentially at this level. People thought of themselves as part of the community and identified themselves with it. Life functioned this way; work was done, politics practiced, and decisions made on the community level, and the army reflected this.

The extension of the community into the army through locally oriented units fused family loyalty and community pride with state and national causes. The home community ended up feeling that it had a stake in the army and in its success. Indeed, the families and local communities never completely gave up control of their men, and when the nature of the army evolved later in the war and became less-community oriented, the experience of the rank and file changed.

The contrast with modern armies could not be more striking. Modern armies are peopled with draftees and volunteers with no local orientation or connection and controlled by a distant, remote centralized authority. They do the bidding of politicians and unelected bureaucrats, and their work usually occurs in far-off places with little or no connection to home. Such an experience would have been totally foreign to the Civil War soldier. The individual isolation would be as unfamiliar to him as companies of friends, neighbors and family members were familiar. Modern armies instill discipline, at least in part, by breaking down an individual's reliance upon others outside the group, then making him reliant upon his fellow soldiers. Civil War armies did not need to do this precisely because the men were already bonded to others in their company and regiment. Life in the Army of Northern Virginia in 1863 was not a departure from a previous life, but an extension of it.

All this had a profound effect on the army's character and the experiences of the soldiers. It served to solidify and reinforce their values, and to make the experiences of army life more intense than they might otherwise have been. Men who fought alongside the men of their family and community took pride in their units, and fought all the harder. This peer pressure reinforced their sense of *elan* and gallantry. It heightened their "will to combat," helped them overcome their fear, and made it easier for the flag to become their symbol. It made their experiences more personal, immediate and exciting.

The women of the community played a key role in the collective *elan*. As one diehard female secessionist remembered, "there were a great many men in the Southern homes that were disposed to be more conservative and to regret the threatened disruption of the Union, but the ladies were all enthusiastically in favor of secession . . . and if the Southern men had not been willing to go I reckon they would have been made to go by the women."[25] One soldier commented on the irresistible pressure from the women. "They vowed they would themselves march out and meet the Yankee scoundrels," he said. "In a land where women are worshipped(sic) by the men, such language made them war-mad."[26]

The unity of soldier, family and community was frequently underscored and strengthened by the experience, widespread during the early part of the war, of having a mother, sweetheart, wife or sister, sew a flag, often from a wedding dress. The flag was presented to the men of the town when they mustered to go to war, along with urgings of pride and protection. Indeed, during the first part of the war nearly all flags were made by local sewing circles, as were the first battle flags in late 1861. The presentation of a flag to the Desoto Rifles in New Orleans typified the ceremonies that occurred all across the South. The flag had been made by a ladies' sewing circle and was presented by Miss Idelea Collens. She said to the men of her town:

> Receive then from your mothers and sisters, from those whose affections greet you, these colors woven by our feeble but reliant hands; and when this bright flag shall float before you on the battlefield, let it not only inspire you with the brave and patriotic ambition of a soldier aspiring to his own and his country's honor and glory, but also may it be a sign that cherished ones appeal to you to save them from a fanatical and heartless foe.

The color sergeant took the flag and replied in kind:

> May the god of battles look down upon us as we register a soldier's vow that no stain shall ever be found upon thy sacred folds, save the blood of those who attack thee or those who fall in thy defense. Comrades, you have heard the pledge, may it ever guide and guard you on the tented field. In the smoke, glare, and din of battle, midst carnage and death, there let its bright folds inspire you with new strength, nerve your arms and steel your hearts to deeds of strength and valor.[27]

When the Mississippi Rifles, later to become a company of the 18th Mississippi, gathered to accept their flag (probably a First National) from a local ladies' group, the sentiments were similar:

> Ladies of Clinton and vicinity:
>   With high beating hearts and breasts full of emotion, we receive from your hands this handsome flag; proud emblem of our young Republic: which, though but a few months since, was first unfurled to the breeze, now has millions of freemen nobly rallying

around it, and that too with no idle fancy but with a devotion unconquerable, a call unearthly and a love undying.

We prize this flag, ladies, not so much for its intrinsic worth, but for the sake of those who gave it, and while it floats o'er us, fanned by the passing breeze, its every fold shall tell, in terms more eloquent than tongues can speak, of the fair form that bent over it and the bright eyes that followed the fingers as they plied the very stitch; and its every thread shall be a tongue to chant the praise of woman's virtue and woman's worth. . . .

Again, ladies, allow me to acknowledge the honor you have done us and assure you that whether in peace or war your gift shall ever be cherished and guarded, that it never shall trail in the dust disgraced, dishonored. I give you the sacred pledge of our company. Hear it ye gallant few and redeem the pledge as becomes a Mississippian. Today shall long be remembered to those of us whose fate it may be to die a soldier's death, it will recall your kindness and sympathy, and we will include you in the prayer for the loved ones we leave behind and bless you in that trying hour. If our country be invaded and your homes endangered, with your gift streaming o'er us and the fond memories and as-sociations of this day inspiring our hearts and nerving our arms, we'll bare our bosoms for the glorious strife and at our country's call we'll proudly bear this banner to the battlefield. And in that dark and trying hour, in the breaking forth of power, in the rush of steeds and men, may God's right hand protect it then. . . .[28]

A flag presentation in New Orleans in 1861 underscored the links between the flag, Southern communities and religion. On May 26 a flag was given to the Washington Artillery just before they left for Vir-ginia. Half a century later a veteran recalled the ceremony, and began his essay by stating, "My family and friends have often asked me to jot down some of the many experiences of mine while a soldier in the ranks fighting under what we thought the most beautiful banner in the world, the Stars and Bars of the Confederacy." This Gettysburg veteran re-membered the event clearly and in detail:

It would be almost impossible to describe the high pitch of enthusiasm of the citizens of New Orleans at that time. May 26th, a Sabbath morning, our four companies in their gay uniforms, bearing aloft the battalion's beautiful silken flag, a present from the ladies of the city, marched to Lafayette Square, where we were mustered in to the Confederate service. . . The sight was one to be long remembered, for the square was crowded with the relatives and friends of the young men of the command. After the muster the battalion marched to Christ Church . . . The colors of the battalion were placed against the chancel rail and Dr. Leacock, rector of the sacred edifice, delivered his sermon, which mostly contained allusions to the trials and tribulations which we might encounter in the army.

He enjoined all to remember that they were educated to be gentlemen and represented the chivalry of the South and it behooved them to bring back their characters as soldiers and gentlemen unblemished. After the discourse the colors were held aloft before the altar and the benediction pronounced.[29]

On July 4, 1861, nearly the entire population of the community of Little Fork, in Culpepper County, Virginia, turned out to see their local boys, the Little Fork Rangers, who would become Company D, 4th Virginia Cavalry, receive a flag hand-stitched together by 20-year-old Miss Emma Lutham. Their captain drew them up in front of the town and asked them, loud enough for the residents to hear, "Boys, will you follow this banner into the face of the enemy, defending it with the last drop of your blood?" "Yes, yes," they responded. As they jauntily cantered out of town, flag flying in the breeze, the band played "The Bonnie Blue Flag."[30]

Finally, the man who had carried the colors of the 21st North Carolina during its assault on east Cemetery Hill on July 2nd, remembered how the 21st got its flag early in the war. In early June, 1861, the regiment had been drawn up into line near Danville, North Carolina,

with its silken colors (given by the Ladies) waving over them, presenting as fine a body of men as one ever beheld—all young and enthusiastic. Alas! how many of those noble forms now lie mouldering in the dust— on almost every battlefield from Gettysburg, Pa., to New Bern, N.C.?[31]

Confederate women did more than encourage their men to go to war and make flags for them to carry and remember them by. Throughout the war, Southern women formed a primary communications link between the soldier and the community from which he had come, and with which he fought. They were in the men's hearts and minds at all times, and especially before and during battle. This is attested to in letter after letter the men wrote home, and that were written to them. "Martha I waunt you to write often and send me all the nuse for I am one of the Glades[t] fellows you ever seen when I git a letter from you you dont no how much good it dus me to here from you," one Alabaman wrote to his wife.[32]   In addition to the strong emotional bonds that were maintained throughout the war, Confederate women sent the men food and clothes. They played an enormously important role in keeping the army supplied; indeed, they fulfilled many of the functions tha modern armies automatically carry out with large and intricate quartermaster corps.[33]

The Civil War is often referred to as "the brothers' war" because of the popular image of families split over the war and brothers fighting against their own kin. The opposite experience was far more common. While members of the same families did occasionally take opposite sides, it might fairly be called a "brothers' war" for another reason altogether. Perhaps it should even be called a family's war or a community's war. While little research has been done on the subject, it is obvious that very large segments of the male members of local communities participated in the military and that an equally large segment of females supported them. In North Carolina, for example, 125,000 of the 149,000 men eligible for service were in the military during the war. Six percent of the state's entire population and 25% of its adult white male population died during their enlistment.[34]

Moreover, it was not unusual for brothers to sign up together, as well as with cousins, uncles, and even fathers and sons. One recent study of North Carolina concludes that the average family in the state was larger than today and the percentage of soldiers who had at least one brother in the military was high. The author set out to collect and publish the photographs of the men from North Carolina, and realized that there were a significant number of photographs of brothers and other male family members among the collection. He noted that of the 64 brothers he found photographs of, 27 (44%) died in the war. Of the 24 families represented, 14 (58%) lost at least one man.[35] At Gettysburg one private in the 17th Mississippi returned to camp after the battle on the second day to find that in his regiment three sets of brothers, named Ousler, Blackburn and Kandade, had been mortally wounded.[36] Private Albert Batchelor, 2nd Louisiana, wrote home a letter that was probably similar to those written by many other soldiers at Gettysburg. He had been wounded in two places, and wanted to tell his parents that he would recover. In doing so he mentioned that one brother, wounded at Chancellorsville, was probably on his way home. Another, "brother Charley was in the fight and came out safe; he and the Capt. of the next company to ours bore me two or three hundred yds. to the rear, then. . . went back to their commands."[37] The enlistment rolls of Company F, 12th North Carolina, had originally carried the names of five members of the Allen family. Turner, Daniel and Peter were brothers, Hugh and Austin, cousins. Turner was killed at Malvern Hill, Hugh at Chancellorsville. At Gettysburg, Daniel was killed and Austin seriously wounded. Peter would suffer a wound at Petersburg from which he would never recover.[38]

And of course the company and regiment the men served with reflected the strong community ties in that they represented a cross-section of that community. As Bell Wiley pointed out in his study of *The Life of Johnny Reb*, the company they served with included every aspect of the home area. Men from every walk of life, from planters to mechanics, farmers, lawyers, blacksmiths, students, laborers, clerks, doctors, teachers, shoemakers, millers, engineers, butchers, apothecaries, cooks, dancing masters, dentists, sheriffs, stage drivers, and every conceivable occupation were represented, including overseers and slaves.

The men could not forget their ties to home because in a real sense their homes had come with them. Certainly the historian of Hood's Texas Brigade spoke for the vast majority of Confederate soldiers when he wrote that when their flag was unfurled and they saw it "waving in the Virginia breeze it was a sweet reminder of home, a thousand miles away."[39]

Marching up from the South with the army, along the dusty roads of Maryland and Pennsylvania, came men who represented the strong bonds to the home community: thousands of black Southerners. They were integral components of the regiments. Some drove wagons loaded with food and clothing, others carried cooking gear, rode on artillery caissons and on mules and drove cattle. A few carried guns, as they had in the Continental Army during the Revolution.

They were primarily men who had been house servants and had worked closely with whites. They had often grown up with whites and in the daily routine of life they normally had been trusted with the most difficult tasks on the farm or plantation. Many had learned critical skills before the war and become important factors in the lives of white Southerners as cooks, harness makers, carpenters, ironworkers, blacksmiths, wheelwrights, and butlers. A large percentage had been "body servants," assigned to take personal care of one individual or a small group of whites. Almost none had been field hands, picking cotton and tobacco in large gangs on large plantations.

Some of the black Southerners were not slaves at all, but instead were free men of color who had been hired or had volunteered.[40] All were now key elements in the army. These black Southerners were the living, breathing embodiment of the homes and communities the men had left behind and for whom they had come to fight.[41]

Among the 10 million white and black Southerners could be found every sort of human relationship that can be imagined, from hatred to love. The specific attitudes of white Confederate soldiers toward black

Southerners is elusive: no historian has studied that topic or their relationships. The soldiers in the Army of Northern Virginia, and especially those with whom we are most concerned, the men at the rank of captain and below, were by and large not slaveholders.[42] Indeed, in 1860 the typical white Southerner was not a slaveowner. Overall, about 20 to 25 per cent of white Southerners owned one or more slaves. Only 1,800 white families owned 100 or more; out of six million whites just 45,000 families, or less than one percent, owned over one-half of the slaves. Slaveholding was less widespread in Virginia and North Carolina, the two states that furnished the bulk of the men in the Army of Northern Virginia, than it was in the deep South states of Georgia, Alabama and Mississippi.[43]

All in all, only a small fraction of the enlisted men and company-level officers in the Army of Northern Virginia probably had a direct, vested interest in the perpetuation of slavery. Yet that institution so dominated daily life that it affected all aspects of Southern existence.

In recent years historians have learned much about race relations in the Old South. Led by Marxist economic historian Eugene Genovese, they have written about the paternalistic aspects of slaveholders' attitudes toward their chattel. In short, it was not good business to mistreat slaves, and thus the harsher aspects of bondage were often ameliorated by the economic self-interest of the slaveowners.[44] The paternalism engendered by the economic reality of slave owning might lead the Confederate soldier to believe that black Southerners were better off as slaves in the South than as wage earners in the North, a common argument in antebellum debates.[45] He might have any one of a number of other perspectives: we simply have very little evidence to go on.

Yet when Confederate soldiers wrote home about black Southerners in their ranks, they usually talked about them in a matter-of-fact, straight forward way. They were simply a common, obvious, important and integral part of life, at home and in the army. The black Southerners with the army were either owned by the soldiers' parents, relatives or friends, or were hired from wealthy men, or were hired freemen. In general, the white Southern soldier regarded the black Southerner as his property, as part of his community, as part of his family. To the soldier he was an inferior creature, and a living symbol of what could happen to him should the North win the war. On an individual level he might perceive black Southerners as part of his future, as his means of economic success and social ascent, or in many other ways.

Despite slavery and its supporters' rhetoric, and perhaps also because of the paternalism of the slaveowners, some white and black Southerners became life long friends. Many examples of this could be cited, but since this is slightly off the main topic, one example will suffice. Captain S. A. Ashe, a staff officer in Pettigrew's brigade, remarked that his gallant mare had been wounded in Pickett's Charge. Long after the war he made the simple but telling assertion that "her groom," who was with him all during the war, and who "has been my friend and servant for forty years" could verify that she was shot three times. In a footnote he added that her groom was "James R. Norwood, a colored man."[46]

The story of six men from Enfield, North Carolina, serves as an illustration of one community's ties to the army. The Enfield Blues, a militia company first organized in response to John Brown's raid in 1859, eventually became Company D, 43rd North Carolina. When the Enfield Blues marched off to war in 1861, they carried a First National flag, hand stitched by a "noted belle" of the community. Along with much of the Enfield community went two sets of brothers, a cousin and a servant. John Simmons Whitaker, a 31 year-old lawyer and his brother, 29 year-old lawyer Cary Whitaker, signed up. Their friends, "Smiling" Billy Beavens, 21, a store clerk, and his brother Johnny Beavens, an 18-year-old student, were accompanied by their cousin, 18 year-old George Wills. They brought with them Washington Wills, called "Wash," a slave owned by George Wills' father. Billy Beavens and George Wills would be killed in 1864, but all six men were at Gettysburg. Capt. Cary Whitaker and Sergeant George Wills drew commendations from their superiors for their bravery.

During the war the men were constantly in touch with the folks back home, and returned there at every opportunity. News of the lives of the local men in the army was a major part of their letters, and in return they were kept up with all the events at home. They repeatedly asked for food and clothes, and frequently received precious goods sent by mothers, sisters and other women back home. "Wash" played a major role in this network, frequently carrying home valuables and letters, returning with goods and news. When he traveled, he went alone, through dangerous territory and over long distances. On these trips he carried all sorts of valuables, including large amounts of cash. The strength of the trust and respect the whites showed in him was implicit. The men were friends and relatives to numerous men in the 43rd and its sister regiment also raised in their area, the 32nd North Carolina. They knew virtually every man in their company, and all six survived the attack of Brigadier General Junius Daniel's brigade on July 1st.[47] When the Confederate battle flag unfurled over their regiment, it represented all of them, their social and economic relationships, and the society, culture and community to which they belonged.

The Revolution Revisited

Capt. George Hillyer, an officer in a Georgia regiment, recalled an incident that occurred during the cannonade preceding Pickett's Charge. He was lying on the ground with his men.

A shot, evidently fired at the Troup artillery, from the enemy's batteries beyond the historic peach orchard, passed across the left flank of my company. One of my men, the genial and bright young Jackson B. Giles, had been detailed as courier for Gen. Tige Anderson. He was a boy who had been at school with me here in Monroe from the time he learned his ABC's. Always cheerful, bright and willing, he was a favorite with us all. He had at this moment ridden down to our line, and just as he passed around our left flank, dismounted from his horse with the apparent intention of lying down among us. Just then the shell I have mentioned tore away his left leg above the knee and dashed him ten or fifteen feet down the hill. I got up and ran to him and instantly saw, by the pallor of his face and the physical shock he had suffered, being a rather delicate youth anyway, that he would not survive the injury. So I placed him in as easy a position as possible and told him that as soon as the litter corps came to tell them I said carry him back to a hospital, and added, "Jack, you know we are going to make a charge in a few minutes, but if I ever get back to see your father and mother what message do you want sent them?" A distinct animation came into his face as he looked straight at me and said, "Tell them I died for my country."[48]

In 1863, Southerners were no less patriotic than Northerners. As Bruce Catton said of their counterparts, the Confederate soldier "put a special meaning on such a word as 'patriotism'; it was not something you talked about very much, just a living force that you instinctively responded to."[49] A Texan writing to his female correspondent near the end of the war put Southern patriotism in its context. He described the Army of Northern Virginia in the winter of 1865 as "ragged, hatless, shoeless, starving and freezing day and night, and sleeping in huts and dug-outs. . . still undauntedly and resolutely facing a well-fed, well-equipped Federal army" outnumbering them three to one. "If it is patriotism that holds the Yankees in the field," he asked his reader, "how much more noble, self-sacrificing, and enduring must be the conviction which keeps the Confederates there?"[50]

Understanding the significance of the flag to the Southern soldier must include the historical context of the movement for Southern independence. The South played a vital role in the development of the American Union and many Southerners living in 1863 had lived through crucial portions of it. American history formed a much more central

20

Alfred Waud, Prisoners of War After Gettysburg
(Courtesy of the Library of Congress)

part of the public consciousness, rituals, celebrations, social events, and school curriculum for them than it does for us today. People who had not actually lived through those years still knew a good deal about them, and of course Southern schools, writers and public events emphasized the Southern role in the Revolution and in early national development.

Confederates remembered that the Revolution had been led by

Southerners, from Patrick Henry's "give me liberty or give me death" speech to the victories fought and won under the Commander-in-Chief, Virginian George Washington. Southerners had not only risked their lives in battle from Georgia to Vermont, they also suffered through Valley Forge and other terrible winters, and had been present when Lord Cornwallis surrendered on Virginia soil at Yorktown.

The colonial South had in fact been considerably more English in culture and custom than the Northern and Middle Colonies. A hierarchical deference among classes characterized the South's social structure and relationships. Its Episcopalian religion stood only one step removed from the Anglican Church; its language and accents were significantly more English than its neighbors to the North.[51] Thus the break from England was probably more difficult and emotionally scarring for the South than for the North.

And of course, Southerners from Washington, Jefferson and Madison to Andrew Jackson, Zachary Taylor (whose son Richard became an important Confederate general), and John Tyler (whose grandson Robert Tyler Jones carried the colors of the 53rd Virginia in Pickett's Charge) played key roles in the development of the new nation. To Americans of the early 1860s, especially Southerners, the patriotic deeds and events of American history had a distinctly Southern character.

When the Southern states finally broke their ties with the old Union and seceded, it was an emotional act in at least two ways. They rebelled against a Union they had been instrumental in creating and sustaining for over eight decades, severing ties that were very, very strong. Yet they also once again sought their right of self-government as they understood it, and a new national identity.[52]

During the secession crisis and the war, Southerners adopted the language of the Revolution to explain their situation, often citing the colonial secession from England as a model for their own. Their letters and diaries are full of talk of Liberty, and of a distant, tyrannical government whose laws were unfair and oppressive. One Virginia officer invoked his state's motto, *Sic Semper Tyrannis,* to justify secession, and filled his letters with comparisons of the North's "war of subjugation against the South" to "England's war upon the colonies." He spoke confidently of the South's ability to win this "second War for American Independence" because "Tyranny cannot prosper in the nineteenth century" over "a people fighting for their liberties."[53] An enlisted man in a Texas cavalry outfit believed that just as the original patriots had rebelled against King George to establish "*Liberty* and freedom in this western world . . . so we dissolved our alliance with this oppressive foe and are now enlisted in 'The Holy Cause of Liberty and Independence' again."[54] An Alabama infantryman captured at Gettysburg wrote home to his father that the South would eventually win the war because it fought for "the same principles which fired the hearts of our ancestors in the revolutionary struggle."[55] A Virginian summed up this feeling when he wrote that "the Confederate soldier was a mono-maniac for four years. His mania was, the independence of the Confederate States of America, secured by force of arms."[56] A North Carolinian said he was "willing to give up my life in defence of my Home and Kindred. I had rather be dead than see the Yanks rule this country." He got his wish: he was killed at Gettysburg.[57]

The return of a Confederate battle flag after the war prompted Marylander Randolph McKim, an aide to Brig. Gen. George Steuart during the battle, to recall the reasons he felt the men from his state fought for the Confederacy:

> They were compelled to choose between the love of the Union and the love of Liberty. Are they to blame because they preferred Liberty without Union to Union without Liberty? Remember that was the way the issue presented itself to their minds. You may say they were mistaken in their judgment, but you cannot impeach their patriotism. Believing as they did that the war was a war of subjugation, and that it meant, if successful, the destruction of their liberties, I submit that the issue in their minds was clearly drawn as I have stated it, —*Union without Liberty,* or *Liberty without Union.*[58]

That the Southern independence movement was the intellectual descendant of the American Revolution was so widely believed across the South that it was simply assumed. On the flyleaf of his daily journal a Kentucky cavalryman wrote: "To whoever it may concern: Inclosed will be found short records of my life as a soldier, some reflections on the persons & things I have seen, & I hope modest notices of my own unworthy actions—in this great war for Independence."[59] An Alabaman expressed the feelings of many Southerners on July 4, 1862, when he wrote in his diary:

> This is the anniversary o the independence of the U.S. Altho not a citizen of the U.S. now, yet I feel that we of the South are more entitled to celebrate and hold sacred the day than the people of the North. The declaration was the product of the Southern mind, and it was for the principles contained in that instrument that induced me to take [up] arms.[60]

In his first message to Congress after the fall of Ft. Sumter, President Jefferson Davis seemed to sum this up, perhaps better than anyone else. The South was fighting for the same "sacred right of self-government" for which the forefathers had struggled. The Confederacy sought "no conquest, no aggrandizement, no concession of any kind from the States with which we were lately confederated; all we ask is to be let alone."[61]

As will be pointed out in chapter two, the First National flag was directly and consciously derived from the "stars and stripes" of 1776. The Confederate battle flag, in all its variations, became a symbol of rebellion against tyranny—a form of recapitulation of the revolutionary experience—and also a proud symbol of their identity as a new nation, just as the "Stars and Stripes" had been in 1776.

States' Rights and Individualism

As the 13th Virginia, including one company of local boys, marched into Culpepper in 1862, the residents turned out to watch. One resident noticed that "above them the flag chosen by the Confederacy slowly furled and unfurled its stars and bars as the wind rose and fell. . ." She went on to remark that to her the flag symbolized all that the war was about: "As I beheld it my heart beat high, for it seemed a promise of glory and greatness, and of triumph over those who would deprive us of our right to do as we pleased with our own."[62]

Closely tied to, indeed derived from, the revolutionary tradition, the Southern belief in the doctrine of state's rights provided a defining framework within which Southerners analyzed, and ultimately understood, the clash with the Federal government. As far back as the seventeenth century, Americans had developed political structures and an ideology stressing decentralization of political power. Between 1763 and 1775 Americans had grown so distrustful of centralized government in the form of the King and his Court that they resorted to armed rebellion. The Articles of Confederation summarized and embodied this distrust and reliance upon decentralized political power. Republican ideology, growing out of the Revolutionary experience, and forming the bases of politics from 1789 to 1861, stressed the rights of the states and limitations of the central government.[63]

The Constitutional Convention of 1787 had split over this question, and only a series of major compromises, hammered out with great difficulty, had allowed the "founders" to create the national power. We live with this today in the duality of the Senate and House of Representatives. It is one of a series of "checks and balances" in the Constitution that represented the delegates' mistrust of a central power. In order to shackle it, to prevent it from becoming as tyrannical as the King and his minions had become in England, the U.S. would make sure that mountains would have to move before a faction could control enough of the central government to make it a threat to the states.

Between the Revolution and Civil War many divisive issues arose, differing in specifics but essentially centered on the conflict between centralized power and state prerogatives. The question of the relationship between state and national government was the major dividing issue during the Federalist period(1789-1815). The Democratic Party gradually came to represent those who favored state's rights and decentralization, and eventually became the dominant party in the South, while the Federalist and Whig parties, stronger in the North, generally spoke for increasing use of the Federal government in such things as internal improvements and tariffs. Yet always there seemed to be fundamental disagreements over the division of power between the states and central government, and this question provided the wellspring for numerous political battles, some of which included threats of secession. In the Northeast, New England state representatives, meeting in the Hartford Convention of 1814, contemplated leaving the Union over the issue of state versus the central government control of trade and foreign relations. In the Nullification Crisis of 1832, John C. Calhoun led a movement, eventually defeated by Andrew Jackson, in which South Carolina threatened simply to disregard Federal laws that met with its disapproval. During the secession crisis of 1860-61, even New York City contemplated secession from the Union.

The tension between the central authority and the states had been present in the country since the earliest days, and formed the core of antebellum political debate. As the various issues that divided the sections in the years before 1860 gained prominence, Southerners increasingly perceived themselves as menaced by the Federal establishment. As far back as it goes, and as deep down into its roots as one can perceive, Southern society and political ideals stressed reliance on the individual, and the local government as opposed to the centralized state.

Indeed, the belief in decentralized political power was so strong that even during the Civil War, Southern politicians such as Zebulon Vance in North Carolina and Joe Brown in Georgia continually defied the Confederate government by refusing to send troops and military goods from their states to the war effort in Richmond. An entire school of Civil War historians, led by Frank Owsley, has interpreted the Southern loss of the war as a result of the power of the states' rights theory in undermining Confederate nationalism.[64]

Moreover, states' rights had a strong resonance with Southerners on a deeper, more personal level. Much of the South was still relatively unsettled territory, where social institutions were weak and self-reliance was mandatory. This was true for small farmers, homesteaders, even for those who may have owned a slave or two to help out with the work. Not only did they not look to the state or Federal government for assistance, but went forward, got the land and did the work themselves, or so they believed.

"Subjugation" became a code word that could be used to mean the Federal coercion of the states, or the state coercion of the individual, and that word is commonly found in soldier's letters, diaries, etc.[65] Thus a Tennessean wrote in early 1863 that "as long as a yankee can stand the war for my subjugation, I can stand it for my honor and liberty." A North Carolinian justified the growing lists of casualties by saying that it was a "part of the heavy price we must pay for deliverance from servile subjugation and ruin." A Georgian told his wife that "I do not regret the hardships if I can gain my Independance(sic). I consider it a duty that I owe to my children to battle for their liberty as well as my own, for where is the Nation who has ever submitted to the yoke of despotism that have ever gained their liberty[?]"[66] Another Georgian wrote that "i am fiten for a go[o]d cos I fite for my rits and my freedom and for my poor brother and sisters and espe[cial]ly for my s[w]eethart."[67] Another soldier explicitly stated that if he were killed it would be while "fighting gloriously for the underlying principles of Constitutional liberty and self government."[68] A member of the 18th Virginia wrote to his sister from Chambersburg on July 1st that "if the good Lord sees fit to spare my life, I intend to fight the despicable Yankee until the last one [is] killed if they will not keep off our soil. I could rather fight them a hundred years than to be Subjugated by Such a worthless race."[69]

The Southern Code: Honor and Courage

Today we have little understanding of the sense of identity that Southern men held so steadfastly during of the Civil War years. We used to hear a good deal about "Southern chivalry," but we no longer understand what it meant to them. It was in fact much more than simply having good or exaggerated social manners, or being overly sensitive to perceived slights on their manhood, as we now generally view it. The white Southern male of the 1860s had a set of values that are out of fashion and little comprehended today, and indeed values that many segments of American society have publicly disparaged for the last few decades.

The ideals they lived by were not the fantasies of aristocrats and their pretenders, or of those wishing to be Knights of the Round Table. Instead they were the beliefs that gave structure and meaning to the lives of ordinary people, and they were an essential part of the rural, hardworking and individualistically oriented society in which they lived. The ideals the Southern soldier espoused were shaped by a world long gone, one that we can only understand in the abstract, and even then at a distance. Yet the social, economic and legal institutions of the Old South produced and defined the soldier's perception of all aspects of his world, from his own life, the society in which he lived, and the war in which he fought. Today we often see the ideals that made up his code of behavior as irrelevant, certainly unsophisticated and probably naive; something to be stated at a 4th of July speech or in a political campaign, then quickly forgotten amid the reality of modern life.

Regardless of our perception, Southern society instilled in the Confederate soldier a code of behavior that was ascribed to generally across the South, and constituted a powerful element in Southern culture.[70] When one reads the letters, diaries, and other writings of the typical Southern soldier, one cannot help but be struck by his sense that he felt he should, above all else, protect his personal honor, his home, family and state, and that he must have the courage to do so in battle and with his life on the line. It was an essential and deeply rooted part of his understanding of who he was and what his place and role in the world should be.

The ideals of honor and courage provided a guideline for behavior, a set of ethical rules that were ratified by the consensus of the community in which he had been raised. Family integrity, a clearly understood hierarchical social structure of leaders and subordinates, and ascriptive features of individuals and groups guided his evaluation of his own behavior and that of his peers. The Old South was not a monolithic culture; there were striking divisions among whites along lines of class and geography. Yet the consensus in favor of this code held the disparate mass together. Poverty-stricken hillfolk and wealthy urban merchants lived vastly different lives, but generally agreed on these basic values. As one recent historian has said:

> above all, white Southerners adhered to a moral code that may be summarized as the rule of honor. Today we would not define as an ethical scheme a code of morality that could legitimate injustice—racial or class. Yet it was so defined in the Old South. . . . In fact, Southerners saw [the code of honor] as a means of holding fast to the social order that they so deeply cherished. It was threat of honor lost, no less than slavery, that led them to secession and war.[71]

Professor Gerald Linderman, in his study of the lives of men on both sides, *Embattled Courage: The Experience of Combat in the Civil War,* has found these ideas to be central to their experience:

> The young men of the 1860s carried with them into military life a strong set of values that continued to receive reinforcement from home. In a day of simpler assumptions, when one's actions were thought to be the direct extension of one's values, they attempted to apply their values in combat, in camp, and in hospital.[72]

The attitude toward paroles of prisoners of war provides an insight into how the sense of honor shaped the thinking of Confederates. According to the terms commonly offered in 1863, a captured soldier

was given a document stating that he was a prisoner of war being paroled. He was to return to his home and not go back to military service
until he was exchanged. If he was not exchanged, he was required to
make his own way to a designated place in the Confederacy or
Union(depending on which side he was on) and turn himself in. Capt.
Henry Kyd Douglas, a Confederate staff officer, was captured at Gettysburg and then paroled. Soon thereafter he wrote to Washington to
request that he be relieved of his obligation because a year earlier he
had discharged a Federal Major from his parole. In the letter Douglas
included a letter of testimony from the Federal officer.[73]

James F. Crocker grew up in Virginia, attended Gettysburg College and became the valedictorian of the Class of 1850. He was practicing law in Virginia when the war broke out. He joined the 9th Virginia in Armistead's brigade and served as its adjutant during the battle.
Wounded and captured during Pickett's Charge, Crocker was sent to
the 12th Corps hospital. While recuperating he was given a pass to go
into town and purchase some new clothes, with the sole provision that
he present the pass at the Provost office and have it countersigned. "I
went alone, unattended," Crocker later remembered. "The fields and
woods were open to me. They somehow knew—I know not how—that
I could be trusted; that my honor was more to me than my life." Crocker
walked into town, had the pass authorized, and went about his business, without trying to escape.[74]

When Capt. Wayland Dunaway of the 47th Virginia was captured at Falling Waters along with most of his regiment, he was among
a small number of officers invited to dinner by their captors. They
enjoyed the meal in captivity and talked with their captors, who were
"as friendly as men who had been campanions (sic) from childhood."
Dinner over, the Confederates were asked to pledge their good behavior, and upon doing so were allowed to return to their tents without a
guard, in open country. "It was nearly midnight when the Col. told us
that if we would promise to go back and deliver ourselves up, he would
not call a guard to escort us," Dunaway recalled, "and we gave him our
word, and bade him goodnight." What happened next reveals much
about the belief system held by these men and the acknowledgment of
it by their erstwhile enemies:

> There we were in the darkness, our limbs unfettered,
> our hearts longing for freedom, no Yankee eye upon us;
> and it is not strange that there flitted across our minds
> the temptation to steal away and strike out for Virginia;
> but though our bodies were for the moment free, our
> souls were bound by something stronger than manacles
> of steel,—our word of honor. We groped our way back,
> entered the circle of soldiers who were guarding our
> fellow-prisoners, and went to sleep on the ground, while

our late entertainers reposed upon comfortable cots.[75]

In 1863 Southern soldiers expected these values to be held by their enemy as well as themselves. When Gen. Pickett's division was chosen to guard the prisoners on the return to Virginia, he instructed his men to parole the captured officers. They were to return to Federal camps with a document "binding them to render themselves prisoners of war at Richmond if they were not duly recognized [as exchanged] by their government."[76] Having given them a small piece of paper to sign and carry with them, he let them go. He did not think it a significant risk to ask men who were unexchanged and living in the North to make their way to the Confederate capital and turn themselves in if they were not exchanged.

The origins and depth of the roots of these values were revealed by a comment made by a Southern woman at the end of the war. The diarist Mary Chesnut summed up the attitude toward personal honor and courage so widespread throughout the Old South: "Are you like Aunt Mary? Would you be happier if all the men in the family were killed?" she was asked. "To our amazement quiet Miss C took up the cudgels—nobly. 'Yes, if their life disgraced them. There are worse things than death.'"[77]

The Confederate soldier (like his Federal counterpart) believed that it was essential to have the courage to fight effectively in battle. According to Linderman, the soldiers understood courage to mean "heroic action taken without fear," and it was the central focus of a constellation of values including manliness, duty and several others.[78] Pvt. Carlton McCarthy noted that the soldier was expected to display his courage under fire. "In a thousand ways he is tried . . . every quality is put to the test. If he shows the least cowardice he is undone," he remarked. "His courage must never fail. He must be manly and independent."[79] Soldiers commonly felt that combat was the test of their manhood. Others might speak about the connection between courage and godliness, or duty. All meant the same thing.[80]

Failure to live up to these ideals in combat was among the Confederate soldier's most dreaded experiences. One must remember that he was most likely fighting alongside his family, neighbors and members of his community, and this put a good deal of social pressure on him. Cowardice, said one, "is the one sin which may not be pardoned either in this world or the next."[81]

Evangelical Protestantism

Nineteenth century Americans were a religious people, in all respects Christian and predominantly Protestant. The rural South, more English than the Northern urban landscape, was probably even more thoroughly Protestant than the North, or even the Northwest, with its

German-Catholic populations. And during the war, an evangelical revival spread throughout the Southern armies.

Evangelical Protestantism formed an essential element in the life of the Confederate soldier and provided the framework for understanding much of the world in which he lived, and much of what occurred on the field of battle. His religion taught him to believe in God in a direct, personal way. The Almighty provided order in an otherwise chaotic universe. God was omnipotent and controlled all aspects of the soldier's daily life, and intervened whenever He desired.

Beginning after the battle of Antietam in 1862 the Southern armies experienced a significant revival of religion. Early in the war, Southerners had not believed it would cost many lives, but as the war went on, more and more blood flowed. Relatives, friends and neighbors were wounded and killed, while the number of revival meetings and subsequent conversions increased. Chaplains in Southern armies preached that the Confederate cause was righteous and divinely blessed, and that the soldier's duty was to fight for the Confederacy and for the Lord. Vigorous evangelical preaching in the days between Chancellorsville and Gettysburg resulted in widespread individual conversions.[82]

Parents and evangelical societies sent the men religious tracts to read, many of which instructed them to fight for God and the South. One of the most widely read was called "A Mother's Parting Words to Her Soldier Boy," in which a mother told of giving her son to the army. She did so willingly because he went to support a righteous cause. He must be a good soldier, she said, obedient to his superiors and courageous in battle.[83]

J. A. Strikeleather, who carried the flag of the 4th North Carolina at Gettysburg, wrote a long reminiscence after the war. In it he tried to tell his children and grandchildren what his experiences in the war were like. He recalled that religion played an important role in the soldier's lives:

> And, from Gen. [Stonewall] Jackson down through all the grades of rank to the humblest private, many were found who trusted in more than an arm of flesh when they went into battle. Many of the soldiers carried with them Bibles and Testaments, gifts of loved ones at home, and along with the gifts were prayers, that they might be read and their teachings be heeded. I am satisfied that many were brought to a proper sense of their obligations to their Maker, to their fellows, and to themselves through this instrumentality. Often did the soldiers find comfort from a perusal of God's Word. They learned the secret of being alone in the midst of company. Three times a day could [a] Christian soldier go into his closet and pray, . . . but, in the midst of his

comrades, he could open his Bible and read a chapter without embarrassment, and at the close of the reading lesson, with his book open before him, offer up his prayers and none of those present ever suspect but what he was still reading. Many no doubt had these stated occasions of prayer there as well as at home; and, the world knew nothing of it; but the privilege of those who availed themselves of it, was one of much comfort.[84]

Scholars have estimated that there were 50,000 evangelical conversions in the Army of Northern Virginia during the war, with 1,500 coming in the weeks preceding Gettysburg.[85] Private Joe Shaner of the Rockbridge Artillery reported his conversion to his mother and explained the importance of this in a letter written on the march towards Gettysburg.

I told [his sisters] Liza and Becca in my last letter that there was a meeting going on in the company and that the men ware[sic] a taking a greate[sic] interest in the meetings and that meeting has still bin[sic] agoing on and I am happy to say that the Lord has bin doing greate work for us there has bin some 20 or more that has come forward and made a public profeshion[sic] that they intended to follow Christ and I supose[sic] that you both will be glad to hear that I have not bin left out of that number. yes[sic] by the help of the Lord I intend to lead a new life[.] I fell[sic] as though I was a new man[.] some[sic] 10 or 12 of that number have joined the church[.] capt[.][sic] Graham has also expressed a desire to become a member of the Church. I hope that this good work may continue untill[sic] evry[sic] man in our company may become a Christain[sic] and oh what a happy company we wold[sic] have then[.] Just think of a company of all christains[sic] there[sic] is the majority of our company now christains[sic][.][86]

The connection between religion and combat, and its attendant experience of the death of friends and comrades, was obvious. As one Confederate soldier said in 1862:

Probably at no period of the war has the religious element in the army been more predominant than at present. In many instances, chaplains, missionaries, colporteurs, and tracts, have accomplished great benefits, but by far the most cogent influences that have operated upon and subdued the reckless spirit of the soldiery are those which are born in the heart itself upon the field of battle. There is something irresistible in the appeal which the Almighty makes when he strikes from your side, in the twinkling of an eye, your friend and comrade, and few natures are so utterly depraved as to entirely disregard the whisperings of the "still small voice" which make themselves so vividly heard at such a moment. Every man unconsciously asks himself, "Whose turn will come next?" and when, at the termination of the conflict, he finds himself exempted from the awful fiat that has brought death to his very side, and all around him, his gratitude to his Creator is alloyed, though it may be but dimly, with a holier emotion, which for the time renders him a wiser and a better man. In this respect, the recent battles have done more to make religious converts than all the homilies and exhortations ever uttered from the pulpit. A man who has stood upon the threshold of eternity, while in the din and carnage of a fight, has listened to eloquence more fiery than ever came from mortal lips.[87]

Pvt. John Moseley of the 2nd Alabama was mortally wounded and captured on July 3rd. No more traumatic event could happen to a Civil War soldier than to face certain death far from home, family, or friends. As he lay dying behind enemy lines, those emotions and ideas that were of supreme importance to him dominated his mind. In his final moments he wrote a farewell letter to his mother. In it he communicated the essence of his life at that moment: his innermost thoughts, his strongest, perhaps even heretofore subconscious beliefs. All of that was represented by the flag: courage, family, Confederate victory and God.

Battlefield, Gettysburg Penn. July Fourth, 1863

Dear Mother

I am here a prisoner of war & mortally wounded. I can live but a few hours more at farthest— I was shot fifty yards [from] the enemy's lines. They have been exceedingly kind to me.

I have no doubts as to the final results of this battle and I hope I may live long enough to hear the shouts of victory yet, before I die.

I am very weak. Do not mourn my loss. I had hoped to have been spared, but a righteous God has ordered it otherwise and I feel prepared to trust my case in his hands.

> Farewell to you all. Pray that God may receive my soul.
>
> Your unfortunate son John[88]

Another soldier, Sgt. David Hunter of the 2nd Virginia infantry, wrote a letter to his mother in the middle of the battle, and in it he revealed much about the attitudes the men held about themselves, the combat they found themselves in, and the hand of God:

> Line of battle near Gettysburg, Pa. July 2nd. /63
> We are in all probability on [the] eve of a terrible battle. The two contending armies lie close together and at any moment may commense[sic] the work of death. Great results hang upon the issue of this battle. If we are victorious peace may follow if not we may look for a long and fierce war. We trust in the wisdom of our Gens. and the goodness of our Father in Heaven who doeth all things well. He has time and again vouchsafed to give us victory and I know He wil[l] not forsake us in the hour of trial. If it is the Lord's will I am, I trust, prepared to go. He is able to save to the uttermost. I have prayed to Him and I hope and believe he will forgive all my sins. O how awful to die without this hope, but with it death is but a step from this world of trouble and sin to another bright and glorious, where all is happiness.
> I trust I may be spared to my country and my dear mother, but if not-Thy will be done O Lord I put my trust in Thee and am content.[89]

Hunter's letter reveals that evangelical Protestantism was important on another level as well. It allowed men to go into combat unafraid or with little fear of being wounded or killed. Many of the Confederates at Gettysburg went into battle convinced that God directed events, and that if his time to die had come, nothing could stop the bullet heading for him. It was God's will. But if it was not yet his time, he would live through the battle. The result was that the Southern soldier could go into battle feeling free to be as aggressive as he wanted. Another Southern soldier described the inner role of religion in combat:

> In the battle of Seven Pines, in which we lost one-third of our regiment in about twenty minutes, amidst the most terrific shower of shot and shell of this whole war, the Lord not only so far sustained me as to enable me to stand up and do my duty to my country, but to do it

without the least fear of anything man can do unto me. Nor did I, as many men seem to do, lose sight of my personal danger. My mood was so calm that my calculations were perfectly rational. I felt that the Lord's hand was with me, that his shield was over me and that whatever befell me would be by his agency or permission, and therefore it would all be well with me. It was a period of positive religious enjoyment, and yet of the most vigorous discharge of my duties as a soldier.[90]

The belief that God could protect an individual in combat if He so chose was a powerful concept, allowing him to go into a fight with less fear that he might otherwise experience. At the beginning of the march to Gettysburg, Private Alexander "Ted" Barclay of the 4th Virginia wrote to his sister: "I think before you hear from me again we will in all probability have had a battle. I fear not the result, am confidant that we through God will be victorious. Fear not for my safety, God can protect me amidst the storm of battle as well as at home and if I should fail I trust that I will go to a better world and is that not gain?"

After the battle he wrote again, and his attitudes were consistent with his previous letter. "Since last I wrote we have pulled through trying scenes," he told his sister. "Through all of which, by the mercy of God, I have been spared whilst others have been cut down. . . My dear sister how differently I feel now exposed to death and danger with God as a protector! I care not what may be the privations and dangers knowing that God can bring me through them all."[91]

Even a Northern minister who engaged in lengthy discussions with prisoners recognized the influence of religion in the Army of Northern Virginia. Describing the battle of Gettysburg he noted a source of their strength:

Every [Confederate] soldier is taught to feel that the cause in which he contends is one that God approves; that if he is faithful to God, His almighty arm will protect and his[sic] infinite strength insure success. Thus believing that God's arm of protection is thrown around him, that God's banner of love is over him, that God's eye of approval is on him, the southern[sic] soldier enters the field of battle nerved with a power of endurance and a fearlessness of death which nothing else can give. . . .[92]

Pvt. David Ballenger of the 26th Alabama lived through the battle and firmly believed that only God's grace had preserved his life. After the battle he wrote home to his mother and explained how strongly he believed in God's protection:

> I was also glad to be alive to hear from you again; for I feel every degree of assurance that no other hand than that of a God of infinite wisdom and power could have taken me safely through what I did go through without being slain. By and through his divine agency of God I am still alive and able to go about, though I feel very badly, both as to health and rest. But I hope to be thankful to God for His mercies to me, even for my last breath, and for having so signally preserved me in the midst of ten thousand dangers.[93]

Finally, colorbearer J. A. Strikeleather recalled his conversion in terms that specifically linked it to his experiences in battle and his fears of future combat. At the beginning of the spring 1864 campaign Strikeleather foresaw the long and bloody struggle that would soon begin. It seemed to him that

> the chances of escape unharmed were fewer than at any time in the past. The contemplation of that which seemed to be lying immediately before us, was, to say the least of it, a serious one. With feelings in my breast that such a contemplation might inspire, (on the first night of battle . . .) an intense desire took possession of me to *re*-commit myself then and there into the hands of my Divine Master. At nine o'clock that night, after most of my comrades had wrapped themselves in their blankets, I went off some hundred paces from camp and was literally alone with God. I kneeled behind a large tree, and tried in a spirit of trustfulness to humble myself before Him who knoweth the secrets of all hearts. The Lord most graciously looked upon me in my low estate. I scarce had time to give expression in words to the desires that were in my breast, ere I felt that in a most gracious sense that His everlasting arms were *around me*. My prayer was short, a desire to praise rather than pray filled my breast. Tears of gratitude and joy streamed down my cheeks. I did not feel that my life would or would not be spared through the coming campaign, but, I did feel, that whatever might happen, would happen for the best. With this feeling I returned to my comrades, most of whom were asleep around their campfires.

Strikeleather's conversion had transformed the scene around him and relieved his fears of combat. Death no longer mattered:

> Oh! How changed the scene, and how changed my
> feeling in one short hour. I could lie down now with a
> feeling of indescribable restfulness and trustfulness
> pervading my whole being. Never shall I forget how
> sweet was that nights[sic] rest. In the morning when I
> awoke I remembered what had passed, not as a dream,
> but as a reality, and its strengthening influences were
> with me still, nor did I a few hours later when hurried
> into battle, fail to catch inspiration from a remembrance
> of my experience, the night before. And, through the
> whole of the subsequent campaign a pleasant memory
> of that night's scene remained with me, and, its
> presence to me, was sweet and uplifting as that of a
> guardian angel.[94]

Here lies part of the secret of success of the Army of Northern Virginia in mortal combat.

Elan and Fear

In July of 1863 the Army of Northern Virginia's sense of itself as a community, pride in its accomplishments, confidence in its abilities, and conviction of its destiny were perhaps at an all-time high. The victories at Fredericksburg and Chancellorsville and the march through the lush enemy territory of ripe cherry, apple and peach orchards, large stone barns overflowing with goods and verdant fields had invigorated them. Brig. Gen. Richard Garnett thought his Virginians were in "fine condition."[95] A North Carolinian noted that "the spirit and morale of the army were superb."[96] Another officer stated that his brigade "never knew more spirit and elan among the men." Still another noticed that the army was larger than ever, its successes having brought back to it men who had been sick or wounded or who had gone home for spring planting. The "passionate ardor" of the men had reached a high point.[97]

These men were by and large combat veterans, ready to fight again; the shirkers and malingerers had been weeded out. Over half a century later the spirit they had carried into Pennsylvania still burned brightly in the memory on one South Carolinian. Thomas Littlejohn had been a 20-year-old private, fairly representative of the rank and file:

> We passed through several little hamlets, the names of
> which I can't recall now. The women showed their
> colors, and our boys would guy them unmercifully. We
> were in the best of spirits, just as though we were going

36

to see our girls. I don't believe there was ever an army of finer soldiers than General Lee led across the Potomac to Gettysburg. The morale of the men was all that could be desired. If there was one deserter from our Army, I never heard of it.[98]

In Armistead's brigade a field officer described his troops' attitude just before the assault on July 3rd and noted the role of the flag:

The *esprit de corps* could not have been better; the men were in good physical condition, self-reliant and determined. They felt the gravity of the situation, for they knew well the metal(sic) of the foe in their front; they were serious and resolute, but not disheartened. None of the usual jokes, common on the eve of battle, were indulged in, for every man felt his individual responsibility... I believe the general sentiment of the division was that they would succeed in driving the Federal line from what was their objective point . . . every man felt that it was his duty to make that fight; that he was his own commander, and they would have made the charge without an officer of any description; they only needed to be told what they were expected to do. . . . Many of them were veteran soldiers, *who had followed the little cross of stars from Big Bethel. . .* : they knew their own power, and they knew the temper of their adversary; they had often met before and they knew the meeting before them would be desperate and deadly.[99]

Adjutant James F. Crocker's heart burst with pride in the army as he lined up to make the charge on July 3rd. The Confederate battle flag helped him find the courage to go forward, and his view was probably typical of most of those with him: "As the lines cleared the woods that skirted the brow of the ridge and passed through our batteries," he noted, "with their flags proudly held aloft, waving in the air, with polished muskets and swords gleaming [it was] an inexpressibly grand and inspiring sight."[100]

Yet the battlefield of the Civil War, perhaps even above all others that American men have fought on, was a landscape of terror and fear. In World War II Dwight David Eisenhower learned that fear and elan were universal and often related: "The things that create fear in man create *elan*, create morale, make a leader confident and bold," he said. "The man that fought under Alexander was just as subject to the same kind of fears and the same kind of emotions and prejudices and sentiment that they are today."[101] A veteran of Pickett's Charge remembered the fear and those who could not overcome it: "We rise to our feet, but not all," he wrote. "There is a line of men still on the ground with their faces turned," some of whom are dead, wounded, or with sunstroke. Yet there were others, "men in whom there is not sufficient courage to enable them to rise. . . Some are actually *fainting* from the heat and dread. They have fallen to the ground overpowered by the suffocating heat and the terrors of that hour." He described his own fear and acknowledged its power, even though he made the charge:

> When you rise to your feet as we did today, I tell you the enthusiasm of ardent breasts in many cases *ain't there*, and instead of burning altars and firesides, the thought is most frequently, *oh*, if I could just come out of this charge safely how thankful *would I be!*[102]

A member of the 5th Texas recorded an incident at Gettysburg that reveals the interplay between an individual's fear of combat, his sense of honor, courage, and the peer pressure of fighting beside members of his community. The 5th Texas was part of the Texas Brigade, made famous under the command of John Bell Hood and made up largely of men from Texas. The incident took place amid the rocks in the Devil's Den/Houck's Ridge area on July 2nd:

> While behind the rock protection in the evening of the second day, word passed along the line to get ready to change the front. The order shocked me, and my feelings were indescribable; in fact, I had a bad case of cowardly horror. I felt sure if I retraced my steps of the evening before, it would be the ending of me. I could see no object in the move, only to sacrifice the extreme left[of the brigade] to save the army on retreat, as I felt we had gotten a good whipping all along the line and I was considering which was preferable— disgrace or death, for I felt as one feels when fright and disgrace at one and the same time has possession. I tried to force manhood to the front, but fright would drive it back with a shudder. I was in this state of torture for at least fifteen minutes. I was laying[sic] behind rock protection and dropped asleep with fear and disgrace to be my portion. . . .
>
> When I awoke my fears had gone and when I heard the countermanding order I had a feeling of regret, thinking what a great relief we could be to our wounded by dropping our water canteen by their sides as we went forward; and possibly through some unforeseen condition we might be able to remove them

to the rear. I think my feeling about the necessity of aid was felt as much as those who needed it, and I have often thought: What is mind, and what causes its changes? for[sic], in this instance when the order was received for the forward move, I at once was a transformed being; feeling all the pangs of horror that one could have flash over him, feeling as I once had great pride, knowing that I had done my duty under any and all conditions to the best of my ability, and now all was lost, if I did not go into the charge and be shot down to avoid disgrace; for I knew I had been as far to the front the day before as anyone I could see to my right or left, and I well knew that the enemy had the night previous to arrange or strengthen their position, if such was needed; but this was not needed, for nature had long ages since done the work . . .[103]

Most of the Confederate soldiers at Gettysburg managed, by and large, to stifle their fear, even though approximately ten per cent of those who were assigned to participate in Pickett's Charge did not do so because of their inability to control their terror.[104] The mechanisms for suppressing that fear were several: the close-knit feelings of support and loyalty that came from an organization raised on a local level containing friends and family members; the role of officers and their conspicuous displays of valor and courage, and carrying forward the flag that symbolically represented their comrades.[105]

Comrades: The Army As A Subculture

When the battle was over, the dead buried and the wounded sent to the rear, those who survived returned to camp to see who was left. They swapped war stories, made up new messes with new partners and mourned those who had not returned. Sometimes those left behind were literally their sons, fathers, brothers and cousins. For example, in the 28th Virginia Capt. Michael P. Spessard had his son Hezekiah in his company, and the boy was hit during the advance across the field on July 3rd. Another officer noticed the captain seated on the ground, his son's head in his lap, obviously severely wounded. The captain looked up and implored him to "look at my boy, Colonel." Spessard then kissed his son tenderly, laid his canteen beside him, rose to his feet with his sword in hand and resumed command of his company. It was observed that he fought with ferocious intensity and was one of those who got inside the wall.[106] Thus the social and personal bonding that took place in those severely traumatic experiences gave a special intensity of emotion to the flag, for it came to represent not only home, family, honor and courage. It became the spiritual embodiment of those comrades who had been killed or wounded, and those who still fought by his side.[107]

War changed men. They entered the army as civilians, as products of the shaping influences of home, family, church and community. But the experience of being a soldier—of army discipline designed to mold them into a cohesive, obedient, Napoleonic fighting unit; the shared danger of combat; the long boring hours of camp life—were common experiences that gave them a different perspective. They met people and experienced things that they as civilians had not even known existed.

It was not long before soldiers began to see themselves as a group apart from the mainstream of civilian life. As time passed, the men became increasingly aware that the experience of combat and endurance of the hardships of army life were entirely different from life as they had known it before the war. The people at home, for whom they continued to fight, could not comprehend the experience and stress of seeing men horribly slaughtered in battle. Men who stayed home seemed to retain their economic status, avoid their duty, and not comprehend or sympathize with the soldier's sacrifices.[108] The bonds of comradeship grew increasingly strong. Only other veterans could understand their experiences, and thus the soldiers formed life long friendships that would be the basis for veterans' organizations after the war. These relationships carried on until the last veterans passed on in the 1930s and 1940s.

This feeling of physical and mental separation from the home community intensified when the army went north into Pennsylvania. "Oh sister you folks at home can form no idea of what a soldier has to endure," wrote a young Georgian just after the battle. "I thought I knew it all, but this last campaign exceeds in hardships anything I ever experienced." He then went on to enumerate all the difficulties he had put up with, and how dramatically different they were from what the people at home experienced.[109]

In Pickett's division on the evening of July 2nd, with portents of the next day's fight in the air, Sgt. Randolph Shotwell received a letter from home, and recorded his response in his diary:

> A few minutes ago I was handed a letter from home. It had been nearly three weeks on the way. I wish I had not received it. How strange a contrast between the simple home affairs in the backwoods of North Carolina—of which the letter speaks—and the stirring, exciting situation in which it finds me. Here are thousands of weary soldiers lying on the grass, the light of countless camp fires illuminating the grove, the rumble of long trains upon the turn-pike, and the sullen "Boom!" "Boom!" "Boom!" "Boom!" of artillery in the

40

distance. There the quiet parsonage is calmly bathed
in twilight, with only the sound of tinkling cowbells, or
the notes of music within hearing. Little did Father
imagine the circumstances under which his letter would
be read; though he bids me do my duty, and trust in
Providence! The one I am doing, the other is rather
more difficult.[110]

Some soldiers came to feel they had more in common with the
men against whom they fought than the men and women at home.
Veteran soldiers could even express admiration for the courage of their
enemies, as did the Confederates who saw the Federals marching up
Marye's Heights, and the Federals who watched the men of Pickett,
Pettigrew and Trimble come across the valley toward them.

During the war each army became a community in and of itself,
and men came to fight for their friends and fellow soldiers. In the
intense and focused passion of combat the Civil War soldier's sphere of
influence, loyalty and devotion shrank from commander to regiment to
his immediate circle of comrades. In the most trying of times the flag
represented home, family, God and country, but perhaps most of all it
stood for the individual soldier and his immediate circle of friends.[111]

Slavery

As we have already seen, slavery was a distinguishing part of
the Old South, one that affected everyone it touched, including those
who were not slaveowners. It twisted and coursed through Southern
life, shaping and altering events and lives in ways that were little understood then, and are not completely comprehended even now. In
their letters home Confederate soldiers seldom wrote about the political, social and economic institution of slavery, and rarely mentioned it
as something they went to war to preserve. Yet slavery was the dominant system of labor in the South, and thus a daily economic reality
that could not be ignored or avoided. If a person wanted to develop a
farm or business, he had to secure additional help; he could not do all
the work himself. With land plentiful, few whites were willing to work
for someone else, let alone as field hands performing the back-break-
ing labor of harvesting crops.

The American dream of economic success and freedom was no
less powerful for Southerners of the 1860s than it is for us today, and
that was true for people of all races. If one wanted to get ahead or even
live comfortably, one had to benefit from the labor of others. Even free
people of color knew that slaves were the only source of labor, and thus
those black Southerners who could, bought slaves. In 1860, 3,000 black
families in the South owned slaves.[112]

White Southerners grew up with black people all around them,

41

and could not avoid seeing the effects of bondage on their lives. Whites were raised to consider themselves the equal of any human being, and this underscored their perception that blacks, in addition to being naturally inferior, were further degraded because they had allowed themselves to become enslaved. This was the other side of the belief in the Civil War as the second American Revolution or a battle for state and individual rights. If the Southerners lost, they could be enslaved by Northern political and economic interests. When they mentioned slavery in their writings, it was often as something the South must prevent happening to itself, not something to protect with their lives.

Furthermore, nothing in the lives of white Southerners led them to believe that any other labor system could or would work in their homeland. During the three decades before the war, Southern political and social leaders—those who had the strongest commitment to slavery and who had the most to lose from its demise—argued forcefully that it was the bedrock of the Southern economy, that it was as good for the slave as for the slaveowner, and that slavery was ordained by God.[113] In their speeches and writings, pro-slavery agitators sought to win and solidify the loyalty of the bulk of white non-slaveholders by portraying whites as physically and morally superior to blacks. It was slavery, they said, that guaranteed their republican society and their own freedom. Thus the white Southerners' future seemed to be tied to slavery, and the perceived attack on all aspects of Southern life by Northern extremists appeared to threaten their future.[114]

White Southerners of the 1860s were not obsessed by race, and could not see the contradiction inherent in white freedom being dependent upon black slavery. Our own obsession with race and racism has made it difficult for us to understand that contradiction or to see beyond it, into the lives of ordinary men and women. The difference in our attitudes toward race is a measure of the distance between our world and the one in which they lived.

Historians have long assumed that the pro-slavery argument was successful, and that all Southern whites supported slavery in the terms used by its strongest supporters. Yet no one has thus far attempted to measure the attitudes toward slavery among the bulk of white non-slaveholders, let alone among the members of the Army of Northern Virginia. We know much about the elite slaveowners and politicians, little about the common people. A major piece of the puzzle is still missing.

One scholarly inquiry now underway promises to reveal some important information on this question. Professor James McPherson has analyzied thousands of letters written by soldiers from both sides. His preliminary conclusion, published as a series of honorary lectures, was that about 20% of a sample of 374 Southerners stated explicit pro-slavery opinions. The documentation limits his ability to measure their depth of commitment, or slavery's relative importance to them. This

20% is, of course, approximately the same as the percentage of white families who owned slaves in 1860. Most of the pro-slavery writers were probably members of slave owning families. The sample included no letter or diary containing an anti-slavery opinion. McPherson's data can also be read in the opposite way: 80% of his sample said nothing about slavery.[115]

The question is not if some white Southerners went to war and followed the flag primarily to preserve slavery, but how many did so. As far as we can tell from the written documentation, most of the men who carried rifles and muskets evidently did not.

For the vast majority of Southern soldiers, slavery *per se* was not high on their list of concerns. To them it was most certainly not the dominant factor in their lives. If we assume that the frequency of appearance of a theme in the written record corresponds at least loosely to the intensity of interest in it, a priority list of the reasons they fought would rank slavery well below issues like family, community, opposition to the encroachment of the central government on any aspect of life, religion and comrades.

Perhaps Randolph McKim summed up the soldiers' response best in a post-war oration, prompted by the return of a Maryland battle flag:

> My comrades, you and I were companions of the men who fought under this banner, we marched by their side, we were familiar with their thoughts, and we know the principles that animated them in the course which they took in that great crisis of 1861. And therefore we are able to repudiate with authority the assertion that these our brothers fought in that great conflict for four years for the perpetuation of slavery. No. A thousand times no! These men did not fight for the perpetuation of slavery, but for the preservation of liberty. When they saw, or thought they saw, that the right of self-government was in danger through the usurpations of power, they sprang to arms with the same spirit, with the same patriotism, and animated by the same love of liberty as the men who fought at Lexington, and at Monmouth, at the Cowpens and at Yorktown.[116]

Long after the war Howard Malcolm Walthall, who had fought with the 1st Virginia as a private and survived Pickett's Charge, wrote his memoirs for his children. He began his essay with this paragraph:

> The younger people of this age generally think it was to save our slave property that we resisted, but that was not the question at all. The older heads know by

the tendency of legislation the disposition of the manufacturing and most densely populated section was to oppress our southern people and make them tributary, by furnishing raw goods to their mills at ruinous rates to us, which with equal rights in making the general laws we preferred separation rather than submission; but when we so decided the government concluded to whip us into submission by sending an army into our territory. This act fired the southern spirit and they made ready to resist the invasion.[117]

Most Confederate soldiers did not march off to war in order that black Southerners would remain in chains. Yet that would be the effect of their victory, and for a few, the cause of slavery was a motivating factor. Slavery was part of their world, and taken for granted, as were the slaves. The Confederate soldier assumed black Southerners' inferiority, but also assumed their loyalty and support, and treated them accordingly.

Summary: For Family, Community, Comrades and God

Many of the themes covered in this chapter were summarized in several letters written after the battle by Pvt. Ted Barclay of the 4th Virginia. In them he expressed the sense of loss of comrades that he had been very close to; the sense of connection to, yet estrangement from, his home community, and the deep religious feeling that served to keep his emotions in check and to hold all else together. Some passages have the quality of nightmares: faces of his friends loomed up out of the darkness, haunting him. He recognized a survivor's guilt; the feel of death approaching, indeed a vision of the dark beyond in his future. These letters reveal so much of the experiences and emotions of a typical Confederate soldier that became bound up in the symbol of the flag that they call for full quotation of one in particular and offer a fitting close to this chapter:

Camp Stephens,
July 14th. 63

Dear Sister:
Here we are once more on Virginia soil. We left Hagerstown on the night of the 13th. Marched all night, forded the Potomac up to our arms, and to one o'clock today when we got to this place, which you will recognize as the first camp we ever had when we came into service. But Oh, how different the camp of '63 compared to that of '61, then we had seventy-three men

whereas today only three of those seventy-three answer the roll call. Where are the others? Many faces come up to my view who now lie slumbering beneath the sod waiting the sound of the "last trumpet" to awaken them to give an account of the deeds done in the body. Among them the form of the noble Mitchell. His prospects were as bright, his hopes as high as those of any of us. In a few weeks he had laid down his life a sacrifice to his country's cause. Why have I been spared those two years of toil and danger whilst many promised to be bright and shining lights have been cut down. I thank God I was not cut off in my sins but spared until, by the mercy of God, I was brought from darkness into light. Now whatever awaits me, whether death upon the bloody battlefield or permitted to breath[e] my last with kind friends around to attend to every want, I feel that I have a bright future before me. I would like to die amidst my friends, but if God has so willed it that I should lie upon the field with nothing to mark the spot where the soldier lies, I feel that when the cold waters of death are ripling(sic) around my feet I can, trusting to the merits of a redeeming Saviour. I can launch my bark upon its dark unknown surface and at last anchor in the harbor of heaven. But I trust that I may be permitted to spend yet many a happy day in the old Stone Cottage in Peace and Safety. Now that we are in Virginia I expect that we will camp here for a week or so, and if Mr. Middleton will come down send me the things that I wrote for and also a box of eatables if possible. But for fear that you may not get my last letter I will give you a list of my wants—two shirts, two pairs of drawers, pair of pants, three pairs of socks, (woolen) boots and jacket, &c &c.

As it is going to rain I will have to close.

Good bye,

Ted.[118]

Perhaps even more succinctly than Barclay, Capt. R. Lewis Rogers of the 57th Virginia summed up what was in the hearts and minds of Confederate soldiers as they followed the Confederate battle flag in 1863. As reports of the Battle of Gettysburg made their way south, with them came rumors of the death of certain individuals. Mrs. Mary Cason heard that her husband had been wounded or killed during Pickett's Charge, and in any case left behind in Pennsylvania. As the commander of Company H, it became Rogers' task to write a letter to Mrs. Cason and confirm her worst fears. He reported that indeed Private William Cason had been killed (although in fact he had been mortally wounded and died in a hospital on July 17th).[119] He then went on to attempt to console the grieving widow by telling her that her husband had fought and died for all the right reasons:

> And while I lament with you the loss of your husband—
> I trust that it will be some consolation to you to know
> that he fell in a good cause—fell fighting for his rights;
> for his home and fireside; for his Country, and for his
> God.[120]

For confirmation of the themes developed in this chapter we need look no further than the commander of the Army of Northern Virginia, the man to whom the rank and file looked for leadership and inspiration. The retreat to Virginia, with its long train of wounded winding its way south through the rain, was not only dispiriting, it was dangerous. Federal cavalry seemed to lurk everywhere, making short, hit-and-run thrusts, pecking away at the exhausted troops. And the threat of attack by the infantry added another dimension of fear.

Robert E. Lee needed his men to gather all the strength and fortitude they could muster. He issued a broadside in which he sought to motivate them to even greater bravery, to summon up every last bit of emotion and commitment to the cause that he could draw from them. The words he used were not accidental, but were well chosen and thoughtfully arranged (probably by an aide, but approved by Lee). Lee knew his men; he knew what was in their hearts and minds, and he tried to appeal to their deepest emotions:[121]

HEADQUARTERS ARMY NORTHERN VA.,

11th July, 1863.

GENERAL ORDER, No. 76.

After long and trying marches, endured with the fortitude that has ever characterized the soldiers of the Army of Northern Virginia, you have penetrated the country of our enemies, and recalled to the defence of their own soil, those who were engaged in the invasion of ours.

You have fought a fierce and sanguinary battle, which, if not attended with the success that has hitherto crowned your efforts, was marked by the same heroic spirit that has commanded the respect of your enemies, the gratitude of your country and the admiration of mankind.

Once more you are called upon to meet the army from which you have won on so many fields a name that will never die.

Once more the eyes of your countrymen are turned upon you, and again do wives and sisters, fathers, mothers, and helpless children lean for defence on your strong arms and brave hearts.

Let every soldier remember that on his courage and fidelity depends all that makes life worth having----the freedom of his country, the honor of his people, and the security of his home. Let each heart grow strong in the remembrance of our glorious past, and in the thought of the inestimable blessings for which we contend; and invoking the assistance of that Divine Power which has so signally blessed our former efforts, let us go forth in confidence to secure the peace and safety of our country.

Soldiers! your old enemy is before you; win from him honors worthy of your righteous cause---worthy of your comrades dead on so many illustrious fields.

R. E. LEE. Gen'l.

Notes

[1] Quoted in Anthony Kellett, *Combat Motivation: The Behavior of Soldiers in Battle* (Boston: Kluwer-Nijhoff Publishing, 1982), 336.

[2] This book is about the Confederate battle flag and its significance, *not* about the development of Southern antebellum life and how it differed from, or was similar to, the rest of the United States. Thus this chapter is by necessity just a sketch, an outline of the factors that made the battle flag a potent symbol for the Southern soldier. Here we can only suggest the highlights of the values, beliefs, and ideals that the Southern soldier took into combat with him, and try to connect them to the flag and his experiences. How Northern society shaped the Federal soldier, and how the two sections and soldiers (or for that matter those of any other period or place) compared, is beyond the scope of this study. That said, my impression is that a chapter on the relationship between Northern soldiers and their flags would be quite similar. Federal soldiers shared several of the cultural attributes described in this chapter. Among the factors that shaped the *differences* would be the impact of immigration, which was heavier in the North than in the South, the growth of industrialization and urbanization, greater cultural diversity, slavery, and the fact that the Federal government invaded the South.

[3] George Fredrickson, *The Black Image in the White Mind: The Debate on Afro-American Character and Destiny, 1817-1914* (New York: Harper and Row, 1974); Walter Taylor, *Cavalier and Yankee: The Old South and American National Character* (New York: G. Braziller, 1961); Frank Owsley, *Plain Folk of the Old South* (Baton Rouge: Louisiana State University, 1982); W. J. Cash, *The Mind of the South* (New York: Alfred A. Knopf, 1943)

[4] And when the community became disillusioned with the war after Lincoln's reelection, Southern soldiers deserted in droves.

[5] See Gabor Borrit, ed., *Why the Civil War Came* (New York, Oxford University Press, 1995). For an older study of this question, see Thomas J. Pressly, *Americans Interpret their Civil War* (Princeton, N.J.: Princeton University Press, 1954).

[6] Bruce Catton, *Prefaces to History* (New York: Doubleday, 1970), 2.

[7] Carlton McCarthy, *Detailed Minutiae of Soldier Life in the Army of Northern Virginia, 1861-1865* (Lincoln: The University of Nebraska Press, 1993) [Privately printed, 1882], 3.

[8] The literature on the Continental Army during the Revolution includes several studies of the socio-economic and ethnic aspects of that army that provide a model that Civil War historians might follow. See Charles Neimeyer, *American Goes to War: The Social History of the Continental Army* (New York: New York Univesity Press, 1996),

for the bibliography.

⁹ James McPherson, *Battle Cry of Freedom: The Civil War Era* (New York: Oxford University Books, 1988). Maris A. Vinovskis, "Have Social Historians Lost the Civil War," in Vinovskis, ed., *Toward A Social History of the American Civil War: Exploratory Essays* (New York: Cambridge University Press, 1990).

¹⁰ Henry Owen, "Pickett's Division," undated clipping from the *South Side Sentinel*, Henry Owen Papers, Virginia State Library.

¹¹ C. Vann Woodward, quoted in Eugene Genovese, *Roll, Jordan, Roll: The World the Slaves Made* (New York: Pantheon Books, 1974), Preface.

¹² Richard Rollins, ed., *Black Southerners in Gray: Essays on Afro-Americans in Confederate Armies* (Murfreesboro, Tn: Southern Heritage Press, 1994) and Ervin Jordan, *Black Confederates and Afro-Yankees in Civil War Virginia* (Charlottesville: University of Virginia Press, 1994). Since we have no statistical data about the black Southerners who bore arms, all data presented is for the white soldiers.

¹³ Wiley, *Johnny Reb.* See also Harrison-Busey, *Nothing But Glory,* and McPherson, *Battle Cry,* 615. Roughly the same profile was found by the authors who studied the Southern troops at Shiloh: Frank and Reaves, *"Seeing The Elephant,"* 19. A study of Cobb's Georgia Legion found that the average age was 24, with the youngest 16 and the oldest 53: John Coski, "The Record Book of 'Cobb's Invincibles,' *The Museum and White House of the Confederacy Newsletter*, Winter/Spring 1994.

¹⁴ Cash, *Mind of the South*, 29.

¹⁵ Owen, "Pickett's Division."

¹⁶ William Fletcher, *Rebel Private Front and Rear* (Austin: University of Texas Press, 1954), 65.

¹⁷ Edwin Forbes, *Thirty Years After* (New York: Fords, Howard & Hulbert, 1890), 274.

¹⁸ Kathleen Georg-Harrison and John Busey, *Nothing But Glory: Pickett's Division at Gettysburg* (Gettysburg: Thomas Publications, 1974), 16.

¹⁹ Quoted in Lee A. Wallace, *Third Virginia* (Lynchburg, Va.: H. E. Howard, 1986), 36.

²⁰ Randolph Shotwell, *Three Years In Battle and Three In Federal Prisons* in J.G. de Roulhal Hamilton, ed., *The Papers of Randolph Shotwell* (Raleigh: North Carolina Historical Commission, 1929-1931), 1-31.

²¹ J. F. J. Caldwell, *The History of a Brigade of South Carolinians, Known First as "Gregg's" and Subsequently as "McGowan's Brigade"* (Philadelphia: King & Baird Printers, 1866), 95-96.

²² Cash, *Mind of the South*, 32-33.

²³ Bertram Wyatt-Brown, *Southern Honor: Ethics and Behavior in the Old South* (New York: Oxford University Press, 1982).

[24] Very little has been written about the community-based nature of Civil War armies. Wayne K. Durrill, *War of Another Kind: A Southern Community in the Great Rebellion* (New York: Oxford University Press, 1990), and Daniel E. Sutherland, *Seasons of War: The Ordeal of a Confederate Community, 1861 - 1865* (New York: Free Press, 1995) are the only applicable studies.. The only significant Northern studies are Thomas R. Kemp, "Community and War: The Civil War Experience of Two New Hampshire Towns," and Reid Mitchell, "The Northern Soldier and His Community" in Vinovskis, ed., *Toward a Social History of the American Civil War.* Speaking of Northern soldiers, Mitchell states that "Combat, military discipline, ideology, and leadership have all been evaluated as determinants of soldiers' conduct during the war, but community values were equally important. In fact, they were crucial to the way in which Americans made war from 1861 to 1865. . . . During combat, could men think of their reputations? The answer is probably yes." (79-80, 85) Robert Gross, *The Minutemen and Their World* (New York: Hill and Wang, 1976) is an excellent study of the development of Concord, Massachusetts, and the experiences of the town and its inhabitants before and during the American Revolution. It provides a useful model of what could and should be done for the Civil War era.

[25] Quoted in Henry Steele Commager, ed., *The Blue and Gray: The Story of the Civil War as Told by Participants* (Indianapolis: Bobbs-Merrill, 1950), Vol. I, 66.

[26] Henry Stanley, *The Autobiography of Sir Henry M. Stanley* ed. Dorothy Stanley (Boston: Little, Brown, 1909), 165.

[27] *Echoes of Glory*, 230.

[28] Manuscript of a speech by Mississippi College Rifles, Charles Vielo Papers, Civil War Miscellaneous Collection, Archives Branch, U.S. Army Military History Institute, quoted in Rod Gragg, ed., *The Illustrated Confederate Reader* (New York: Harper & Row, 1989), 22.

[29] [Anonymous], "A Reminiscent Story of the Great Civil War," Louisiana File, GNMP.

[30] Quoted in Woodford B. Hackley, *The Little Fork Rangers: A Sketch of Company D, Fourth Virginia Cavalry* (Richmond: Privately Printed, 1927), 33-35.

[31] Maj. James F. Beall, "Twenty-first Regiment," Walter Clark, ed., *Histories of the Several Regiments and Battalions from North Carolina. . .* (Raleigh: State of North Carolina, 1901), Vol. II, 9.

[32] Quoted in Wiley, *Johnny Reb*, 193.

[33] With the decline of Confederate military fortunes in the summer of 1863 came a growing discontent back home. Southern women during the last two years of the war exerted a powerful influence by telling their men of their hardships and calling them home. This too is beyond the scope of this study.

[34] Greg Mast, *State Troops and Volunteers: A Photographic*

Record of North Carolina's Civil War Soldiers (Raleigh: North Carolina Department of Cultural Resources, 1995), 159.

[35] *Ibid.*, 183.

[36] William M. Abernathy, *Our Mess: Southern Gallantry and Privations* (McKinney, TX: McKintex Press, 1977), 29.

[37] Albert [Batchelor] to Father, August 20, 1863, Hospital Near Gettysburg, 2nd Louisiana File, GNMP.

[38] Clark, *Histories*, I, 639.

[39] *Hood's Texas Brigade,* 15.

[40] Rollins, ed., *Black Southerners in Gray.*

[41] *Ibid.*, and Eugene Genovese, *Roll, Jordan, Roll: The World the Slaves Made* (New York: Pantheon, 1974) and Wiley, *Southern Negroes.*

[42] See my essay on "Servants and Soldiers: Tennessee's Black Southerners in Gray," in Rollins, ed., *Black Southerners in Gray*, and Fred Bailey, *Class and Tennessee's Confederate Generation* (Chapel Hill: University of North Carolina Press, 1987).

[43] Mark Boatner III, *The Civil War Dictionary* (New York: Vintage Books, 1987), 794; *World Book Encyclopedia* (Chicago: World Book, 1994), 17, 503. See also Kenneth Stampp, *The Peculiar Institution: Slavery and the Antebellum South* (New York: Knopf, 1956).

[44] See especially Genovese, *Roll, Jordan, Roll.*

[45] *Ibid.*

[46] Capt. Louis G. Young, "Pettigrew's Brigade at Gettysburg;" Clark, *Histories,* V, 127.

[47] Manly Wade Wellman, *Rebel Boast: First at Bethel—Last at Appomattox* (New York: Henry Holt and Company, 1956).

[48] George Hillyer, *The Battle of Gettysburg: Address Before the Walton County Georgia Confederate Veterans, August 2nd, 1904* (The Walton Tribune), photocopy, Georgia File, GNMP.

[49] Catton, *Prefaces*, 2.

[50] J. B. Polley, *A Soldier's Letters to Charming Nellie* (New York: Neale Publishing, 1908), 281.

[51] David Hackett Fischer, *Albion's Seed: Four British Folkways in America* (New York: Oxford University Press, 1989).

[52] Richard Beringer, et. al., *Why the South Lost the Civil War* (Athens: University of Georgia Press, 1986).

[53] Quoted in McPherson, *What They Fought For*, 9.

[54] *Ibid.*

[55] *Ibid.*, 10.

[56] McCarthy, *Detailed Minutiae*, 9.

[57] Quoted in McPherson, *Battle Cry*, 310.

[58] Rev. Randolph McKim, *The Second Maryland Infantry: An Oration. . . .* (n.p: n,p, 1909), 19-20.

[59] Quoted in Jimerson, *The Private Civil War*, 5.

[60] Quoted in Michael Barton, "Did the Confederacy Change

Southern Soldiers?" in Harry P. Owen and James J. Cook, eds., *The Old South in the Crucible of War* (Jackson: University of Mississippi Press, 1983).

[61] Quoted in McPherson, *Battle Cry*, 310.

[62] Cornelia Peake McDonald, *A Diary With Reminiscences of the War and Refugee Life in the Shenandoah Valley, 1860-1865* (Nashville: Privately Published 1934), 18.

[63] Gordon S. Wood, *The Creation of the American Republic, 1776 - 1787* (Chapel Hill: University of North Carolina Press, 1969) and *The Radicalism of the American Revolution* (New York: Alfred Knopf, 1992).

[64] See Richard E. Beringer, *Why The South Lost the Civil War* (Athens: University of Georgia Press, 1986).

[65] McPherson, *What They Fought For.*

[66] Quoted in Jimerson, *The Private Civil War*, 19.

[67] *Ibid.*, 24.

[68] Quoted in McPherson, *What They Fought For*, 11.

[69] Willie Miller to Sister, July 1, 1863, 18th Virginia File, GNMP.

[70] Cash, *Mind of the South*; Bertram Wyatt-Brown, *Southern Honor;* Taylor, *Cavalier and Yankee.*

[71] Wyatt-Brown, *Southern Honor*, [3] - 5.

[72] Gerald F. Linderman, *Embattled Courage: The Experience of Combat in the American Civil War* (New York: The Free Press, 1987), 8.

[73] Henry Kyd Douglas, *I Rode With Stonewall* (Chapel Hill: University of North Carolina Press, 1940), 259-260.

[74] Quoted in William Frassanito, *Early Photography at Gettysburg* (Gettysburg: Thomas Publications, 1995), 378.

[75] Wayland Dunaway, *Reminiscences of a Rebel* (New York: Neale, 1913), 98, 101-104.

[76] George E. Pickett, *Soldier of the South: General Pickett's War Letters to His Wife* ed. Arthur Crew Inman (Boston: Houghton Mifflin, 1928), 73-5.

[77] Quoted in Wyatt-Brown, *Southern Honor*, 35.

[78] Linderman, *Embattled Courage*, 17.

[79] McCarthy, *Detailed Minutiae*, 208.

[80] Linderman, *Embattled Courage*, 8.

[81] George Cary Eggleston, *A Rebel's Recollections* (Cambridge, MA: The Riverside Press, 1875), 197.

[82] William W. Bennett, *A Narrative of the Great Revival Which Prevailed in the Southern Armies. . .* (Philadelphia: Claxton, Remsen and Haffelfinger, 1877). See also Drew Gilpin Faust, "Christian Soldiers: The Meaning of Revivalism in the Confederate Army," *The Journal of Southern History* LIII (February, 1987), 63-90; Sidney J. Romero, *Religion in the Rebel Army* (Lanham, Maryland: University Press of America, 1983); John Shepard, "Religion in the Army of Northern Vir-

ginia," *The North Carolina Historical Review*, 1957, 341-376.

[83] Shepard, "Religion," 356.

[84] J. A. Strikeleather, "Recollections of the Civil War in the United States," October 27, 1909, Southern Historical Collection, University of North Carolina, 23.

[85] J. W. Jones, *Christ in the Camp: or Religion in Lee's Army* (Richmond: n.p., 1887), 307; Bennett, *Narrative*, 412-413.

[86] Jo Shaner to Mother, June 4, 1863, GNMP.

[87] Quoted in Bennett, *Narrative*, 173-174.

[88] John Moseley to Mother, July 4, 1863, Virginia State Library.

[89] David Hunter to Mother, July 2, 1863, 2nd Virginia File, GNMP.

[90] Quoted in Bennett, *Narrative*, 175.

[91] Alexander Barclay to Sister, June 3, July 8, 1863, 4th Virginia File, GNMP.

[92] Quoted in Bennett, *Narrative*, 367.

[93] David Ballenger to Mother, July 18, 1863, University of South Carolina Library, photocopy, GNMP.

[94] Strikeleather, "Recollections," 23-4.

[95] Quoted in Harrison-Busey, *Glory*, 16.

[96] Clark, *Histories*, II, 234.

[97] Quoted in Harrison-Busey, *Glory*, 16.

[98] Thomas Littlejohn, 'Recollections of a Confederate Soldier," 13th South Carolina File, GNMP.

[99] Rawley W. Martin and John H. Smith, "The Battle of Gettysburg, and the Charge of Pickett's Division," *Southern Historical Society Papers* [hereafter cited as *SHSP*], 32(1904), 184-185. [emphasis added]

[100] James F. Crocker, "My Personal Experience in Taking Up Arms and in the Battle of Malvern Hill. Gettysburg—Pickett's Charge," *SHSP*, XXXIII, 128-134.

[101] Quoted in Marvin R. Cain, "A 'Face of Battle' Needed: An Assessment of Motives and Men in Civil War Historiography," *Civil War History* XXVIII (1982), 13.

[102] Joseph T. Durkin, ed., *John Dooley: Confederate Soldier—His War Journal* (South Bend: University of Notre Dame Press, 1963), 104-105.

[103] William Andrew Fletcher, *Rebel Private Front and Rear* (Austin: University of Texas Press, 1954), 62-63.

[104] Stewart, *Pickett's Charge*, 171.

[105] John Keegan, *Face of Battle*, 70-71.

[106] Eppa Hunton, *Autobiography of Eppa Hunton* (Richmond: William Byrd Press, 1933), 100. Mortally wounded, Hezekiah Spessard died on July 19. Harrison-Busey, *Glory*, 361.

[107] Linderman, *Embattled Courage*.

[108] *Ibid.*, 216 ff.

[109] Theodore Fogle to Sister, July 16, 1863, 2nd Georgia File,

GNMP.

[110] Shotwell, *Three Years in Battle*.

[111] John Keegan, *Face of Battle*, 46, cites S. L. Marshall's research on World War II but makes it plain that this has always been true, and the material presented here certainly indicates it was so for the Confederates at Gettysburg.

[112] Gary Mills, *The Forgotten People: Cane River's Creoles of Color* (Baton Rouge: Louisiana State University Press, 1977) and Larry Koger, *Black Slaveowners: Free Black Slave Masters in South Carolina, 1790-1860* (Jefferson, N. C.: McFarland Press, 1985).

[113] William Sumner Jenkins, *Pro-Slavery Thought in the Old South* (Gloucester, Mass.: Peter Smith, 1960); Eric L. McKitrick, ed., *Slavery Defended: The Views of the Old South* (Englewood Cliffs, N. J.: Prentice-Hall, 1963).

[114] *Ibid.*; Fredrickson, *The Black Image in the White Mind*.

[115] McPherson, *What They Fought For*, 53-54.

[116] McKim, *The Second Maryland*, 25.

[117] Untitled memoir by Howard Malcolm Walthall, May, 1913, 1st Virginia File, GNMP.

[118] Andrew Barclay to Sister, July 14, 1863, 4th Virginia File, GNMP.

[119] Harrison-Busey, *Glory*, 432.

[120] R. Lewis Rogers to Mary Cason, July 19th, 1863, 57th Virginia File, GNMP.

[121] Order No. 76, July 11, 1863, original in Jedediah Hotchkiss Papers, Library of Congress.

Chapter Two

"Like Our Ancestors We Will Be Free":
The Evolution of the Confederate Battle Flag to 1863

A Federal soldier in Brig. Gen. Alexander Hays' division, examining the captured battle flags after the repulse of Pickett's Charge on July 3, described the banners:

> These "Rebel" flags were mostly home-made affairs like a bed-spread, of pieces of muslin sewed together, and even flannel, calico, and muslin together. Torn by battle, dirty, and cheap looking, no wonder our boys designated them 'rebel rags.' The inscriptions were made by sewing on the letters. Some were more pretentious; when new, no doubt more agreeable to view. Some had a regimental designation only. Seven had the names of battles inscribed on them including among them Frazier's Farm, Malvern Hill, Manassas (Second Bull Run), Sharpsburg (Antietam), Harper's Ferry, Fredericksburg and Chancellorsville.[1]

The flags he described were a variety known as the Army of Northern Virginia pattern: a red square with a blue St. Andrew's (diagonal) cross outlined in white, with 12 or 13 stars bunched together near the center of the flag. Also known as the Southern Cross, this was one of many different patterns of flags carried by Confederate troops during the war. It served as the principal battle flag of the Army of Northern Virginia from late 1861 until the surrender at Appomattox, and is thus known as the ANV pattern battle flag.

The Southern Cross was not the first flag carried into battle by Confederate troops, nor was it the banner most widely flown during the war. It was rarely seen west of the Appalachian mountains. Some Southern men fought and died without ever seeing or marching under it. After the war, even the veterans seemed to forget this, and when the United Confederate Veterans officially adopted as its emblem the battle flag carried by most of the Army of Tennessee in 1864 and 1865, a rectangular version of the Southern Cross, most of the other flags were doomed to obscurity. Today there remains among scholars, reenactors, and Civil War students in general a great deal of confusion and misinformation, and even a significant lack of knowledge about Confederate battle flags.[2] The whole story of the development of the Confederate flag is a subject far too complex to be dealt with in full here, for our scope is limited to the summer of 1863 in the Eastern theater. To place the flags captured in the Gettysburg campaign in their proper context, we must concentrate on providing the necessary information without getting bogged down in too much detail.

The first flags carried into battle by Confederate soldiers looked nothing at all like the Southern Cross. However, they embodied much of the Southern past, not only in their design, but also in the words and symbols placed upon them. Taken together, the color, shape, design and ornamentation comprised the "symbolic language" of a flag that expressed its essential meaning for those who fought under it.

The roots of the Confederate battle flag go deep into the American past and reflect the political thought, social experience, and military history of the English settlements on the North American continent. Since well before the Revolution, American society had been characterized by a deep distrust of European-style centralized authority and its large, coercive standing armies. The tension between colonists and crown after 1763 often touched on this point. For example, England insisted on quartering troops in the colonies and tried to make the colonists pay for them, or at least provide a share of the financial cost of defending the empire in the new world. The colonists bitterly resented this, and steadfastly opposed it. Clashes between townspeople and British troops, epitomized by the Boston Massacre, underscored this situation. For defense, the colonists preferred to rely on militia companies, small units of civilians who practiced soldiering once a month.

The militia system not only served to provide for common defense, its mandatory drilling days and organizational sessions often functioned as community-oriented social gatherings and as excuses for various types of entertainment. In many cases militia units became integral parts of the community, providing a commonality of experience and expectation. When the Revolution began at Lexington and Concord in 1775, these militia companies banded together to drive the Regulars back to Boston, then stayed together at Cambridge to form the New England army.[3]

Between the Revolution and the 1850s the militia tradition continued, though inconsistently and unevenly, across the United States. In some areas it continued to provide a regular gathering point for local communities, while in others it died out. In general, it fared better in the South than in the North. Indeed, in the 1850s, as sectional tensions rose, the militia system grew rapidly, especially throughout the deep South. Longstanding militia units, such as the Richmond Howitzers, Liberty Independent Troop of Liberty County, Georgia, Charleston's Ancient Battalion of Artillery, the Richmond Greys and the Washington Artillery of New Orleans, continued to drill and practice military maneuvers.

After John Brown's raid on Harper's Ferry in 1859, the South virtually became an armed camp. Throughout the presidential campaign of 1860 leading to the election of Abraham Lincoln, Southern communities formed local militia companies and other civil defense forces with colorful names like the "Rough and Ready Guards," "Montgomery Fencibles" and "Creole Guards." Old and new companies were made up of men who had the time, motivation and money to attend the drills and purchase the sometimes elaborate uniforms. Weapons and equipment were often furnished by the state or local government. Units were authorized by the state and in some cases were organized up to the divisional level, although they rarely met on more than a local level. When the war came these organizations readily volunteered as units and formed the bases for state troops.[4]

Since many of the Southern militia units that later became companies in the Confederate army were first organized in 1859 and 1860, and carried flags made in those years into battle in 1861, the origins of the Confederate battle flag might be said to have occurred during this period.

Each militia organization had its own flag. Designed by company members or by females related to them, they were typically sewn by the women of the community. These flags were normally rectangular in shape, usually made of silk, yet also occasionally made from wool or cotton. Their color schemes relied heavily, though not exclusively, on red, white and blue. Yet very few of them resembled the Stars and Stripes of the U. S. national colors.

In addition to color and shape, early militia flags also drew upon another American tradition. During the Revolution it had been common for organizations, including units of the Continental Army, to write, paint or sew political slogans on their flags. "An Appeal To Heaven," "Liberty," "Don't Tread On Me" and similar phrases adorned flags from Georgia to Massachusetts.[5]

In the secession crisis, Southern women also sewed on to the militia flags statements, slogans and symbols as emblems of the major concerns and beliefs of their communities. Some of the emblems were allegorical scenes representing a political theme, such as the overthrow of tyranny. Others represented attributes of the state or local area, such as a cotton plant, or a patriotic theme, such as a portrayal of George Washington. Most common were slogans and symbols which summarized, often in a catchy phrase, the community's feeling about the events of the day. No historian has ever looked at these flags and analyzed their content, but a cursory examination reveals that virtually all the material reflected an opposition to the encroachment of the Federal power upon what the makers perceived to be their rights—that is, the choices they made and the way they sought to order their social, political and economic lives. Southerners would defend with arms their rights to choose how to live. In effect, militia flags represented each community's collective sense of who it was: its own identity as a part of its state and nation.

For example, the Florida Independent Blues, which became

Company E, 3rd Florida Infantry, placed "Any Fate But Submission" on their flag.[6] The Smyth Dragoons, a part of the 8th Virginia Cavalry during the war, carried a flag which read: "From the Smyth Ladies" and "God And Our Right." The Princess Anne Cavalry, later Company C of the 13th Virginia Cavalry, put the slogan "Liberty Or Death" on their flag. The Floyd Guard, a company in the 2nd Virginia, carried a First National with the slogan: "The Price of Liberty is the Blood of the Brave."[7]

Two flags may serve as representative of the rest. The King's Mountain Guards, which became Company F, 5th South Carolina, carried a motto that seemed to sum up the essence of all of them: "Like Our Ancestors We Will Be Free."[8] Perhaps the makers of the flag of the 15th Virginia summed it up even more succinctly. On one side of their flag they painted "15 REG: VA: Vol", surrounded by 10 stars. On the other, surrounded by 10 stars, they placed a single word: "HOME".[9]

Among the local flags carried in 1861 was one design that appeared throughout the South. "The Bonnie Blue Flag" was already a traditional and even legendary part of Southern culture. A simple blue square or rectangle adorned by a single white star, it had first surfaced as the flag of the Republic of West Florida in 1810. It was again seen frequently during the Texas rebellion against Mexico in the 1830s as a symbol of Texan independence, and it became a part of the flag of the Republic of Texas. It continues today as part of the flag of the state of Texas, and was briefly the flag of the Republic of Mississippi in 1861. A Bonnie Blue flag flying over Jackson, Mississippi, in 1861 inspired Harry McCarthy to write the song that virtually became the anthem of Southern troops and Southern patriots during the early days of the war.[10] That song, perhaps the most frequently sung throughout the war by Southern troops, made the connections between politics, culture, and the flag quite explicit:

> We are a band of brothers, and native to the soil
> Fighting for our Liberty, with treasure, blood and toil
> And when our rights were threatened
> The cry rose near and far
> Hurrah for the Bonnie Blue Flag
> That bears a single star
> Hurrah, hurrah, for Southern Rights, hurrah![11]

One incident gives us insight into the potential morale-boosting effect and the symbolic power of the flag. At Spotsylvania Court House in 1864 the men of the 4th and 14th North Carolina regiments found themselves involved in a fight against Federals in the next line of trenches. The firing was heavy and the flags of the two regiments stood not five yards apart. The 4th's colorbearer, J. A. Strikeleather, reported that the flag was hit several times and the staff broken twice:

Just at this time, someone near me commenced singing in a stentorian voice the Bonney[sic] Blue Flag. In a few moments not less than a dozen of us were heartily joining the leader, especially in the chorus, all the while keeping time to the music with our firing at the Blue coats. In a little while the enthusiasm for some distance to the right and left was intense. It reminded me more of one of our old fashioned corn shucking melodies in the midst of a hotly contested race at a corn pile, than anything I saw during the war. . . The leader in the singing, Tisdale Step of the 14th regiment . . . and as fine a specimen of physical manhood as there was in the Brigade, was singing, loading and firing not more than three paces from my position. I watched him with intense interest, his face glowed with enthusiasm and the same feeling was pretty general all around.[12]

Secession brought about the first widespread need for state flags. Few American states had flags before the Civil War. Of the seceding states, only Texas had officially adopted its flag. South Carolina, Georgia, Virginia and Florida had developed flags for use by their military organizations, but they were not sanctioned by state legislatures and were used only sporadically. Upon secession, each of the original seven Confederate states was, briefly, a sovereign republic and during that period each created a flag to symbolize that sovereignty. The Confederacy was, until February 1862, only a provisional country that each republic joined for common defense. Flags with blue fields were popular for states with colonial traditions. Five of the new flags used the Bonnie Blue flag as inspiration in their design.

The newly designed state flags were used extensively during the first few months of secession and the beginning of armed conflict. A few were carried throughout the war in the Western and trans-Mississippi theaters. For example, units of Major General John C. Breckinridge's Army of Southwest Virginia carried Virginia flags in 1864 as did other Virginia units not under the control of the Army of Northern Virginia. North Carolina units stationed in their state for coastal defense carried that state's flag into battle. Three modern state flags date from this era: those of Texas, Virginia and South Carolina. North Carolina's current flag is very similar to the one carried during the war.

When the Confederate States of America was formed in the spring of 1861, one of its first major tasks was to create, from scratch, a flag that would represent the new nation in affairs of state in ceremonies, on the high seas and in military engagements. This was not a unique situation, for it was the same problem faced by the founders of the United States in 1776.

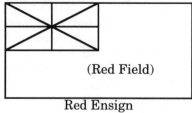

(Red Field)

Red Ensign

Grand Union

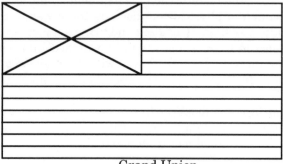

Stars and Stripes

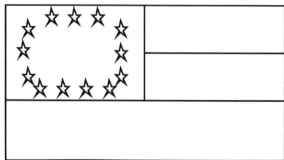

First National

Evolution

As an authority on Civil War flags recently wrote, "National flags are the history and glory of a people expressed in the art of a seamstress."[13] Put another way, flags designed in the midst of an emotional period like the American Revolution or the Southern secession crisis are products of a certain culture at a specific point in its development. They symbolically represent those aspects of that culture that serve as its identifying characteristics. Like their predecessors in the Revolution, the men who formed the Confederacy essentially sought to preserve a set of principles that they believed were being threatened. They debated several design proposals and selected a flag that had a strong cultural resonance with the events and ideals of their past.

The roots of the "First National" or "Stars and Bars" flag could hardly go deeper into the American past. It was a direct descendant of the Stars and Stripes that it replaced in the South. The first American flag had evolved from earlier British and British-American flags. The British flag that had flown over most of the 13 colonies in the 17th and early 18th centuries was known as the "Red Ensign." It appeared everywhere throughout the colonies, on trading ships as well as government buildings. Its red field stood for the Crown, and its canton(upper left corner) bore the "Grand Union," representing the unification of the British Isles under the King. The vertical cross of St. George, for England, and the diagonal cross of St. Andrew, for Scotland, appeared in the canton. In the 1760s, one of the first flags flown by rebellious colonists was quite similar: a red field with a blue canton on which the word "Liberty" replaced the Grand Union. In January of 1776 Americans hoisted the "Flag of Colonial Union," a red-and-white-striped field with the "Grand Union" in the canton. The flag we now know as the Stars and Stripes first flew in 1777.[14]

Thus when the secessionists met in Montgomery in February of 1861, they had a rich heritage of symbolic material to draw upon. The debate in the Confederate Congress reflected their emotional ties to the revolutionary tradition. One delegate argued that the Stars and Stripes should be retained as the emblem of the new nation, since it was *Yankees* who had alienated the South, not the flag or the principles he felt it stood for. Most of the delegates expressed a desire to stay as close to "Old Glory" as possible, and Jefferson Davis wanted simply to keep the old flag. Eventually more than 120 designs were proposed, many of which were very reminiscent of the Stars and Stripes, including one with seven red and white stripes and a blue canton with seven white stars. Others drew on various aspects of Southern and American history. For example, one proposal called for a flag depicting a phoenix shooting out of flame and ashes, with the slogan "We Rise Again."[15]

The flag the delegates eventually flew over the capitol in Montgomery, the First National, was thoroughly *American*. It embodied much of the symbolic language of the old flag, and thus of the old ideals of democracy and self-rule that the previous flag had symbolized. Its red, white and blue colors, a blue canton with white stars in a circle (like the flag of 1777), and red and white stripes, deliberately echoed the stars and stripes. Indeed it had to carry a strong connection to the past if it were to succeed as a symbolic representation of the new nation.

More First National patterns would be surrendered in 1865 than either of the two later official designs. If there was one, single "Confederate flag" that was most widely recognized, most widely flown across the South from 1861 to 1865, and under which the majority or a plurality of Southern troops marched, it was the First National flag, the "Stars and Bars." The similarity to the Stars and Stripes was deliberate, a sharply political statement that the South perceived itself as the true inheritor of the tradition of freedom represented by the American Revolution.

This flag was soon raised over all Confederate government buildings and carried by an uncountable number of military units of all types. It was the First National flag that replaced the Stars and Stripes and flew over Ft. Sumter from 1861 to 1865, and that flew over the *C.S.S. Virginia* during its battle with the *U.S.S. Monitor*. For at least two years, and perhaps throughout the entire war, Robert E. Lee's headquarters flag was a First National pattern with the stars in the shape of the "arch of the constitution."

While the First National flag would turn out to be the one most often carried into battle during the next four years, it would not become "the Confederate flag," or "the Confederate battle flag." No single design ever became the dominant type of emblem representing the Confederacy.[16] The flag that we now think of as that flag, the rectangular Johnston pattern introduced in late 1863, which will be described later, was in fact a major type in terms of the number of men who bore it only in the Western theater in 1864-5, and even then it was not carried exclusively. Indeed more Western theater Confederate soldiers in that period probably carried other flags. Confederate armies fought under at least 20 different flag patterns, and that does not count the unique local flags and state flags.[17] The Army of Tennessee, the principal army in the Western theater, carried at least eight different patterns in 1863, and possibly as many as 11 or 12, again not counting local and state flags. In the winter of 1864 an entire division threatened to quit when told it would have to give up its old, solid-blue "Hardee-pattern" flags in favor of the rectangular St. Andrew's cross flag preferred by its new commander.[18]

The diversity of flags was not accidental, but revealed the essential characteristics of Southern culture. It underscored the Confederacy's decentralization of political power, the local allegiances of its people, their democratic heritage and the evolution of its sense of its own identity.

The national color continued to evolve throughout the war. A Second National flag was introduced in the spring of 1863. As late as

March of 1865, a few weeks before the surrender at Appomattox, the Confederate government adopted yet another pattern known as the Third National flag.[19] These flags will be discussed later in this chapter.

The design of the First National flag was partially responsible for the development of what we today think of as "*the* Confederate battle flag." On a battlefield, seen from a distance and often obscured by smoke, the First National was difficult to see, and even more difficult to differentiate from the "Stars and Stripes."

At Manassas in 1861, several incidents of mistaken identification of troops caused by the flag they carried led to friendly troops firing on each other. With any number of state and local flags appearing on the field, confusion was the order of the day. Jubal Early, then a colonel commanding a brigade in the Confederate Army of the Potomac (as the principle army in the Eastern theater was then known), reported one incident of confusion over a flag. An aide had gone to the top of a hill in front of Early's men and spotted a body of troops approaching, carrying what he believed was a Confederate flag. The troops fired on Early's men, but the aide identified them as the 13th Virginia regiment:

> This turned out to be a misapprehension, and in the mean time a considerable body of the enemy appeared to the right of my position. . . bearing what I felt confident was the Confederate flag. It was soon, however, discovered to be a regiment of the enemy's forces, and was dispersed by one or two well-directed fires from the artillery on our left.[20]

Col. R. E. Withers, commanding the 18th Virginia, ordered an artillery piece temporarily under his command to sight in "a large number of men who were congregated near a two-story house beyond the turnpike." But, "just as we were about to fire I discovered among [the enemy] the Confederate flag, and ordered them not to fire. I know in this I am not mistaken, as it was first recognized by the naked eye, and an examination with a good fieldglass confirmed my first opinion." While debating what to do he watched as two other bodies of troops with U.S. flags clearly visible joined the first, so he concluded that the first group had raised a Confederate flag with the intention of deceiving him.[21]

After Manassas Gen. P. G. T. Beauregard decided that something must be done, and spoke to Congressman William Porcher Miles about the situation. Miles reminded Beauregard of the design he had submitted months earlier, a red flag with a blue St. Andrew's cross and white stars affixed to the cross. Beauregard liked it and showed it to Gen. Joseph E. Johnston, commander of the Army of the Potomac. Johnston liked the design, but suggested that it be made in a square pattern, rather than rectangular. Johnston also recommended that it

"The Damned Red Flags Of The Rebellion"

Don Troiani, "Emblems of Valor"
(Courtesy of Historical Art Prints)

be made in different sizes for the infantry, artillery and cavalry.

Beauregard had in mind a distinct flag, a *battle flag,* one that would be used only in combat. In September of 1861 he wrote to Johnston specifying this point:

> Colonel [William Porcher] Miles informs me that the flag committee voted down any change of our flag by a vote of four to one, he being alone in favor of it. I wrote to him then to propose that we should have two flags, a peace or parade flag and a war flag, to be used only on the field of battle; but, Congress having adjourned, no action will be taken on the matter. How would it do for us to address the War Department on the subject for a supply of regimental war or badge flags, made of red with two blue bars crossing each other diagonally, on which shall be introduced the States, the edge of the flag to be trimmed all around with white, yellow, or blue fringe. We would then on the field of battle know our friends from our enemies. . . .[22]

This can reasonably be called the genesis of the Southern Cross, the Army of Northern Virginia pattern of the "Confederate battle flag."

Miss Constance Cary and her cousins Hetty and Jenny Cary, originally from northern Virginia and Maryland but then "refugeeing" in Richmond, were asked to make three prototype flags. This was done and one each was presented to Beauregard, Johnston and Gen. Earl Van Dorn. Made in September, 1861, each flag featured 12 gold five-pointed stars on an 5-inch-wide blue cross outlined in white, made of silk and carrying a gold fringe. This pattern was quickly adopted by many units in the Army of the Potomac. In 1862, when Gen. Robert E. Lee became its commander, this force was renamed the Army of Northern Virginia. Each regiment was ordered to carry only one flag, the Army of Northern Virginia pattern "battle flag."[23]

Between October, 1861, and the end of the war, the Army of Northern Virginia battle flag was issued in nine distinct variations. (See Appendix B for an outline of the variations and an analysis of the captured flags still in existence). At Gettysburg, the army carried several of these: flags made of silk, cotton or wool; some had 12 stars, others 13. Some had a five-inch blue cross, on others it was eight inches wide. This diversity probably accounts in part for the "home made" part of the description quoted at the beginning of this chapter.

While this flag continued to be the primary banner of the Army of Northern Virginia for the remainder of the war, it was not carried exclusively. Some units carried the First National flag until Appomattox, while others, late in the war, again carried state flags. At least two "Hardee" pattern flags, a blue field with a white circle in the middle, and one "Polk" flag, a blue field with a red upright cross, both carried predominately in the western theater, were captured at Petersburg.[24] They had belonged to regiments that came east with Longstreet in the fall of 1863. The Army of Northern Virginia pattern flag was rarely carried in the Western theater, though the flag adopted by the Department of South Carolina, Georgia and Florida was quite similar.[25]

By the spring of 1863 little emotional attachment to the old Union remained in the South. The blood of many battles had seen to that. The dissipation of this sentiment, coupled with much dissatisfaction with the design of the Stars and Bars, led to a movement to redesign the national flag. The result was the Second National flag, often referred to as the Stainless Banner. It consisted of a white field with the Army of Northern Virginia battle flag in the canton. The first example made of this flag was draped over the coffin of Lt. Gen. T. J. "Stonewall" Jackson at his funeral in May. The flag was used primarily after Gettysburg. In the Army of Northern Virginia it was normally a headquarters flag, but at least one was carried as a regimental banner during the battle. It was used extensively in the Western theater as a regimental battle flag.

The Stainless Banner represented the evolution of the Confederacy's sense of identity. The citizens of the South were no longer concerned about symbolizing their allegiance to the original Union. They now had an entirely new design, one born of their own experiences, representing their own country and its ideals. While it remained red, white and blue, it no longer reminded them of the stars and stripes. Now its white field represented the purity of their cause. In its canton, the Southern Cross, the battle flag itself, spoke of their determination to win their independence by force of arms.

However, from a distance the Second National flag could be easily confused with a white flag of surrender, and this was unacceptable. In March, 1865, the Confederate government approved a Third National flag. It was simply the Second National with a wide red vertical band attached to the fly end. Very few were manufactured or flown in combat. During the wave of surrenders in the spring of 1865, more First National flags were turned in than either of the other two designs.[26]

Over the course of the war, Confederate troops carried flags with a wide range of words and symbols, referred to as "battle honors," added to them to designate and commemorate their experiences in combat. Several of the Confederate flags captured at Gettysburg carried battle honors. Soon after the first engagements, regiments had the name of battles in which they had fought written, sewn or painted on their flags, either by individual members of the regiment or by more skilled artists paid for their services. In the West, several units painted an inverted cannon or two inverted crossed cannon to commemorate their capture of one or more enemy artillery pieces. On July 23, 1862, the War Department issued order No. 52, allowing flags to be marked with the names of battles that units had fought in, thus officially recognizing a practice already common.[27]

Beginning with Gen. Longstreet's Right Wing in June, 1862, honors were painted on strips of white cloth, in black letters, for Seven Pines and Williamsburg.[28] These strips where then sewn on the red field of the ANV pattern flags, usually after the flags were issued. Some regiments continued to add honors in their own style, and others added the number of their regiment. The Richmond Depot began issuing flags with honors in late 1862.

In the spring of 1863, the Confederate government began issuing flags to entire divisions. Maj. Gen. D. H. Hill's division (commanded at Gettysburg by Robert Rodes) received "fourth issue" (also known as "third bunting") Army of Northern Virginia flags in April, with honors applied. Originally released in the summer of 1862, these flags were made of wool bunting, had a five-inch-wide blue cross and white border. Maj. Gen. A. P. Hill's division (divided into two divisions commanded by Henry Heth and William Dorsey Pender at Gettysburg) received new flags in May, with honors applied, and Maj. Gen. Pickett's division received theirs in June, with unit numbers and state abbreviations painted in gold lettering but no battle honors.

Some regiments, the 8th, 14th and 38th Virginia, for example, continued to use the flags issued earlier.[29] Quartermasters at some level—brigade, division or corps—must have carried extra flags with them as part of the normal military supplies. These were probably flags that had been previously issued and either not used or returned when a new flag was received. While no official documentation has been found among the quartermaster records, at least five regiments engaged in the battle of Gettysburg lost their flags early in the battle and subsequently carried a different flag at Gettysburg. Whether the second flag was an old flag that had been stored in a quartermaster's wagon, or a new one issued to a Quartermaster by the government and carried along, then given out when the first flag was lost, is probably impossible to determine.

During the Gettysburg campaign the Army of Northern Virginia carried two types of flags into battle. Of the 42 flags still in existence that were captured during the campaign, 40 are of the Army of Northern Virginia battle flag type, while two are First National or Stars and Bars. At least one Second National flag was carried by a regiment as its battle flag. It is possible that other Second Nationals were used as headquarters flags for various units, but highly unlikely. I have seen no documentation that would substantiate this point.

Notes

[1] Quoted in G. T. Fleming, ed., *Life and Letters of Alexander Hays* (Pittsburgh: n. p., 1919), 463. This description is somewhat ironic, since none of the flags captured in Pickett's Charge were homemade. All were professionally made government issue flags. Those carried by Scales' brigade, such as the 28th North Carolina, were among the most aesthetically attractive of all Civil War flags. Hays' comment, made as the fire of battle was still smoldered, is probably an indication of how sensory perception can be distorted during battle, or how memory can be affected by the passage of time.

[2] For example, on July 3, 1996, I watched as a group of reenactors portrayed Pickett's Charge. They carried 16 flags, including three First Nationals, one Second National, two Third Nationals, three Virginia flags, four Army of Northern Virginia flags, one Army of Tennessee flag, one Hardee pattern and one Texas flag.

[3] David Hackett Fischer, *Paul Revere's Ride* (Boston: Little, Brown, 1994). See also John Galvin, *The Minute Men* (New York: Hawthorne Books, 1962). For a study of the difficulties the militia system posed for the Continental Army and how the military leaders tried to overcome the militia system's weaknesses, see Robert K. Wright, *The Continental Army* (Washington: Center For Military History of the United States, 1989).

[4] For an interesting analysis of how the organizations in Tennessee and Virginia provided the foundation for the Army of Tennessee and Army of Northern Virginia, and how the state political culture shaped each army and affected its military success, see Richard McMurry, *Two Great Rebel Armies: An Essay in Confederate Military History* (Chapel Hill: University of North Carolina Press, 1989).

[5] Edward W. Richardson, *Standards and Colors of the American Revolution* (Philadelphia: The University of Pennsylvania Press, 1982).

[6] [Time-Life Editors], *Echoes of Glory: Arms and Equipment of the Confederacy* (Alexandria, Va.: Time-Life, 1992).

[7] *CV*, 8(1900), 25.

[8] Crute, *Emblems of Southern Valor*.

[9] *Fifteenth Virginia* (Lynchburg: H. H. Howard, 1985).

[10] G. Ward Hobbs, "Lone Star Flags and Nameless Rags," *Alabama Review* 39(October 1986), 271-301.

[11] See the original sheet music in Devereux Cannon, *The Flags of the Confederacy: An Illustrated History* (Memphis: St. Luke's Press and Broadfoot Publishing, 1988), [93-94].

[12] Strikeleather, "Recollections," 26.

[13] *Ibid.*, [1].

[14] Boleslaw and Louise D'Otrange Mastai, *The Stripes and*

Stars: The Evolution of the American Flag (Ft. Worth: Amon Carter Museum, 1973).

[15] William C. Davis, *"A Government of Their Own": The Making of the Confederacy* (New York: The Free Press, 1995), 241-242.

[16] For a look at the variety of flags carried by Confederate troops during the war, see Rollins, ed., *The Returned Battle Flags.*

[17] *Ibid.*

[18] Madaus, *Army of the Tennessee.*

[19] Crute, *Emblems of Southern Valor.*

[20] Report of Col. Jubal Early, August 1, 1861, *OR*, Ser. I, Vol. 2, 557.

[21] Report of Col. R. E. Withers, n. d., *OR*, Ser. I, Vol. 2, 547.

[22] G. T. Beauregard to General J. E. Johnston, September 5, 1861, *OR*, Series I, Vol. 40, 272.

[23] Conversation with Howard Madaus, August 30, 1994. The order directing that each regiment carry a single flag, and that it should be the Army of Northern Virginia pattern, has not been located. Letters accompanying the return of state flags with the note that the order had been issued have been located, and the records of captured flags are consistent with the order. See "Letter" and "Record."

[24] "Record."

[25] Madaus, *Army of Tennessee*, and Crute, *Emblems of Southern Valor.*

[26] See "Record."

[27] Philip Katcher, *Flags of The American Civil War, No. 1: Confederate* (London: Osprey Publications, Limited, 1992), 20.

[28] In early 1862 the army was organized into two wings, the other commanded by Gen. Gustavus W. Smith. This evolved into the organization by corps.

[29] Conversation with Howard Madaus, August 30, 1994.

Chapter Three

"Where the Colors Are the Regiment Is Supposed To Be:"
The Battle Flag and Napoleonic Tactics

The Civil War battle flag had a specific use on the battlefield that modern Americans rarely recognize or seldom remember. In current military jargon this is called Command and Control. Officers used the flag to identify and maneuver large bodies of troops. Without it, major maneuvers like Pickett's Charge would have been exceedingly difficult, if not impossible.

In order to comprehend its tactical importance, one must first understand that the flag was carried by a specific type of unit within the overall structure of the army. Furthermore, the unit it represented—called a *regiment*—was made up of smaller ones—*companies* and *platoons*—and was in turn a part of larger organizations—*brigades, divisions* and *corps*.

The shape of Nineteenth Century warfare in Western civilization had been solidified during the early part of the century, when Napoleon Bonaparte used his armies to dominate Europe. Napoleonic warfare featured rapid maneuvering by large concentrated bodies of troops (the principal tactical organization was the corps), massed artillery battalions and rapid cavalry pursuit. The essence of Napoleonic tactics was summed up in his famous maxim: "God is on the side of the heaviest battalions."

This was emphasized in American military thought at West Point, where Dennis Hart Mahan taught military theory in the years before the war. Mahan in turn based his ideas on the writings of a Frenchman, Baron Antoine-Henri de Jomini, who essentially summarized European tactical ideas in his classic work *Summary of the Art of War*.[1] During the war Confederate Gen. Beauregard put this into an order on the level of the ten commandments when he wrote that:

> The whole science of war may be briefly defined as the art of placing in the right position, at the right time, a mass of troops greater than your enemy can there oppose you.
>
> PRINCIPLE NO. 1—to place masses of your army in contact with fractions of your enemy.[2]

The task of a commander in an offensive maneuver, no matter what level of troops he commanded, was to bring the largest number of troops to bear on a given point in the enemy's defenses. To do this each army was organized into groups or blocks of men, called (in order from largest to smallest) *corps, divisions, brigades, regiments* (made up of 10 or more companies; units of less than 10 companies called *battalions*), and *companies*. The smoothbore or rifle-musket that each soldier carried was meant to be aimed at the enemy's line, not necessarily aimed at an individual. Standing shoulder to shoulder in front of the enemy's line or fortifications, with guns leveled, the men would fire by volley, by file or "at will," in effect sending sheets of lead into the enemy line. The more men in line, the more destructive the fire.

The battle flag flying above the battle line was what officers relied upon to see where the center of the line lay, and the location of the regiments and brigades next to them. Alignment was essential for the fire of a line of muskets to be effective. If the line was not straight, the full impact of the simultaneous fire of a hundred, five hundred or even thousands of muskets would be diminished. Instead of tearing into their target, the bullets would scatter, and this would minimize the destructiveness.

After the first volley, the colors were often the only thing that could be seen through the smoke. The muskets and rifles used what we today call "black powder." When exploded, it created a cloud of thick, greyish, acrid smoke. The more guns fired, the denser the cloud of smoke surrounding the men.

Thus in the eyes of the men and officers, the flag was the material embodiment of the regiment. If the line broke and fell back, or charged ahead, each man would see the flag and try to rally around it. In the heat of battle, when a man's life was most vulnerable, he looked to the flag for guidance and this further strengthened his attachment to it.

If in combat the colorbearer was hit, one of the color guard had to pick up the flag and move forward. If he survived, he would normally remain the colorbearer until he, too, went down. Some colorbearers carried the flag through several engagements, others for only a brief moment.

Since both sides had the same drill in the correct position of the flag and its color guard, all Civil War soldiers understood how important the flag was to their enemy as well. The fact that the flag was usually one of the easiest things to see on a battlefield meant that it was always a focal point of enemy fire. It was an easy and vital target and the men who carried the flag, and those around them, suffered a higher mortality rate than the rest of the unit. If a man carried the flag, or picked it up when it fell, he could be sure that he was being lined up in the sights of the enemy. Thus assuming the role of colorbearer often required significant courage.

To bring an effective force together, large numbers of troops had to be moved from one point to another. This often required some fairly sophisticated maneuvers, such as changing from a column of four men abreast, marching side by side, into a line of battle extending across several hundred yards. When in line of battle, each soldier aligned himself by keeping elbow-to-elbow contact with the man on each side.

Army commanders needed full control of the various units, and this was accomplished through a command structure, or chain of command. At Gettysburg, Maj. Gen. George Gordon Meade had just taken command of the Federal *Army of the Potomac*, with some 93,000 men. Gen. Robert E. Lee commanded the Confederate *Army of Northern Virginia*, with roughly 70,000. The Army of the Potomac was divided into seven infantry *corps*, each commanded by a major general and averaging more than 10,000 men. The Army of Northern Virginia consisted of just three *corps*, each led by a lieutenant general with some 20,000 or more men. In both armies, each corps had two or more *divisions* of 4,000 to 8,000, and each division had two or more *brigades* of about 1,000 to 2,000 men each.

At Gettysburg, most brigades had four or five *regiments*, and that is the level of organization with which this study is most concerned.[3] A regiment normally began its service at "muster-in" with approximately 1,000 men, headed by a colonel, a lieutenant colonel, and a major. The regiments that fought at Gettysburg had been raised primarily in 1861 in the South, and 1861 or 1862 in the North. By the summer of 1863 the typical regiment was from 350 to 700 men, although many were considerably smaller. On July 3rd, several Southern units would go into Pickett's Charge with only 150 to 200 men.

Within each army difficulties in communication, and thus in combat effectiveness, changed at each level. At the level of army, corps and division command, most orders went out by courier on horseback. The commander simply had too many men, spread out over too much space, to see and hear everything and to talk to each significant subordinate. At the brigade level a commander might be able to ride from regiment to regiment, to where each flag could be seen, and give orders or discuss problems. The regimental commander could usually see everyone under his command and ride or even walk to where he was needed, and a company commander could almost always yell commands to his men, one of which was to "rally around the colors."

As previously mentioned, regiments and companies, especially early in the war, were raised on the community level. In the years before the Civil War it was normal, especially in the South and in rural areas and small towns in the North, for each town, village, or local region to sponsor militia companies. The type of military establishment that we have today, with its distance from the lives of the common population matched by its heavy influence in the halls of Congress and the central administration, was simply unimaginable before the Civil War.

When war broke out in 1861, the militia companies quickly volunteered and were mustered into the service by their states. They became the foundation on which armies were based. In addition, individuals, because of their wealth, social leadership in a given community, political position or military background, would raise a company of 80 to 100 volunteers who also sought to join state service. When a state government had ten companies—and in 1861 there were typically more volunteers than the state could uniform and equip—they were formed into a regiment and given a number. Thus the regiments that fought at Gettysburg were mainly composed of volunteers who came from the same area as the rest of the men in their company and regiment.

The relationship between community and army has already been discussed, but this point cannot be stressed too much, for it shaped the very character of the army, and thus the experience of the Civil War soldier. They were not only "citizen armies," made up almost exclusively of volunteers.[4] They were in fact constructed upon the reality that the men in them usually knew virtually every other man in their companies, and a sizable number in their regiments.

A process of socialization helped produce the armies of 1863. It often started with pre-war militia service, and in any case included living through the political debates and other social events that preceded the split between the sections. A young man with a rural, individualistic background now experienced volunteering and recruitment, followed by the life of a soldier: of drill, camp life, being away from home (often for the first time), living with other men away from the well-known and ordered routines of home, and finally combat, loss of friends and family, and death. The army forced the soldier to live a dramatically different way of life, and he could not avoid changing because of it.

This process normally caused the Civil War soldier to identify himself with his comrades, with his regiment, and thus with its flag. This identification furthered the process of unification and solidification, from a mass of individuals to a coherent, living and breathing organization of human beings. Loyalty, comradeship, and social bonds, already significant, were further strengthened. And above them always waved the flag.

Close order drill, the method used to move bodies of men from place to place, was one of the most important aspects of life in a Nineteenth Century army. It contributed significantly to the process of socialization. Each man stood and marched with his elbow and/or shoulder in contact with the men next to him on each side. Much of the time spent early in the war in training camps or "camps of instruction" was devoted to practicing these drills. Citizen-soldiers learned to maneuver on a field of battle, from column into line of battle, around houses and through gates. There were company drills in the morning, battalion, regiment, brigade or even division drill in the afternoon.

From the repetitive marching together and maneuvering came a sense of unity with the group. It created a feeling of belonging that would be of utmost importance when it came time to execute orders and commands under fire, amid the smoke and din of actual combat. One South Carolinian remembered the long-term effect of the drill, as well

74

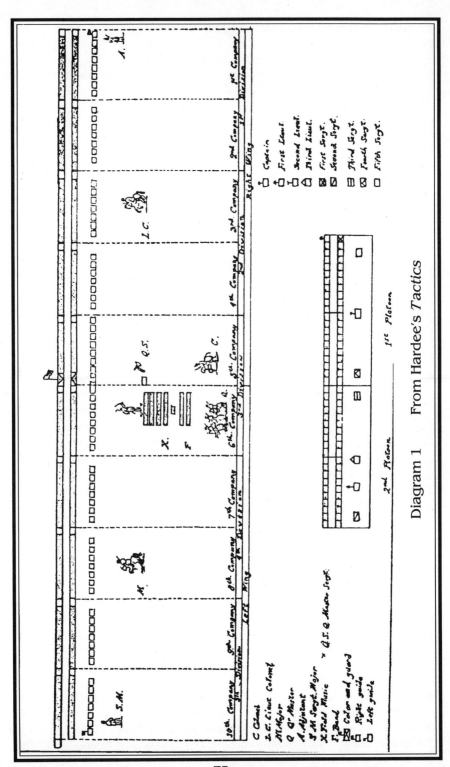

Diagram 1   From Hardee's *Tactics*

as the importance of the battle flag in all this:

> For the battlefield is not a drillroom, nor is a battle an occasion for drill, and there is the merest semblance of order maintained. I say *semblance* of order, for there *is* an under-current of order in tried troops that surpasses that of the drillroom—it is that order that springs from the confidence comrades have in each other, from the knowledge that these messmates of yours whether they stand or lie upon the ground, close together or scattered apart, in front of you three paces, or in rear of you six, in the open or behind a tree or rock—that these, though they do not 'touch elbows to the right,' are nevertheless keeping dressed upon the colors in some rough fashion, and that the line will not move forward and leave them there, nor will they move back and leave the line.[5]

The South Carolinian pointed out that during battle the entire well-trained regiment fought with a sense of unity and confidence in itself, and again the battle flag played a key role in its experience:

> With a burst of yells, a long, wavering, loose jointed line sweeps rapidly forward, only now and then one or two stopping to fire, while here and there drop the killed and the wounded; the slightly wounded . . . giving no heed but rushing on, while others run hurriedly, half bent to the rear. The colors drop, are seized again—again drop, and are again lifted, no man in reach daring to pass them by on the ground. Colors, not bright and whole and clean as when they came fresh from the white embroidering fingers, but since clutched in the storm of battle with grimy, bloody hands, and torn into shreds by shot and shell.[6]

The flag pinpointed the regiment. Indeed the military instruction manuals of the day, used by both North and South, emphasized the role of the flag in guidance and alignment. As one Gettysburg veteran said when asked if there was any regimental organization among the Federal troops defending the Angle during Pickett's Charge, "The colors were there and where the colors are the regiment is supposed to be; the men rallying under these colors."[7]

The bible of the drill-master was the manual written before the war by William J. Hardee, one of the pre-war U.S. Army's professional soldiers, who became one of the Confederacy's leading generals in the Western theater. This little book, *Hardee's Rifle and Light Infantry Tactics*, or one of its variations was used by nearly all officers in drilling

76

their troops throughout the war.

Hardee dictated that a color guard be chosen from the best men the unit had to offer, those who were "most distinguished for regularity and precision, as well as in the positions under arms as in their marching . . . The latter advantage and a just carriage of their person are to be more particularly sought for in the selection of the color-bearer."[8] The color guard should consist of nine men, a sergeant who carried the flag and eight corporals. Perhaps in some Federal regiments in 1863 the color guard may have been that large. In Southern forces, however, it was usually smaller: two to five men, chosen for their bravery and coolness under fire.

The standard size of the Army of Northern Virginia pattern was 48" (4') square, with the artillery version a bit smaller at 36". By regulation cavalry guidons were supposed to be 28" square, but in actuality all existing examples are the same size as infantry flags. The flag was carried, often by the largest and most physically imposing men in the regiment, on a staff that measured as least eight feet in length, making certain its visibility. The flagstaff normally carried a metal finial at the top, sometimes a very elaborate one.[9]

According to Hardee, the color guard was posted on the left of the right-center (Fifth) company of the regiment, which meant it would be as close to the center as possible (see Diagrams 1 and 2).

When the regiment went forward in line of battle, the colors were posted six paces in advance of the front line of the regiment (see Diagram 3).[10] As an older manual still in use during the war stated, "It is of the utmost importance, in marching in order of battle (or line), that the color-sergeant should be thoroughly habituated to preserve the precise length and cadence of step, and in his own person, to prolong a given direction, without deviation."[11] During actual combat, the color-bearers would step back one pace to avoid being shot by their own line (see Diagram 4).[12]

The colorbearer must be among the best men in the regiment. When George Nutting, colorbearer of the 5th Alabama, was killed on

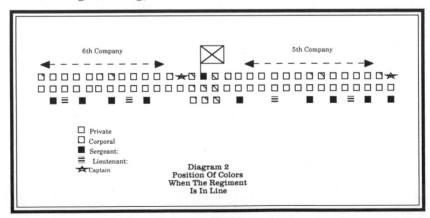

Diagram 2
Position Of Colors
When The Regiment
Is In Line

July 1st, his lieutenant, E. P. Jones, wrote to his sister:

> Our loss was not heavy compared to what the loss was
> in some other companies in the regiment; but still we
> feel deeply and mourn much the death of poor "Tone." I
> know of no one in the Company who would have been
> missed more and talked of as much as he, in fact, he was
> the life of the company, always in good humor, full of fun
> and as brave as a lion. Every one in the Company liked
> him, and feel that we have not only lost a brave soldier,
> but a friend whose place cannot be filled.[13]

Pvt. Stephens C. Smith of the 15th Virginia Cavalry recognized
the danger inherent in being the one carrying the flag or even marching
next to it. "Calhous Sparks is safe and well; he is color bearer of our
regiment," he said in a letter home. "I have been appointed color guard
with him, our position is one of danger and honor."[14] J. A. Strikeleather
of the 4th North Carolina recalled that in 1864 his regiment picked nine
of their best men for the colorguard, "to protect (the colors) with their
lives, to bear them forward in case the color bearer should fall . . . All

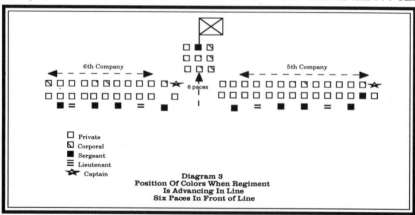

Diagram 3
Position Of Colors When Regiment
Is Advancing In Line
Six Paces In Front of Line

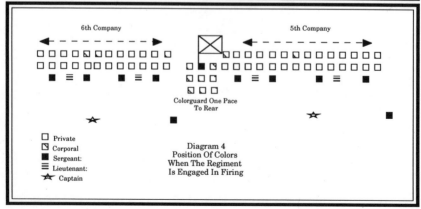

Diagram 4
Position Of Colors
When The Regiment
Is Engaged In Firing

heroes of whom any people may well be proud . . ." He went on to describe the quality of the men chosen for this duty. He felt that in describing their character he was "treading on sacred ground. I doubt if there was a nobler hero in the war, North or South." One of them, Pvt. Martin Snow, was Strikeleather's friend, and what Americans of former times might have called an "all-American boy." He was of humble birth and uneducated, a "natural man, . . . a born gentleman, and, in his make-up, there was as embodied as much of true and noble manhood as anyone I have ever known."[15]

The story of the 26th North Carolina on July 1st underscores the role of the flag and the Southern soldier's intense devotion to it. By two o'clock in the afternoon of July 1st, the 26th North Carolina infantry had spent several hours waiting to go into battle near McPherson's Ridge. They listened to the sounds of battle grow louder. Finally the waiting ended with the command "attention!," and the entire regiment stood up to face the enemy. Their 21-year-old colonel, Henry Burgwyn, stood in front of the center of the line; the colorbearer, Pvt. J. B. Mansfield, with a small color guard, was six paces in front of the regiment. With the command "Forward, March!," the lines moved forward, shoulder to shoulder, "as pretty and perfect a line as ever a regiment made, every man endeavoring to keep dressed on the colors."[16]

As if on parade, they moved toward near-certain death across Willoughby Run, into the muskets of the 24th Michigan and the 19th Indiana. Nearly as soon as the Carolinians stood up, the Michigan men fired a volley straight into them and cannon fire struck their left. Mansfield was shot in the foot in the opening volley, and two others in the colorguard went down. Sgt. Hiram Johnson picked up the colors, but he was shot before reaching Willoughby Run, and as he fell the banner was grabbed by Pvt. John Stamper. As they crossed Willoughby Run the Federal cannon, now almost on their flank, fired again, and down went Stamper. Pvt. George Washington Kelly grabbed the flag, but was quickly hit. His friend, Pvt. Larkin Thomas yelled at him to get up, but Kelly checked his ankle and found he had been hit by a piece of an artillery shell, and pleaded with Thomas to recover the shell. Instead, Thomas picked up the colors and continued on.

The Tarheels paused after crossing the stream to realign in the face of direct enemy fire. Thomas was shot down and as he fell he passed the flag to Pvt. John Vinson. Vinson was instantly hit and another man, Pvt. John Marley, grabbed the flag but was immediately killed. Another soldier, his name now lost, picked up the flag and carried it forward. By now they were close enough to the enemy that their orders could be heard by the Federals. The Rebels fired a volley and the blue line broke. As the 26th charged, the colorbearer waved the flag aloft. He carried it to the front and center of the line, whereupon a few Union soldiers took aim and fired a volley at him. He fell on top of the flag, pierced through the heart and drenching it in his blood. It was quickly picked up by Capt.

Don Troiani, "The Boy Colonel"
Col. Henry Burgwyn, 26th North Carolina
(Courtesy of Historical Art Prints)

W. W. McReedy; he, too, was shot down and fell to the ground with the flag beneath him.

Lt. George Wilcox pulled the blood-soaked flag from beneath McReedy, lifted it skyward and cheered the Tarheels onward. He took a few steps and quickly fell with two chest wounds. But the 26th had broken a second Federal line and was 20 paces from the third, being fired at from point-blank range.

Col. Burgwyn took the flag from Wilcox, began to advance again, and shouted out an order for the men to align themselves on the flag in the center: "Dress on the Colors!" (see "The Boy Colonel") What was left of the regiment fell into line and Pvt. Frank Honeycutt rushed to Burgwyn and requested the honor of carrying the flag. As the colonel turned to give the flag to him, Burgwyn was hit in the side, the bullet passing through both lungs. The blow jerked him to his left and wrapped him in the blood-soaked banner. Burgwyn fell on the flag and as Pvt. Honeycutt bent down to take it from beneath him, a bullet entered Honeycutt's brain.

Lt. Col. John R. Lane took command of the regiment and pulled the flag from beneath Burgwyn. As he did he asked Burgwyn if he was severely hurt, but the colonel could not speak. Lane then ordered his men to close to the left: "I am going to give them the bayonet." He was soon hit, and the 14th man to carry the flag, Capt. W. S. Brewer, took the banner, heavy with symbolism and blood, from Lane. As Brewer led the regiment forward yet again, Lt. Blair rushed forward out of the ranks and shouted, "No man can take these colors and live!" Brewer yelled back: "It is my time to take them now! Forward the Twenty-Sixth!" He carried them for the rest of the day, and when the 26th regrouped that evening, only 216 men remained out of the 800 who had gone into battle that morning.

As Burgwyn was carried off on a stretcher, he realized he was mortally wounded, but said, "The Lord's will be done. We have gained the greatest victory in the war. I have no regrets at my approaching death. I fell in the defense of my country."[17]

The story of the 26th North Carolina and its colors on July 1st underscores the dual function of the flag and the central role it played in the experience of combat. It served as both a means of inspiring troops and of controlling them in the midst of the most severe combat. It also highlights the incredible valor of these men. Everyone who picked up the flag must have known that the men in blue would be aiming at him, and that his chances of being wounded or killed became much greater with the flag in his hands than they were when he was just another uniform in the ranks. Yet they kept coming, indeed even asked for the honor of carrying the flag. Their opponents recognized the importance of the flag not just by concentrating their of their fire upon it, but also by explicitly honoring the men who reportedly captured them.

Notes

[1] For a discussion of Mahan and Jomini and their influence on military tactics, see Grady McWhiney and Perry D. Jamieson, *Attack and Die: Civil War Military Tactics and the Southern Heritage* (University, Alabama: University of Alabama Press, 1982). This is an excellent introduction to Civil War tactics, even though its most notable assertion, that Confederates more often launched frontal attacks and did so because of their Scots-Irish culture, is essentially unconvincing. See also Archer Jones, *Civil War Command and Strategy: The Process of Victory and Defeat* (New York: The Free Press, 1992), 256-278.

[2] *Ibid.*, 275.

[3] The Army of Northern Virginia also contained units called *Legions.* These were outmoded organizations named after Roman legions. When they were first raised they contained infantry, artillery and cavalry units, but by Gettysburg they had been divided and each group assigned to an appropriate infantry, artillery or cavalry unit.

[4] Conscription had begun in 1862 but had not yet reached levels significant enough to affect this aspect of army life.

[5] Susan W. Benson, ed., *Berry Benson's Civil War Book* (Athens: University of Georgia Press, 1962), 22.

[6] *Ibid.*, 23.

[7] Testimony of Capt. William H. Hill (19th Mass.), *Supreme Court of Pennsylvania. Middle District. May Term, 1891, Nos. 20 and 30. Appeal of the Gettysburg Battlefield Memorial Association From the Decree of the Court of Common Pleas of Adams County,* 211. (Hereafter cited as *Supreme Court*)

[8] Bvt. Lt. W. J. Hardee, *Hardee's Rifle and Light Infantry Tactics, for the Instruction, Exercises and Maneuvers of Riflemen and Light Infantry* (New York: J. O. Kane, 1862), 8-9.

[9] The Museum of the Confederacy has 125 flagstaffs captured during the war and returned in 1905. They range from 96" to 102", and are 1 1/4" to 1 1/2" in diameter. Rebecca Rose to author, July 12, 1995.

[10] Hardee, *Tactics*, 8.

[11] *Abstract of Infantry Tactics; Including Exercise and Maneuvers of Light Infantry and Riflemen; for the Use of the Militia of the United States. Published by the War Department, Improved Edition of 1861* (Philadelphia: Moss, Brother and Company, 1861), 15-16.

[12] Hardee, *Tactics*, 8.

[13] E. P. Jones to Sister, no date, published July 24, 1863, *Alabama Beacon.* Photocopy in 5th Alabama File, GNMP.

[14] Stephens Smith to Sophia and Julia, [June, 1863], Stephens Calhous Smith Papers, Virginia State Archives, photocopy GNMP.

[15] Strikeleather, "Recollections," 30.

[16] George C. Underwood, *History of the Twenty-Sixth Regiment*

of the North Carolina Troops in the Great War, 1861-1865 (Goldsboro: Nash Brothers Printers, 1901); Mrs. B. A. Emerson, "The Most Famous Regiment," *CV* 25(1917), 352-255; R. Lee Hadden, "The Deadly Embrace: The Meeting of the Twenty-Fourth Regiment, Michigan Infantry and the Twenty-Sixth Regiment of North Carolina Troops at McPherson's Woods, Gettysburg, Pennsylvania, July 1, 1863," *The Gettysburg Magazine* (hereafter cited as *GB*), 5(July 1991), 27.

[17] Recollection of Pvt. William Cheek, quoted in Time-Life, *Voices of the Civil War: Gettysburg* (Alexandria, Va.: Time-Life, 1996), 55.

Chapter Four

Prologue:
Carlisle and Hanover

After the victory at Chancellorsville and the death of Stonewall Jackson in May, 1863, President Jefferson Davis met with the leadership of the Confederacy in Richmond to discuss what should next be done. They discussed several possibilities, but, at Gen. Robert E. Lee's urging, settled on another campaign in the Eastern theater. The Army of Northern Virginia would move north into Maryland and Pennsylvania. The campaign plans were not written down and thus today seem a bit vague. An offensive battle, like Chancellorsville, might take place, or perhaps a defensive one, like Fredericksburg, might occur. Numerous Eastern cities would be threatened. Perhaps merely a successful invasion, with no major engagement with the enemy, might suffice to bring the Yankees to the negotiating table, where wily Southerners could at last attain their ultimate goal: independence. With that in mind, Vice President Alexander Stephens was scheduled to sail to Washington about the same time the army entered Pennsylvania.

Yet whenever battle erupted, Gen. Lee's aggressive instincts took over and he became his most aggressive and creative self. So it would be in Pennsylvania. After Confederate victories at Second Manassas, Fredericksburg and Chancellorsville, Lee's opponents had merely crawled back to Washington, refitted, reorganized and emerged even stronger and more difficult to deal with. They had been essentially hollow victories, and bloody ones at that, costing the South thousands of casualties. Lee did not want another such victory, so this time all restraints would be removed.

As the Rebel forces crossed the Mason-Dixon line and entered Pennsylvania, panic spread throughout the area. Where were they headed? Harrisburg? Baltimore? Philadelphia? New York? Speculation and rumors ran wild, and people crowded the roads, fleeing in terror of the advancing Southerners. "Ja, the rebels eat babies," claimed one of the rumors that spread ahead of them.[1]

Southern Pennsylvania was familiar territory to Lt. Gen. Richard Ewell. Newly appointed commander of the bulk of Stonewall Jackson's old II Corps, Ewell been stationed before the war at the Carlisle Barracks in Carlisle, about 30 miles north of Gettysburg. On June 27th some of Ewell's men moved into Carlisle and took over the military post, which had been abandoned two days earlier. Led by a brigade of cavalry under the command of Brig. Gen. Albert Jenkins, they looked fearsome to the townspeople. These deeply tanned, lanky, men collected supplies and prepared to attack Harrisburg.

"The Damned Red Flags of the Rebellion"

On the afternoon of Sunday, June 28th, Gen. Ewell held a flag-raising ceremony in Carlisle on the grounds of the post where he had once served in the U.S. Army. Most of the division of Maj. Gen. Robert Rodes, battle-hardened men from the deep South, lined up for the event. The Confederate Congress had recently authorized the Second National flag, the white "stainless banner" with the Army of Northern Virginia's St. Andrew's Cross in the canton. Brigade, division and corps headquarters would soon begin to fly it.

Two conflicting accounts of the origins of the 32nd North Carolina's flag exist. In the most widely cited one, a group of ladies in Richmond had sewn one of the new flags and had given it to President Jefferson Davis. Davis had handed it to Lee and Lee had decided to have it presented to a regiment in his army singled out for its courage and "most worthy of receiving and carrying it,"[2] as one of the members of the regiment who received it remembered. The flag was given to Ewell, who in turn presented it to Rodes, who gave it to Brig. Gen. Junius Daniel, commander of one of the four brigades in his division. Daniel chose the 32nd North Carolina for the honor of raising the flag. He presented them with "the only regular Confederate [national] flag that was in the corps (all other flags were battle flags) and the Thirty second Regiment carried that flag in the battle of Gettysburg," the brigade historian recalled. [3]

The second version, reported by one of Ewell's staff, Maj. Campbell Brown, differs markedly. Brown recorded in his diary that when the Confederates got to Carlisle and saw the flagstaff still standing, they decided to raise a Confederate flag on it. The Second National sent by Lee to Ewell was raised, but the corps commander decided it was too small to impress the "ignorant citizens" of Carlisle. The battle flag of the 32nd was available, so they made it the "ground work"[canton] of a new flag. They found two or three tailors "and in an hour or two we had a handsome flag ready for hoisting."[4] Thus a large Second National Confederate flag fluttered over the U. S. Army barracks in Carlisle, Pennsylvania.

A cask of whiskey and/or beer, apparently part of the government stores, was hidden in a haystack. The men found and opened it, and soon everyone began to feel relaxed.[5] Someone produced a quantity of mint, sugar and ice, and soon mint julips were plentiful. Two regimental bands broke out their instruments and struck up "Dixie," and "The Bonnie Blue Flag." Songs were sung and speeches were made by senior officers including Ewell, Rodes, Daniel and Maj. Gen. Isaac Trimble, who was currently without a command, having just returned to the army after recovering from wounds. All the officers apparently consumed a goodly amount of the brew. They spoke of what had been and what was to come, of freedom and liberation. The soldiers responded with storms of applause. The residents of Carlisle were friendly—the Confederates had been well-behaved so far—and the men

86

were given food and drink; it was, according to one witness, an "animated scene."

Assistant Surgeon William Marston recorded in his diary that they "raised our new flag today in the Barracks—great cheering and speech making."[6] One Confederate wrote that the ceremony made him feel like marching straight for New York. The northern most U.S. military base to be captured during the campaign was duly sanctified with the Confederate flag. The entire North seemed to stand open to the Rebels.[7] After the battle of Gettysburg Brig. Gen. Stephen D. Ramseur would compliment the 32nd for its work around the McPherson barn on July 1st, saying that the finest thing he saw during the battle was "the conduct of that regiment that carried into the fight that flag with the long white tail to it."[8]

* * *

While Rodes' men frolicked at Carlisle, Maj. Gen. J. E. B. Stuart's cavalry rode on the east flank of the army, protecting the flank and gathering in Yankee supply wagons caught behind the lines. Two days after the 32nd raised the flag at Carlisle, a Union cavalry division under the command of Brig. Gen. Judson Kilpatrick wound its way through the countryside east of Gettysburg. Kilpatrick's men had gotten between Stuart and Lee's army, and their mission was to stay there and separate the two. Among Kilpatrick's units rode Brig. Gen. Elon J. Farnsworth's outfit, men who would meet their fate in the rocky fields south of Gettysburg on the afternoon of July 3rd. During the march north, the reception these troopers received in the small towns of Pennsylvania had been wonderful. Citizens of all sorts greeted them with cheers, patriotic songs and even good food and cold water. The men were soon relaxed and enjoying themselves.

Part of Farnsworth's brigade—the 5th New York and the 18th Pennsylvania cavalry regiments—moved into Hanover, a small town about 14 miles east of Gettysburg. Their reception was similar to that in other towns, with children waving flags and singing songs and women putting out cold water, coffee, sandwiches, fresh pies and fruit for troopers weary from a long week in the saddle. Even some fresh cigars were passed out; the cavalrymen began to loll about in the shade, talk to the local citizens and all in all to feel safe and proud of themselves.

Suddenly a cannon opened fire. For a moment men reacted as if it were just another salute from some local militia. Then a cavalry troop charged out of the woods at them, "a battle flag at their head." An adjutant yelled out "don't fire, they are our men," but someone else said that "our men don't carry that flag."[9]

In a flash they realized it was Jeb Stuart's cavalry and horse artillery. The flag they saw belonged to the 2nd North Carolina Cavalry of Brig. Gen. W. H. F. Lee's brigade.[10] While the civilians ran screaming to their homes, Maj. John Hammond of the 5th New York Cavalry ordered his men back on their horses, quickly organized them into column and led them out of town to an open field near the railroad depot, where they deployed in line and charged back into the town. They met Lee's brigade—the 2nd North Carolina and 9th and 13th Virginia cavalry regiments—on Frederick Street in the middle of town. Soon men on horses were swinging sabers and firing pistols and carbines at point blank range. It was a brutal but short fight, with bodies falling off horses and into the dust, and in just a few minutes the gray-clad troopers turned around and rode back from where they had come, with Stuart himself on his thoroughbred charger jumping a high fence to barely escape capture.

As the Rebels scattered, Corporal James Rickey and Sgt. Thomas Burke of the 5th New York spotted the flagbearer of the 13th Virginia Cavalry riding with a second trooper. The Federals turned to charge and as they did the unnamed Confederates began to ride away. It quickly became a race, the Federals firing their carbines as they rode and other Confederates firing back at them. Rickey's horse was shot after about 200 yards but Burke continued chasing the colorbearer. "I gained on my prize," he recalled, "and closing in on the men, as I used my carbine with good effect, I called on them to surrender." Burke's efforts were rewarded: the Confederates stopped and turned over their pistols, carbines, swords and the regimental battle flag.

Burke herded them back to Federal lines as fast as their horses would go and promptly took the flag and prisoners to Gen. Kilpatrick, who by now had ridden back from the head of the column.[11] Thus the first Confederate battle flag captured in the Gettysburg campaign was lost by Jeb Stuart's cavalry. It would be the only Confederate cavalry standard lost in Pennsylvania.

Notes

[1] McKinley Kantor, *Gettysburg* (New York: Landmark Books, 1952).

[2] Harry A. London, "Thirty-Second Regiment," Clark, *Histories*, II, 525.

[3] "Daniel-Grimes Brigade," Clark, *Histories*, IV, 514. The entire story of the presentation to a regiment based on their courage is probably apocryphal: the 32nd had only recently joined the division, had not fought with the Army of Northern Virginia in previous battles, and had not been cited for valorous or outstanding service. The story was written by the regimental historian long after the event. The 32nd, raised in April, 1862, was stationed in Richmond during the Fredericksburg and Chancellorsville campaigns.

[4] Journal of Campbell Brown, Tennessee State Archives, Nashville. I find this story much more convincing, as it was recorded in the

diary at the time of the event, was not meant for publication and was written by a person not involved in the history of the 32nd.

[5] Journal of Campbell Brown. Also quoted in J. D. Hufham (pseudonym), "Gettysburg," *Wake Forest Student*, April, 1897, 452.

[6] Diary of William Marston, Woodruff Library, Emory University.

[7] Diary of Jed Hotchkiss, entry for June 28, 1863, in Archie McDonald, ed., *Make Me a Map of the Valley* (Dallas: Texas Christian University Press, 1988); Wellman, *Rebel Boast*, 119-120. A North Carolina newspaper published a small article in 1863 suggesting that this flag was used as Ewell's headquarters flag on July 2nd or 3rd. I doubt this. Among other things, the author put the 32nd in Daniel's brigade, not Ramseur's. *State Journal*, n.d. (1863), 32nd North Carolina File, GNMP.

[8] Quoted in London, "Thirty second," 526.

[9] Horace K. Ide, "History of the First Vermont Cavalry," in Elliott W. Hoffman, ed., "The First Vermont Cavalry in the Gettysburg Campaign," *GB*, 14(December 1995), 12.

[10] Report of Maj. Gen. J.E.B. Stuart, *OR*, 2, 695.

[11] W. F. Beyer and O. F. Keydel, eds., *Deeds of Valor From the Records of the United States Government* (Detroit: The Perrier-Keydel Co., 1907), 218; Rev. Louis Boudrye, *Historic Records of the Fifth New York Cavalry, First Ira Harris Guard. . .* (Albany: S. R. Gray, 1865), 64-65; Kilpatrick's Reports, June 30, 1863 *OR*, 1, 70 and August 10, 1863, 992; Report of Maj. Gen. Alfred Pleasonton, *OR*, 3, 469; Report of Maj. John Hammond, 5th New York Cavalry, *OR*, I, 1008-9; Daniel T. Balfour, *13th Virginia Cavalry* (Lynchburg: H. E. Howard, 1986), 21-2; George R. Powell, *Encounter at Hanover: Prelude to Gettysburg* (Hanover: The Historical Publication Committee of Hanover, 1963); "Record" #17, incorrectly states it was captured on July 1st; G. W. Bealel, *A Lieutenant of Cavalry in Lee's Army* (Boston, 1918), 114-115. This flag is currently in the Museum of the Confederacy, Richmond, Virginia.

Chapter Five

"Their Battle Flags Looked Redder and Bloodier
In the Strong July Sun
Than I Had Ever Seen Them Before":
July 1

The village of Gettysburg and its 2,400 residents lay nestled among the green fields and wooded hills of southern Pennsylvania. Ten important roads met there, giving the town a strategic significance out of proportion to its size. Travelers from Baltimore, Harrisburg and other points east and north passed through on their way west and south. Prosperous farmers, some with thick German accents hinting at European origins, brought crops to market in Gettysburg and sold them to buyers who had come to town on the railroad that connected Gettysburg to the larger Eastern cities.

The earth here was rich and fertile; the farmland shaded by the surrounding hills produced bountiful yields of hay, barley and corn. Orchards with trees bearing cherries, apples and peaches dotted the countryside. Both armies had spent the previous two years in northern Virginia, and had virtually stripped the area of livestock, crops and timber, giving it a desolate look. The contrast between southern Pennsylvania and northern Virginia was striking and many soldiers wrote home glowing accounts of Pennsylvania's abundance and beauty. Farmers worked large fields, well-tended and ordered, with stone, rail or strong post-and-rail fences. Beautiful large barns with stone foundations and walls gave the area a solid, bountiful ambience. The town itself looked prosperous. White clapboard houses sat next to brick storefronts, stone churches and public buildings.

The rolling fields surrounding the town rose into several ridges that seemingly protected it. On the west and running north to south lay Seminary Ridge, wood-covered and crowned with the Lutheran Seminary that gave it its name. Farther west the land rose and fell into three more wooded ridges approximately a mile apart, the closest known as McPherson Ridge, followed by Herr Ridge and Schoolhouse Ridge.

South of town a large hill jutted up and then trailed off into rocky fields. On top of the hill lay Evergreen Cemetery, just a few years old, from which Cemetery Hill took its name. Cemetery Ridge ran south from there, gradually vanishing into woods before rising again at another hill now called Little Round Top.

* * *

The battle began west of town, with the lead elements of the Army of Northern Virginia crossing the ridges and moving down the Chambersburg Pike toward Gettysburg. The fighting opened early in the morning when Confederate Brig. Gen. James J. Archer's brigade of Maj. Gen. Henry Heth's division, A. P. Hill's corps, attacked Brig. Gen. John Buford's cavalry along McPherson's Ridge. All day long the struggle grew as various commanders fed newly arriving troops into the fray. By the end of the day most of Hill's corps and some of Ewell's corps opposed the Federal I and XI Corps.

Combat occurred all day along the ridges west and north of the town until the late afternoon, when the Confederates broke the Federal lines and pushed them back helter-skelter through the town. Armed action closed late in the afternoon with the collapse of the XI Corps north of town and the I Corps along Seminary Ridge and Oak Ridge. On Cemetery Hill Federal officers constructed a strong defensive position into which the Union men fled and regrouped at the end of the day.

Just after dawn the first column of Confederates came marching down the Chambersburg Pike. Pvt. E. T. Boland of the 13th Alabama in Archer's brigade remembered that their colonel, Birkett D. Fry, rode out ahead of the column. When Fry "rode back to the color bearer and ordered him to uncase the colors, [it was] the first intimation that we had that we were about to engage the enemy."[1] As the Confederates came over Herr Ridge Lieutenant John Calef, commanding a Federal artillery battery west of Gettysburg, saw the first battle flags. "Their battle flags looked redder and bloodier in the strong July sun," he remarked, "than I had ever seen them before. At those flags the firing was directed, and my gunners succeeded in making excellent shots, throwing the lines into some confusion."[2]

Calef had seen the 13th Alabama's flag leading the Confederate advance, carried by its colorbearer, Tom Grant. Archer's brigade was soon engaged with Calef's battery and Buford's dismounted cavalry. Grant, a tall, double-jointed man had "imbibed freely of Pennsylvania rye or apple juice," and led the regiment into battle, waving the flag and yelling at the top of his voice. Another man in the color guard noted that he made a "fine target," and drew fire toward them. Pvt. W. T. Moon told him "Tom, if you don't stop that I will use my bayonet on you!" At that moment a volley of Federal rifle fire rang out, and "Tom needed no further admonition from me."[3] Pvt. W. A. Castleberry picked up the 13th's flag and carried it forward. As the battle progressed Archer's brigade got into a terrible fight and was surrounded by Federal troops along Willoughby Run. Just as Archer and his colorbearer were about to be captured Castleberry decided to save the flag. He recalled that,

> I thought of what my Colonel, Aiken, had told me when
> he gave me the colors at Chancellorsville. He said:
> 'Don't let the Yankees have them.' So, in order to keep
> the Yankees from getting them, I tore the flag from the

staff and put it in my bosom. As I started off a Yankee struck me with his sword and cursed me, telling me to come back. I told him I would die if I did not get a drink of water soon, for I claimed to be very sick.

Castleberry crawled through a wheatfield to escape, and watched the battle from behind a cord of wood.[4] The 13th's flag survived only to be lost on July 3rd.

* * *

The first Confederate battle flag lost at Gettysburg may well be the most famous and well-known of all those captured during the campaign. It was taken from the 2nd Mississippi by men from the Iron Brigade, one of the most famous fighting outfits in the Army of the Potomac. The incidents surrounding its capture were some of the most dramatic and violent of the entire campaign.[5] (See Map I)

Formed of five regiments from the "Old Northwest," one each from Michigan and Indiana and three from Wisconsin, the Iron Brigade fought valiantly at Brawner's Farm and all through the battles of 1862 and early 1863. On July 1st the men were awakened before first light for reveille, built their fires, boiled coffee and ate their breakfast of hardtack early enough to be on the march shortly after daylight.

On the way up the Emmitsburg Road from Marsh Creek they were cheered by the rumor that Maj. Gen. McClellan was back in command of the army, and as they neared Gettysburg they could hear the sound of the guns, and learned that Buford's cavalry had gotten the army into a skirmish with the Rebs. A regimental band struck up "Red, White and Blue," and off they went to meet the enemy.

The 6th Wisconsin was at the end of the column as they turned northwest off the Emmitsburg Road near the Codori farm and crossed the fields toward the Seminary. Lt. Col. Rufus Dawes had to shout out his orders so they could be heard above the din of the band playing "Yankee Doodle." Looking west from Seminary Ridge the soldiers saw one battle in front of them and another off to their right, so Dawes sang out "by company into line, on right company," thus changing the regiment from a column of fours into a line of battle. They crossed the fields to the west and moved north, up a slight rise to the Chambersburg Pike that runs northwest out of Gettysburg. As they reached the pike they saw a line of Confederates at the crest of the rise, their red flags waving overhead, already engaged against the Federal right to the north of the pike and railroad cut.

The Confederate line they faced was made up of three regiments of a brigade led by Brig. Gen. Joseph Davis. This brigade was an anomaly in several ways. It was one of only two in Hill's corps with troops from more than one state (Longstreet and Ewell each had one brigade of mixed troops). None of the nine regimental officers had formal military training and the brigade commander—nephew of the president—was a beneficiary of nepotism. Most of the officers lacked significant combat experience. Finally, the 11th Mississippi had been left behind to guard the supply trains, so the brigade brought to battle only three regiments.

Davis' men had begun their attack near the Chambersburg Pike west of an unfinished railroad cut, advanced up a gradual slope and were now in line parallel to the cut just north of the Pike. They were fighting with three regiments of Brig. Gen. Lysander Cutler's I Corps brigade. In the first volley the 76th New York had shot down two of the 55th North Carolina's colorbearers. A third, Sgt. Galloway, was hit, and Colonel J. K. Connally, commanding the 55th, seized the flag and rushed out in front of his men, waving it aloft. He made a conspicuous target and drew an immediate volley from the Pennsylvanians and New Yorkers, wounding him in the arm and hip. Near him was Major Belo, who leaned down and asked him if he was badly wounded. Connally replied that he was, and added, "but do not pay any attention to me; take the colors and keep ahead of the Mississippians."[6] The Southerners kept going and Cutler's men turned around and retreated several hundred yards.

Coming up on the south flank of Cutler's retreating line, the Wisconsin men halted at the Chambersburg Pike, then began loading and firing at their enemy. They saw the unfinished railroad bed that disappeared into a hill on their left flank, between them and the enemy. The Federals to their left retreated, and the Confederates seemed to be swallowed up by the earth.[7]

Davis's brigade had not disappeared, but about half of them had jumped into the unfinished railroad cut which ranged in depth from a few inches up to 10 feet. They had already been engaged with and defeated the 76th New York, 56th Pennsylvania and the 147th New York regiments of Cutler's brigade, and had even traded volleys with Capt. James Hall's 2nd Maine artillery battery, forcing it to retreat and nearly capturing one of its fieldpieces.

Now the Iron Brigade's 6th Wisconsin, with about 420 men in line, found themselves facing the 2nd Mississippi Infantry, in the center of Davis' line. William Murphy, senior corporal of the 2nd's colorguard, carried the flag because Sgt. Christopher Columbus Davis, the usual colorbearer, was sick that morning. Murphy stood about 50 paces east of the cut and about 10 paces south of its east end, toward Gettysburg. "There was no ditch there at all," Murphy remembered, "the ditch was not more than two feet deep where I passed over the railroad."[8] Most of the men west of Murphy jumped down into the cut where it was deeper, and let loose devastating volleys at the 6th Wisconsin.

The Chambersburg Pike had rail fences on each side, and the Mississippians' bullets could be heard thumping into them as well as into the bodies of the Wisconsin men. The fences were quickly torn down, and the men stood firing away at any Confederates they could see. It was a "murderous" situation, and soon the Wisconsin men began to chant "Charge!," "Charge!," "Charge!" The only way the men on the left could see the enemy was "by their flag, which was planted on the edge of the excavation, and by the smoke of their muskets as they gave us volley after volley."[9]

The 95th New York and 84th New York (also known as the 14th Brooklyn) joined the 6th Wisconsin and Dawes yelled out for the combined force to charge the cut. Across the field they went into a storm of lead bullets, with men falling at almost every step. One Badger remembered that he felt the Rebels hold their fire for a moment as they got near the railroad cut, then let loose a tremendous volley, seemingly knocking down half the charging men at a distance of about 18 feet.[10] As the Wisconsin men approached the enemy line, they noticed that the Confederate battle flag seemed to stand alone in front of the line. In fact, Murphy held the flag of the 2nd Mississippi by himself, and recorded that it was struck at least 12 times, and the staff was splintered in two or three places.[11] The rest of the colorguard had been shot down in the first five minutes of the fight.

Lieutenant William Remington of the 6th Wisconsin saw the flag and decided to capture it. So did several others at about the same moment. Remington ran for the flag but was wounded within 15 to 20 feet of it:

> I got hit at this time on the left side of my neck. It was not of enough account to hardly draw blood. I got quite near the flag, was changing my sword to my left hand, where my revolver was, when I saw a soldier taking aim at me from the railroad cut. I threw my right shoulder forward and kept going for the flag. He hit me through the right shoulder and knocked me down. I crawled forward, got up, walked backward until I got through our regiment, spoke to Major Hauser, got d——d for going after the flag and started for the rear on my best run. Flag-taking was pretty well knocked out of me.[12]

Another Badger, Cpl. Cornelius Okey, also went for the flag:

> I remember seeing Lt. Wm. Remington, Drummer L[ewis] Eggleston and myself—there may have been others, but we were close together and making for the rebel flag at the top of our speed, Remington in the center, Eggleston on the right and I on the left. At this time the firing from both sides was very hot, and as we got well out between the two lines it seemed almost impossible to breathe without inhaling a bullet. Lt.

Remington was wounded through the right shoulder and Eggleston and myself pressed on, expecting every moment to be shot, but it was too late to turn back. I reached the flag a little in advance of Eggleston and bending over grasped the staff low down, but he was so close to me that before I could draw it from the ground, the staff having been driven well down in the dirt, Eggleston had also got a hold of it. As I straightened up, I noticed a rebel corporal on his knees, right in front of me in the act of firing, his bayonet almost touched me; as quick as thought almost, I made a quarter face to the left, thus pressing my right side to him and bringing Eggleston, who still retained his hold on the flag, as well as myself, at my back. The rebel whom I had noticed fired. His charge, a ball and three buck-shot passed through the skirts of my frock coat in front and lodged in my left fore-arm and wrist. Almost at the same instant Eggleston fell to the ground, having been shot through both arms. . . .[13]

Pvt. John Johnson of the 6th had a fouled musket, his ramrod stuck halfway down the barrel as he watched the struggle for the flag. He tried to save Eggleston:

As I arrived at the edge of the railroad cut, I saw that the rebel color sergeant had stuck the end of his flag staff into the ground and was holding on it with both hands. Louis [sic] Eggleston, one of my mess-mates, whom I loved as a brother, also had hold of the staff and was trying to wrest it from the rebel's grasp. Seeing other rebels raising their guns as if to shoot or bayonet Eggleston, I stepped in front of him and raised my musket to defend him as best I could. While thus in the act of striking, I received a wound that disabled my right arm. Poor Eggleston also went down, and I think from the same bullet that wounded me.[14]

At that moment some of the 6th gained the top of the cut and began yelling at the Confederates, ordering them to surrender. Another group gained the left flank of the Mississippians and fired into the line. Earl Rogers remembered the scene:

Bayonets are crossed. The fight was hand to hand amidst firing and smoke. The men are black and grimy with powder and heat. They seemed all unconscious to the terrible situation; they were mad and fought with a

96

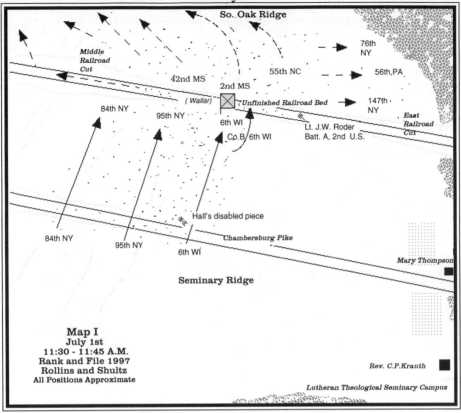

So. Oak Ridge

Middle
Railroad
Cut

76th
NY

55th NC

56th, PA

42nd MS

2nd MS

147th
NY

(Wallar)

Unfinished Railroad Bed

East
Railroad
Cut

84th NY

95th NY

6th WI

Lt. J.W. Roder
Batt. A, 2nd U.S.

Cp. B 6th WI

84th NY

95th NY

Hall's disabled piece

Chambersburg Pike

6th WI

Mary Thompson

Seminary Ridge

Map I
July 1st
11:30 - 11:45 A.M.
Rank and File 1997
Rollins and Shultz
All Positions Approximate

Rev. C.P.Krauth

Lutheran Theological Seminary Campus

desperation seldom witnessed.[15]

As the Confederates in the deeper part of the cut threw down their guns, gave up their swords and began to surrender, the fight over the flag of the 2nd Mississippi continued unabated. Pvt. Bodley Jones of the 6th managed to grasp the flag but was instantly shot down. A friend of Eggleston, "Mountain Man" Anderson swung his musket like a club and bashed in the head of the man who had shot Eggleston. Around the flag men from both sides fought viciously with guns, bayonets and fists. Cpl. Frank Wallar and his brother Sam of the 6th lunged towards the flag. As a Rebel took aim at Frank, Sam managed to knock the gun off target, then brain the Rebel with the butt of his own gun. John Harland reached for the flag but was knocked down by a bullet and fell into the cut, stopping at the feet of the man who had killed him.[16]

Through all this Cpl. Murphy held on to the flag and fought off everyone who tried to take it from him:

> Just about that time a squad of soldiers made a rush for
> my colors and our men did their duty. They were all
> killed or wounded, but they still rushed for the colors

97

Don Troiani, "Fight For The Colors"
(Courtesy of Historical Art Prints)

with one of the most deadly struggles that was ever witnessed during any battle of the war. They still kept rushing for my flag and there were over a dozen shot down like sheep in their mad rush for the colors. The first soldier was shot down just as he made for the flag, and he was shot by one of our soldiers. Just to my right and at the same time a lieutenant made a desperate struggle for the flag and was shot through the right shoulder. Over a dozen men fell killed or wounded, and then a large man made a rush for me and the flag. As I tore the flag from the staff he took hold of me and the color. The firing was still going on, and was kept up for several minutes after the flag was taken from me. . . .[17]

The "large man" described by Murphy was Cpl. Frank Wallar of the 6th, and, as Wallar relates, he successfully wrestled the flag out of Murphy's grasp:

I had no thought of getting the flag till at this time, and I started straight for it, as did lots of others. Soon after I got the flag, there were men from all the companies [of the 6th] there. I did take the flag out of the color bearer's hand . . . My first thought was to go to the rear with it for fear it might be retaken, and then I thought I would stay, and I threw it down and loaded and fired twice standing on it. While standing on it there was a 14th Brooklyn man took hold of it and tried to get it, and I had threatened to shoot him before he would stop. By this time we had them cleaned out. . . . [18]

Wallar's company commander described the action:

Major Blair, of the Second Mississippi, finding no way to escape, ordered his men to surrender, and springing to the ranks of th 6th, gave his sword to Colonel Dawes. In the terrible confusion of this moment, it seemed impossible for the men to hear the orders to cease firing, when Cpl. Frank A. Waller[sic], of Company I, after several attempts by others to seize the flag of the Second Mississippi had failed, jumped into the Confederate ranks and seized the flag which was firm in the bearer's hands and wrenched it from him. He jumped back upon the embankment and threw the flag upon the ground and stood upon it, took his gun and again commenced firing. . . . [19]

Wallar gave the flag to his commander, Lt. Col. Dawes, who in turn gave it to a wounded Sgt., William Evans, who was headed for a hospital. Dawes wrapped the flag around Evans' body and instructed him to take care that it not be recaptured. Evans then hobbled into town and went to the home of a woman in Gettysburg.

After the war a Northern man wrote to William Murphy and asked why the color guard did not protect him and the flag. To this impertinent question Murphy gave a simple but telling answer: "They did all that mortal man could do in the defense of the flag, as they all lost their lives in the defense of their country."[20] After the battle the flag was forwarded to the War Department and in 1905 returned to Mississippi, where it now rests in the state historical museum.[21]

* * *

About three hours later, a series of events took place that led to the capture of five more Confederate battle flags. Maj. Gen. Rodes and his division of Ewell's corps had marched from Carlisle and spent the night of June 30 near Heidlersburg. They had started toward Gettysburg in the morning, marching down the Carlisle Road, and soon heard the sound of guns off in the distance to the southwest. Rodes moved his division off the road to the right, and formed a line with three brigades:

Survivors of the 2nd Mississippi with the Captured Flag
(Courtesy of the Mississippi Dept. of Archives and History)

Colonel Edward Asbury O'Neal's Alabama Brigade on the left, Brig. Gen. Alfred Iverson's North Carolina Brigade in the center, and Brig. Gen. Junius Daniel's Tarheels on the right. Rodes' idea was to attack simultaneously with these brigades while Brig. Gen. Stephen Ramseur's North Carolinians came up behind and Brig. Gen. George Doles' Georgia Brigade was held in a defensive posture.

The Federals in their front and right belonged to Brig. Gen. Henry Baxter's brigade of Brig. Gen. John Robinson's division of the I Corps. They formed the right of a line that stretched all the way back past the railroad cut and McPherson's barn to some nearby woods. Baxter's men had been on the march since early morning, pounding up the dusty roads from Maryland. Their faces were bright with high hopes once again, for they too had heard the rumor that McClellan was back in command, and he was the one man in whom the army had faith.

Baxter's men had just hurried into position, double-timing the last two miles to the Lutheran Seminary. After a short rest they moved north along Oak Ridge with their right stopping at the Mummasburg Road.[22] The 11th Pennsylvania and 97th New York filed into a field which they characterized as a "rank growth of timothy." From here they could see puffs of smoke in the distance. The brigade moved another 200

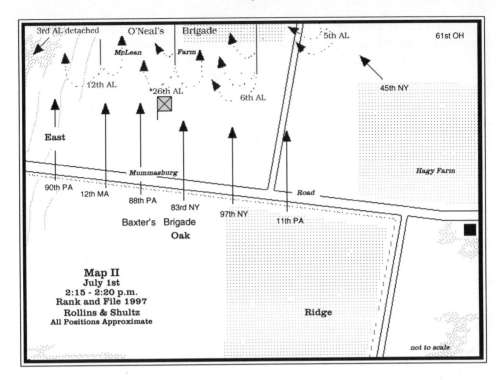

3rd AL detached   O'Neal's   Brigade   5th AL   61st OH

McLean   Farm

12th AL   45th NY

26th AL   6th AL

East

Mummasburg   Hagy Farm

90th PA   Road

12th MA

88th PA   97th NY   11th PA

83rd NY

Baxter's Brigade

Oak

Map II
July 1st
2:15 - 2:20 p.m.
Rank and File 1997
Rollins & Shultz
All Positions Approximate

Ridge

not to scale

yards forward and lined up behind a rail fence running parallel to the Mummasburg Road. They looked out at a nearby hill and saw a bright red battle flag and part of a Confederate line of battle.

It was O'Neal's Alabama Brigade, approaching the Mummasburg Road with the 6th Alabama on its left, the 26th in the middle and the 12th on the right. O'Neal's other two regiments, the 3rd and 5th, were separated from the line and essentially out of the fight. On O'Neal's right, Iverson had waited for a nearby battery to shell the Federal line, but was now moving forward. A considerable gap existed between O'Neal's right and Iverson's left. The Confederate attack was not well coordinated, and when the Alabamans approached the Mummasburg Road they were on rough ground, marching uphill, slowed down by thick brush and rock fences.[23] As one Alabaman remembered:

> In places the regiment moved through full-grown wheat, in others over plowed ground, through orchards, gardens, over wood and stone fences, which, with the rapidity of the march, fatigued the men, causing many of them to faint from exhaustion.[24]

When the Confederates approached the McLean house east of the Mummasburg Road they ran into the right flank of Baxter's line, with the 11th, 88th and 90th Pennsylvania, 12th Massachusetts, and 83rd

and 97th New York behind fences along the road. O'Neal's men stopped
and opened fire, and for 15 to 20 minutes each side traded volleys. It
quickly became a "desperate and bloody" fight, but the two lines did not
come close enough to engage in hand to hand combat.[25]

In Baxter's brigade Pvt. Hershel Pierce saw a friend get hit, and
then a Confederate battle flag and its colorbearer, perhaps from the
26th Alabama, appeared in front of him:

> The Rebel color bearer . . . flaunted his defiant flag in the
> faces of our men about the time [his friend] was shot.
> Both causes operated so strongly upon me that I could
> not resist any longer but unslung my carbine from my
> shoulder[.] I shot him dead in his tracks. And I felt the
> better for doing it.[26]

Soon appeared the lead elements of the XI Corps coming up from
Gettysburg. They opened fire, enfilading the Alabamans from the left,
as did an artillery battery, and the fight was over. Half an hour after
they opened fire, O'Neal's men made for the rear, out of the battle with
severe casualties. At some point they left behind one battle flag,
probably from the 26th Alabama, which was picked up by Lt. Eldridge
Leven of the 88th Pennsylvania.[27]

As O'Neal's men retired, Iverson's brigade crossed the Mummasburg Road and the farm of John Forney, moving toward Baxter's left and
rear. There was real danger here for Baxter's brigade—in a few short
moments the Confederates would reach their objective and scatter
Baxter's men to the wind. But Baxter saw the Rebel threat coming and
immediately ordered his brigade to run up the crest of the hill to their
left and form line behind the low stone wall that farmer Forney had set
out to define the boundary of his field. Despite their having marched all
morning and having been in a hot fight, they charged up the steep hill
to the crest and got down behind the stone wall. The 90th Pennsylvania
anchored the Federal right, with the 12th Massachusetts and 88th
Pennsylvania, 83rd and 97th New York and 11th Pennsylvania in order
to their left.[28] Baxter's men laid down behind the stone wall, rammed
cartridges home and capped their rifles.

Now Iverson's men were in their front, marching not straight at
them, but diagonally across their line of fire. Their leader stayed back
in the rear, and the men found themselves leaderless. The historian of
the 23rd North Carolina recalled that they advanced "southeast against
the enemy, visible in the woods at that corner of the field, exposing our
left flank to an enfilading fire . . . that was fatal. Yet this is just what
we did. And unwarned, unled as a brigade, went forward Iverson's
deserted band to its doom."[29] The 5th North Carolina was on the
Confederate left, nearest the Federals, followed by the 20th, 23rd, and
then the 12th on the extreme right of the Confederate line.[30] Most of

them apparently could not see the Federals behind the fence, for a member of the 12th recalled that they "bounded forward" almost blindly "for his whole line, with every flag, was concealed behind the rock wall. . . Not one of them was to be seen."[31] (See Map III)

The men of the 88th Pennsylvania saw the Confederates "sweeping on in magnificent order, with perfect alignment, guns at right shoulder and colors to the front." Bunched together and in lines in good Napoleonic style, "as straight as if on parade," they made a perfect, nearly unmissable target:

> They reached and descended a little gully or depression in the ground, and moving on ascended the opposite slope as orderly as if on brigade drill, while behind the stone wall the Union soldiers, with rifles cocked and fingers on the triggers, waited and bided their time, feeling confident that they could throw back these regiments coming against them.[32]

Word was passed to aim low. When the Confederates got within 100 yards of the wall, Baxter's men and some of Cutler's brigade to their left rose up and let loose a tremendous, destructive volley. The "sheet of flame and smoke burst from the wall with the simultaneous crash of the rifles," knocking down hundreds of Confederates,

> plainly marking their line with a ghastly row of dead and wounded men, whose blood trailed the course of their line with a crimson stain clearly discernible for several days after the battle, until the rain washed the gory record away.[33]

"We delivered such a deadly volley at very short range," said Major A. J. Sellars of the 90th Pennsylvania, "that death's mission was with unerring certainty."[34] They continued to pour a "withering fire" into the Confederates with "terrible effect." What was left of Iverson's brigade soon broke for the rear, took cover in a small creek bed, and there managed a weak return fire. Some pulled out white handkerchiefs and waved them in surrender as Iverson watched, horrified. He saw the bodies lying in line, and thought they were refusing to fight.[35] Another recalled that the bodies formed a line "perfectly dressed . . . the feet of all these dead men were in a perfectly straight line."[36]

Despite the destruction unleashed by Baxter, three or four Confederate battle flags still waved over Iverson's men, and some Rebels continued to fight back. Behind the stone wall, Sgt. Evans of Company B, 88th Pennsylvania crouched next to Pvt. John Witmoyer of Company H, firing steadily at the Confederates. Evans spotted a battle flag waving in plain sight, the colorbearer "defiantly flaunting his flag," and

103

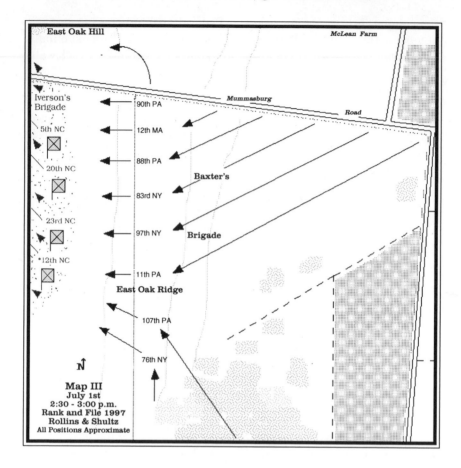

East Oak Hill

McLean Farm

Iverson's
Brigade

90th PA

Mummasburg
Road

5th NC

12th MA

88th PA

20th NC

Baxter's

83rd NY

97th NY

Brigade

23rd NC

12th NC

11th PA

East Oak Ridge

107th PA

N

76th NY

Map III
July 1st
2:30 - 3:00 p.m.
Rank and File 1997
Rollins & Shultz
All Positions Approximate

brought his musket to his shoulder, saying to Witmoyer, "John, I will give those colors a whack." The last word reached the ears of Witmoyer followed quickly by a dull thud of lead striking bone and flesh. Witmoyer turned to ask Evans if he had been hit. Evans was looking straight ahead, his musket still in firing position, but slowly being lowered. Then Evans toppled over dead, his heart pierced by a bullet.[37]

Riding behind the wall on his horse, Baxter ordered his men to fix bayonets and charge: "Up, boys, and give them steel."[38] Led by the 88th Pennsylvania, the entire line crossed over the wall and ran toward Iverson's men with Lieutenant Colonel Spofford of the 97th New York yelling out: "Boys of the 97th, let us go for them and capture them."[39] The entire brigade charged up to Iverson's line, and face-to-face combat briefly occurred. Sgt. Sylvester Riley of the 97th New York grabbed the flag of the 20th North Carolina from its bearer and immediately handed it to his lieutenant.[40] Running with the 88th Pennsylvania, Capt. Joseph H. Richard found the colorbearer of the 23rd North Carolina and engaged him in a desperate hand-to-hand struggle over the flag. The Confederate fought off Richard and held onto the flag until Sgt. Edward

Gilligan smacked him in the head with the butt of his musket and then grabbed the flag.[41]

The Confederates were stunned. Unable to retreat or advance, they fought as best they could, then began to surrender. "I believe that every man who stood up was either killed or wounded," said an officer in the 20th North Carolina.[42]

As they surrendered Cpl. William Miller of the 83rd New York spotted a Confederate battle flag planted in the ground, "with the red Southern cross hanging limp in the hot summer air." He broke into a run for the flag, outdistanced some others from his regiment, and got near the flag when he realized someone else was running next to him. Miller redoubled his efforts, and his comrades cheered him on. The two men reached the flag at the same moment, and each grabbed the staff. "I'll take care of this color," said Capt. Erastus Clark of the 12th Massachusetts. Miller, terribly disappointed, turned his attention to corralling prisoners, while Capt. Clark walked off with the flag of the 5th North Carolina.[43]

Iverson's brigade suffered about 900 casualties, including several hundred taken prisoner. Baxter's brigade, out of ammunition and replaced by another, marched them to the rear. Along with the regimental flag of the 20th North Carolina, the 97th New York captured 213 men, more than they had in their own regiment at the time of the action.[44] They also reported that a Southern regiment had hidden its flag in the bushes in order to avoid surrendering it.[45]

After the battle, Maj. Gen. John Newton reported that a flag had been captured by a private in the I Corps, then taken from him and secreted away by an unnamed colonel.[46] This may have been a reference to the incident involving Col. Charles Wheelock of the 97th New York cited below.

Brig. Gen. Cutler's brigade had been involved in fierce fighting with Davis's brigade near the railroad cut, and in midafternoon he reformed two of his regiments, the 76th New York and 56th Pennsylvania, in the woods along Seminary Ridge north of the cut. They moved back out to their old ground, held it for half to three-quarters of an hour, then fell back to the woods.[47] They soon moved a short distance to their right oblique, through the woods, and came up on the left of Brig. Gen. Baxter's brigade, which was engaged with Iverson's North Carolinians. Here the 76th New York obtained "a good position," and poured fire into the right flank of the enemy, silencing them. They shot down a colorbearer and captured an unidentified battle flag, probably from the 12th North Carolina.[48]

In the midst of the chaos Colonel Charles Wheelock of the 97th New York was waving the 20th North Carolina's flag at the enemy while organizing his men when Gen. Baxter spotted the captured flag and ordered it to the rear for safekeeping. Wheelock objected and refused the directive, claiming that "my regiment captured these colors and will keep them." Baxter promptly ordered the colonel put under arrest. Wheelock responded by giving the flag to a captain in his regiment to hold while he ran his sword through it in defiance and anger, tearing it from its staff. The captain holding the staff was promptly struck by a bullet and killed.[49]

Later in the afternoon, when the I and XI Corps broke and retreated through town to Cemetery Hill, a man from the 97th New York carrying the 20th's flag to the rear was accosted by a Confederate soldier. Capt. Alexander of the 45th North Carolina saw the 20th's flag and went for it. The two men struggled, and in the fight the flag was torn into two roughly equal pieces.[50] When they separated each took half with him.[51]

The flag remained in two halves until the 50th anniversary of the battle, when Sgt. Henry M. Fitzgerald of the 97th New York strolled into the camp of the veterans of the 20th at the reunion in Gettysburg. He was introduced to the 20th's colorbearer, J. D. Irvin. "The colorbearer!" cried Fitzgerald. "That's better than I hoped for. I've got the other half of your flag that we took away from you fifty years ago today, and I wanted to return it to somebody from that regt., but I didn't hope to be able to give it to the very man we took it from." The two halves were united, and it was noted that the half still owned by the 20th had 27 bullet holes in it.[52]

At about the same time that the 20th North Carolina's flag was being ripped in half, the men of the 88th Pennsylvania also tried to rally to stem the tide of retreat. It was no use, and when they began to flee through town Capt. Joseph Richard reportedly tore the 23rd North Carolina's flag up into small pieces and distributed it among the regiment.[53]

*   *   *

By 4 p.m. the Federal forces had retreated to Seminary Ridge, where they formed a hastily constructed line with a breastworks of rails and dirt on the slope fronting the west of the Ridge. Here men from the I and XI Corps lined up, along with several of the I Corps batteries, under the command of Colonel Charles Wainwright.

The Confederate brigades of Brig. Gen. James Lane, Brig. Gen. A. M. Scales and Colonel Abner Perrin, in Maj. Gen. Dorsey Pender's division of Hill's corps, charged across an open field and then up the slope, encountering a storm of shot and shell from the batteries and the muskets of the infantry. One Federal saw that "they maintained their alignment with great precision. In many cases the colors of the regiments were advanced several paces in front of the line."[54] Despite taking severe casualties, they pressed on as ordered, without firing "until the line of breastworks in front became a sheet of fire and smoke, sending its leaden missiles of death in the faces of men who had often,

Levi and Henry Walker

(Courtesy of the North Carolina Museum of History)

but never so terribly, met it before."[55]

One of the most incredible events of the battle occurred here, according to John B. Gordon, who fought with the army throughout its entire existence. Pvt. William Faucette, colorbearer of the 13th North Carolina, had the colors in his right hand when he received a mortal blow that almost severed his arm, tearing it from its socket. Without halting or hesitating,

> he seized the falling flag with his left hand, and, with his blood spouting from the severed arteries and his right arm dangling in shreds at his side, he still rushed to the front, shouting to his comrades, 'forward, forward!'[56]

A few minutes later Pvt. Levi Walker, the fifth colorbearer of the

13th to be hit during this charge, was shot in the left leg and knocked down. His brother, Lt. Henry J. Walker, escaped the battle, even though the regiment lost 59 killed out of about 230 who went into the fight.[57]

As hand-to-hand combat took place, Col. Wainwright saw that "a big fellow had planted the colours of his regiment on a pile of rails within fifty yards of the muzzles of [Capt. James] Cooper's guns at the moment he received his order to limber up."[58] This was most likely the color-bearer of the 13th or 14th South Carolina of Perrin's brigade.[59] Some-time in this action R. Owen, colorbearer of the 14th South Carolina, was killed along with all but one of his colorguard. In the 12th South Carolina one colorbearer after another was shot dead until all four were down. Lt. Col. Joseph Brown, commanding the 14th, noted that "a scarcely less fatality attended the colors of the other regiments." Referring to the Irish-born men in his regiment, he stated that "The land of the Shamrock, as in other fields, contributed its quota on the strongly contested ground."[60] Every one of the colorbearers that went into battle with Perrin's brigade was killed, and several regiments had several men pick up the flag and then be wounded or killed.[61] Perrin later stated that "better conduct was never exhibited on any field than was shown by both officers and men in this engagement."[62]

The charge broke the Federal lines, and panic ensued. Federal troops fled off the entire line of the I and XI Corps, headed back to the village of Gettysburg and the safety of Federal reinforcements on Cemetery Hill south of town.

Perrin's brigade followed the Federals into Gettysburg, with the 1st and 14th South Carolina in the lead. The two regiments entered "simultaneously with flags unfurled."[63] Perrin and the 1st South Carolina reached the center of the town, planted the 1st's flag in the diamond, and appeared eager to go further in pursuit of the Federals. But Maj. Gen. Pender, commanding the division, ordered them to halt. One of the men remembered Pender "pulling off his hat to our regimen-tal colors—said our Regiment had done enough for one day."[64]

The Federals ran through the town of Gettysburg in a mad dash to escape capture. Chaos reigned in the streets, and men who had sought shelter and aid in the residences of citizens found themselves in danger of being taken prisoner. In a brief rear-guard action near a brickyard, Capt. Hugo Siedlitz of the 27th Pennsylvania, (Col. Charles Coster's brigade, Brig. Gen. Adolph Von Steinwehr's division, XI Corps), captured an unidentified Confederate battle flag from a regiment in Rodes' division.[65]

Sgt. William Evans of the 6th Wisconsin had possession of the flag of the 2nd Mississippi captured earlier in the day. Evans found refuge in the home of the Hollinger family, and became worried as he heard the Confederates going house to house in search of Federals. Evans talked two young women into slicing open his mattress and hiding the flag in it, and there it remained until after the battle. On July 4th Dawes took it to Meade's headquarters and had inscribed upon it the significance of the flag: "Captured by the 6th Wisconsin together with the entire regiment. Kept by Sergt. Evans for two days while a prisoner in the hands of the Enemy."[66]

Notes

[1] E. T. Boland, "Beginning of the Battle of Gettysburg," *CV*, XIV(1906), 308.

[2] John Calef, "Gettysburg Notes: The Opening Gun," *Journal of the Military History Institute*, 40(1907), 48.

[3] W. T. Moon, "The Beginning of the Battle of Gettysburg," *CV*, XXXIII(1925), 449.

[4] W. A. Castleberry, "Thirteenth Alabama—Archer's Brigade," *CV*, XIX(1911), 338.

[5] D. Scott Hartwig, "Guts and Good Leadership," *GB* 1(July 1989), 5-14; William K. Beaudot, "Francis Ashbury Wallar: A Medal of Honor at Gettysburg," *GB* 4(January 1991), 16-21; Terrence J. Winschel, "The Colors Are Shrouded In Mystery," *GB* 6(January 1992), 77-86; Lance J. Herdegan and William J. K. Beaudot, *In the Bloody Railroad Cut at Gettysburg* (Dayton: Morningside Press, 1990), 279-285. The commander of the 6th Wisconsin told the story in Rufus R. Dawes, *Service With the Sixth Wisconsin Volunteers* (Dayton: Morningside Press, facsimile, 1984). A. A. G. Townsend's official tally of flag captures and Medals of Honor awards incorrectly lists this as the flag of the 20th Mississippi in his Report, July 29, 1863, *OR*, II, 282. "Record" #40 incorrectly dates this as having been captured on July 2.

[6] This story is told by one of the survivors, Sgt. J. A. Whitney, in *The Galveston Daily News*, June 21, 1896. See also Charles M. Cooke, "Fifty-Fifth Regiment," Clark, *Histories*, III, 297, and S. A. Ashe, "The First Day at Gettysburg," *CV*, 38(1930), 379.

[7] J. P. "Mickey" Sullivan, "The Charge of the Iron Brigade at Gettysburg," *Mauston* [Wisconsin] *Star*, February 13, 1883, photocopy, 6th Wisconsin File, GNMP.

[8] William Murphy to Dr. F. A. Dearborn, June 29, 1900, E. S. Bragg Papers, Box 1, State Historical Society of Wisconsin Archives.

[9] C. W. Okey, quoted in Herdegan and Beaudot, *Bloody Railroad Cut*, 186.

[10] Loyd Harris, quoted in *Ibid.*, 194.

[11] Murphy to Dearborn. It should be noted that the flag, now in the Mississippi State Archives and Museum, bears only a few marks that could be considered bullet holes.

[12] Quoted in Herdegan and Beaudot, *Bloody Railroad Cut*, 194.

[13] Quoted in *Ibid.*, 195.

[14] *Ibid.*, 195-6.

[15] *Ibid.*, 196.

[16] *Ibid.*, 200.

[17] Murphy to Dearborn.

[18] Quoted in Herdegan and Beaudot, *Bloody Railroad Cut,* 200. See also Meade's statement, October 17, 1864, *OR*, Series III, Vol. 3, 817.

[19] *Ibid.,* 282.

[20] Murphy to Dearborn.

[21] "Record" #40.

[22] Report of Capt. Edmund Y. Patterson, 88th Pennsylvania, August 22, 1863, *OR*, I, 311.

[23] John D. Vautier, *History of the 88th Pennsylvania Volunteers in the War for the Union* (Philadelphia: J. B. Lippincott Co., 1894), 134. Hereafter cited as Vautier, *88th PA.* Vautier was not at Gettysburg, so his information is second hand. See "Attack and Counter-Attack," *GB* 12(January, 1995).

[24] Report of Colonel J. M. Hall, 5th Alabama, July 9, 1863, *OR*, II, 596.

[25] Report of Maj. Gen. Robert E. Rodes, [undated, 1863], *OR*, II, 545-561; Report of E. A. O'Neal, 26th Alabama, July 24, 1863, *OR*, II, 591-594.

[26] Hershel Pierce to Brother, July 11, 1863, in James McLean, ed., *Baxter's Brigade at Gettysburg* (Baltimore: Butternut and Blue, 1995), 138.

[27] This was most likely the flag of the 26th Alabama, though it could have belonged to another regiment, possibly the 6th. Report of Capt. Edmund Y. Patterson, 88th Pennsylvania, August 22, 1863, *OR*, I, 311, incorrectly lists this as the flag of the 16th Alabama. The 6th and 26th were in O'Neal's brigade, the 16th was in the Army of Tennessee. Oscar W. Blacknall, "Memoir of Chas. Blacknall," North Carolina Dept. of Archives and History, photocopy, North Carolina File, GNMP, also reports it incorrectly as the 16th. George W. Grant, "The First Army Corps on the First Day at Gettysburg," *The Gettysburg Papers*, [hereafter cited as *Papers*], V.1., Ken Brady and Florence Freeland, eds., (Dayton: The Morningside Bookshop, 1986), 262, states that it was captured by Lieutenant Eldridge Leven of the 88th. See also Vautier, *88 PA*, 107. The flag probably carried by the 26th Alabama *after* Gettysburg is now in the Alabama Department of Archives and History. It has a Gettysburg battle honor and was given to the Alabama Archives in this century by the O'Neal family, with the statement that it was never captured. Rodes' division, then commanded by D. H. Hill, had been issued new flags in April, 1863. The 6th's flag from the same issue was captured on May 10, 1864. Neither the "Record" nor "Letter" carry any trace of the flag captured by Leven. Even more confusion reigns here because the account by Grant and the history of the 88th read as though this flag was captured a little later when Baxter's brigade fought against the 5th, 20th, and 23rd North Carolina of Iverson's brigade. In

any case, it was apparently not turned over to the War Department and disappeared from the record. See also Vautier, *88th PA*, 135-136.

[28] Three regimental histories give conflicting accounts of the exact order of the regiments in the line of battle. See Vautier, *88 PA*; Isaac Hall; *History of the Ninety-Seventh Regiment New York Volunteers ("Conkling Rifles") in the War for the Union* (Utica: C. C. Childs and Co., 1890); and Benjamin Cook, *History of the Twelfth Massachusetts Volunteers (Webster's Regiment)* (Boston: Privately Printed, 1882).

[29] "The Twenty-third Regiment," Clark, *Histories,* II, 235.

[30] Oscar W. Blacknall, "Memoir."

[31] Clark, *Histories,* II, 225.

[32] John Vautier, "At Gettysburg: The Eighty-Eighth Pennsylvania in the Battle," *Philadelphia Weekly Press*, November 10, 1886. Since Vautier was not at Gettysburg, this must be the recollection of others as told to him.

[33] Vautier, *88 PA*, 135.

[34] Quoted in John P. Nicholson, ed., *Pennsylvania at Gettysburg: Ceremonies at the Dedication of the Monuments Erected by the Commonwealth of Pennsylvania,* 2 Vols (Harrisburg: William Stanley Ray, State Printer, 1904), 1, 488.

[35] Report of Brig. Gen. Alfred Iverson, July 17, 1863, *OR*, II, 579.

[36] Henry R. Berkeley, *Four Years in the Confederate Artillery: The Diary of Private Henry Robinson Berkeley*, ed. William H. Runge (Chapel Hill: University of North Carolina Press, 1961), 50.

[37] Vautier, *88th PA*, 106-7.

[38] Grant, "First Army Corps," *Papers*, 262.

[39] Hall, *History of the 97th Regiment*, 138. See also "Fighting Them Over," *National Tribune*, September 24, 1885.

[40] Ibid., 141. All during this action Baxter's men received fire from O'Neal's brigade on their right and Ramseur's brigade on their left.

[41] *Deeds of Valor*, 223. The ANV pattern flag is now in the North Carolina State Archives, Raleigh. "Record" #46, incorrectly says this was captured on July 2. See also Report of Maj. Gen. Abner Doubleday, December 14, 1863, *OR*, I, 248-9, and Gilligan's letter of March 31, 1892, RG 94, Box 328, National Archives; "Twenty-third Regiment," Clark, *Histories*, II, 237.

[42] Clark, *Histories*, II, 119. For more information on this clash see Gerard A. Patterson, "The Death of Iverson's Brigade," *GB* 5(July 1991), 13-18.

[43] *Twelfth Massachusetts (Webster) Regiment Association*, December 1911, 10-11. I thank Gary Kross for this citation. Three months later Miller and Clark chanced to meet in Philadelphia, where both were seeing about replacing limbs shot off during Gettysburg. Clark had the flag wrapped around his body, and swore to Miller that he would never take it off. Long after the war Clark was killed in a duel, and reportedly had the flag still wrapped around him. Miller's story

appeared originally in the *National Tribune*, October 15, 1885. Miller did not remember Clark's name, but it was confirmed by an unidentified member of the 12th in a letter to the *National Tribune*, December 10, 1885. The flag disappeared, so we cannot be sure what pattern it was, nor even if the events reported are true. A flag of the 3rd issue ANV, of the kind issued in the spring of 1863, was captured from the 5th North Carolina on March 25, 1865. Several possibilities exist. The regiment may have carried an earlier issued flag at Gettysburg, and used the 1863 issue later.

[44] Report of Charles Wheelock, 97th New York, [n.d.], 1863, *OR*, I, 310.

[45] Hall, *97th New York*, 136.

[46] Report of Maj. Gen. John Newton, Sept. 30, 1863, *OR*, I, 263-4.

[47] Report of Brig. Gen. Lysander Cutler, July 9, 1863, *OR*, I, 282.

[48] Report of Capt. John Cook, 76th New York, July 11, 1863, *OR*, I, 286. I conclude that this was the 12th's flag because the 12th was the closest regiment to the 76th, and all other flags from Iverson's brigade are accounted for. However, a 3rd issue flag like those issued in the Spring of 1863 was captured from the 12th at Cedar Creek on 12 October 1864, so this flag may have been an earlier issue.

[49] Grant, "First Corps," 263.

[50] Report of Lieut. Gen. Richard Ewell, [n.d.] 1863, *OR*, II, 451. See also *88 PA*, 136, and Report of Capt. J. A. Hopkins, 45th North Carolina, July 17, 1863, *OR*, II, 575.

[51] See Hopkins' report, *OR*, II, 575. The struggle over the 20th North Carolina's flag between the man from the 97th New York and Capt. Galloway took place either in or near the railroad cut east of the one in which the flag of the 2nd Mississippi had been captured a few hours earlier. The eastern cut was the same one recently destroyed by the National Park Service and Gettysburg College. Part of their justification for the destruction of the cut was that nothing of historical significance occurred there.

[52] *New York Times*, July 2, 1913. See also Ewell's report, *OR*, II, 451. The flag disappeared from the record at this point.

[53] Samuel G. Boone, "Personal Experiences," USAMHI. As the photograph of the flag clearly indicates, it shows no signs of being torn apart.

[54] Dawes, *Service With the Sixth*, 175.

[55] Varina Davis Brown, *A Colonel at Gettysburg and Spotsylvania* (Columbia, S.C.: The State Company, 1911), 78-79.

[56] John B. Gordon, *Reminiscences of the Civil War* (New York: Charles Scribner's Sons, 1903), 114. Faucette, according to John W. Moore, *Roster of North Carolina Troops in the War Between the States* (Raleigh: Ashe and Gatling, 1882), Vol. 1, 487, was mortally wounded.

[57] Mast, *State Troops and Volunteers*, 183.

[58] Allan Nevins, ed. *A Diary of Battle: The Personal Journals of Colonel Charles Wainwright, 1861 - 1865* (Gettysburg: Stan Clark Military Books, 1962), 236. This was the 1st Pennsylvania Light Artillery, Battery B.

[59] Brown, *A Colonel at Gettysburg and Spotsylvania*, 78-79.

[60] *Ibid.*, 85.

[61] Abner Perrin to Governor, July 25, 1863, in Milledge Louis Bonham, ed., "A Little More Light On Gettysburg," *Mississippi Valley Historical Review* XXIV(March, 1938), 519-525.

[62] Report of Brig. Gen. Abner Perrin, August 13, 1863, *OR*, II, 663.

[63] Brown, *A Colonel at Gettysburg and Spotsylvania* , 78-79.

[64] Capt. Walter Shooter to Lt. McIntyre, 20 July 1863, 1st South Carolina file, GNMP.

[65] Maj. Gen. George Meade to Brig. Gen. Lorenzo Thomas, July 28, 1863, *OR*, I, 102. No report was filed for the 27th. This was probably from Avery's brigade and could be WD# 83, an unidentified flag of the 3rd ANV-wool issue of spring 1863 with no regimental number or battle honors. It is now in the Museum of the Confederacy, Richmond.

[66] Rufus Dawes to Mary Dawes, July 4, 1863, Wisconsin Historical Society Archives. See also Report of Lieutenant Colonel Rufus Dawes, July 17, 1863, *OR*, I, 276, and Report of Colonel Edward R. Fowler, 84th New York[14th Brooklyn], July 9, 1863, *OR*, I, 286. Also note that Report of Maj. Gen. Abner Doubleday, December 14, 1863, *OR*, I, 246, says two flags were taken from Davis' brigade. The second flag is not substantiated by any other report, and therefore I have decided not to count it. It is possible that the flag of the 55th North Carolina was captured. They had several colorbearers shot down on July 1st, and much fighting occurred over their flag, but I have found no report of it being lost or captured. I believe it was more likely captured on July 3rd.

Chapter Six

"This Flag Never Goes Down
Until I Am Down":
July 2nd

Early on the morning of July 2nd Brig. Gen. Henry Jackson Hunt, Chief of Artillery, Army of the Potomac, and a group of Federal officers stood amid the strong defensive position they had organized on Cemetery Hill and looked south along Cemetery Ridge. They peered out over a mile-wide valley of fields of wheat and hay spreading off to the west, where the dark mass of South Mountain and the Blue Ridge dominated the horizon. No Rebels appeared to be in this country. Across the valley Seminary Ridge seemed a barely perceptible rise in the landscape. This was misleading, for in fact there was little if any flat ground immediately west of Cemetery Ridge. Instead the land undulated between deep swales and rises, the latter averaging about 40 feet above the depth of the swales.

Behind the observers, the northeastern face of Cemetery Hill looked out upon the Confederate lines in the town. The Union lines would soon take the form of a giant fishhook. The shank would begin at Little Round Top and run north along Cemetery Ridge, curve northeasterly, easterly, and southeasterly around Cemetery Hill and end up along the crest of the Culp's Hill, probably the dominant geologic form on the battlefield. Hard fighting would take place this day and into the night on the eastern face of Cemetery Hill and along the slopes of Culp's Hill.

But at the moment the Federal officers were most interested in the land between the two principle ridges, and about one mile south and west of Cemetery Hill. In this area the ridge declined as it ran south from Cemetery Hill, then rose up to form two smaller hills, the first of which the local residents called by several names, but which we know today as Little Round Top. If one stands on the rocks and boulders on the crest of Little Round Top, one can see a fine view of the entire Union as well as of the valley and Seminary Ridge to its west. Directly west of Little Round Top are the large boulders of Devil's Den, followed by the rocky face of Houck's Ridge, at an elevation somewhat lower than Little Round Top. Just west of Houck's Ridge are woods, followed by a wheat field and peach orchard, about half way between the ridges.

As the Federal officers examined the landscape, the Confederate leadership met just north and west of Gettysburg to discuss plans for the coming day. Lt. Gen. James Longstreet, commanding Lee's I Corps, wanted to march around the flank of the Federal line and head toward Washington, but Lee disagreed. He ordered Longstreet to march south of Gettysburg, then turn east and attack up the Emmitsburg Road which ran northeast toward the town and between Cemetery Ridge and Seminary Ridge. He would be supported by troops from Hill's III Corps.

Longstreet's march from Herr Ridge to the southern end of Seminary Ridge, over winding roads and with other distractions, took most of the day. By 4 o'clock his men were lined up facing east with the right wing, Maj. Gen. John Bell Hood's division, facing the two hills. The line coursed north and crossed the road, stretching to a point directly west of the Peach Orchard. Hood's division began the attack. Maj. Gen. Lafayette McLaws' division formed on Hood's left and moved east across the Emmitsburg Road toward Cemetery Ridge. After them came two brigades from Maj. Gen. Richard Anderson's division of A. P. Hill's Corps.

Battle flags were intended to be used in battle, and thus were wrapped around a staff and encased in a canvas or oil cloth bag while the men marched to the point of action. Brig. Gen. Evander Law's brigade anchored the right of Hood's division and as the men prepared for combat, they unfurled their battle flags.

During the battle of Sharpsburg the previous September, the 1st Texas had carried an Army of Northern Virginia flag and a silk Texas state flag. The latter featured a blue vertical bar on the left with a single white star reminiscent of the Bonnie Blue flag. Red and white horizontal stripes(one of each color) extended to its right. Both flags were captured, but the regiment had been given replacements for each. The new Texas flag included a black border in mourning for the men slaughtered in the Cornfield.[1]

Just before the attack began, Hood and Texas Brigade commander Brig. Gen. Jerome Robertson rode in front of the 1st Texas. The color guard had unfurled the regimental battle flag as well as the regiment's Texas flag. Color Sergeant George Branard, who had been given the Texas state flag because of his gallantry in combat, had fixed to the top of its staff a 7 x 13-inch First National variation, with a single white star in the canton.[2] Hood made a short speech, then rose in his stirrups "to the full height of his manhood." In a loud voice he called, "Fix bayonets, my brave Texans; forward and take those heights." Lt. Col. Philip Work, commanding the regiment, pointed to Little Round Top and gave the order to "Follow the Lone Star flag to the top of the mountain."[3]

The 1st Texas attempted to carry Houck's Ridge twice by itself, but was repulsed in bloody fighting. Brig. Gen. Henry Benning's Georgia Brigade came up as reinforcements, with the 20th Georgia in the lead. The Georgians opened fire by mistake into the Texans' line, and Branard "stepped out in the open space and waved our state flag to and fro."[4] The Georgians ceased fire, and together they made one more charge up the ridge.

Sgt. Branard led the 1st Texas, running ahead of the line and vying with the colorbearer of the 15th Georgia for the lead.[5] Branard carried his flag so far in front of the main line and with such gallantry in front of the Yankees that in recognition of his bravery the Northerners shouted out, "Don't shoot that color-bearer—he is too brave!" When Branard got behind some rocks he was joined by colorbearers from several Georgia regiments, and they drew the concentrated fire of the enemy. Branard then called his colorguard to follow him and, mounting the rocks, dashed forward toward the Federal lines:

> It was here that the Federal infantry sought to spare him; their artillery, however, could not be so magnanimous, and the bursting of a shell carried away all but the lower part of the flagstaff, and laid Branard unconscious upon the ground. At first it was thought he was killed, but that was a mistake. He revived in a few minutes, and, if his friends had let him, would have attempted to whip the whole Yankee nation by himself—he was so mad.[6]

According to the Texas Brigade historian:

> As he lay by his flag his color guard, [Private] Willis James Watts, [Corporal] James Williams, [Private] Elias Newsome and [Color Sergeant] David Bronaugh, were by his side to preserve the unblemished honor of the sacred colors and hoist them afresh, high up in the bright firmament above the mountain top, that friend and foe from a distance could see the lone star standard of our Texans shining with the effulgence of heavenly glory.[7]

Slowly the men moved forward up the slope, "undismayed by the terrors that seemed to awake from the infernal region." The enemy infantry and artillery seemed to concentrate their fire on the first line. "Down the plunging shot came, bursting before and around and everywhere tearing up the ground in a terrific rain of death." Still the men moved on "in a solid beautiful line the red star-gemmed cross floating defiantly in the midst," recalled a Georgian.[8] In this action the 20th Georgia of Benning's brigade lost seven colorbearers and its flag had 87 holes torn in it. Its colonel, John A. Jones, was killed, and it was remembered that "he was an excellent officer and devoted patriot, and a braver spirit never fought beneath a flag."[9]

> Branard apparently reached the top of Houck's Ridge, for Pvt. James Bradford of the 1st Texas recalled that "The Lone Star Flag crowned the hill and Texas was

there to stay."[10]

Just north of Benning's men, more Georgians in Brig. Gen. George Thomas "Tige" Anderson's brigade moved into the Plum Run Valley headed toward Little Round Top. They had fought through the Wheatfield and Rose's woods, and from a rise they could see the Confederate attack developing on both their flanks. A captain in the 9th Georgia, George Hillyer, looked in both directions and saw "thirty-five or forty battle flags, and only from thirty to fifty men with each."[11] As they crossed Plum Run, the colorbearer of the 8th Georgia got mired in the mud. He sank up to his waist, and in struggling to get free was mortally wounded. As he fell to the mud he continued to hold the flag as best he could.[12]

While the 1st Texas and Benning's brigade fought up Houck's Ridge, two other Texas regiments, the 4th and 5th, along with a portion of Law's Alabama Brigade moved up Round Top and toward Little Round Top. The Texans made several charges up the slope of the smaller hill, but Federal rifles knocked them back. The flag of the 5th Texas was carried by colorbearer T. W. Fitzgerald, who was severely wounded. The flag was picked up by Cpl. J. A. Howard, who was killed instantly. Maj. J. C. Rogers, commanding the regiment, reported that as soon as Howard went down the flag was grabbed by Sgt. W. S. Evans, "who planted them defiantly in the face of the foe during the remainder of the fight, always advancing promptly to the front when the order was given."[13] A Federal soldier defending the hill watched as "a regiment of Rebels came on waving their flag and came quite near and stopped. I counted nine men shot down while trying to keep their flag up but someone would pick it up as fast as it dropped."[14]

The fighting just to the right of the Texans was fierce, and has been depicted in numerous accounts including the recent film *Gettysburg*. Several attacks were made by the Alabamans on the position held by the 20th Maine under the command of Col. Joshua Chamberlain. At one point, as Col. William C. Oates of the 15th Alabama charged up the slope of Little Round Top, he was about 15 feet from his regiment's flag when he saw a Maine soldier grab for it. The colorbearer, Ensign John Archibald, saw him coming and dodged, whereupon Sgt. Pat O'Connor of the 15th jabbed his bayonet into the Federal's head, saving the flag.[15] Major George Cary of the 44th Alabama, seeing the flag of his regiment knocked down, picked it up and "bounded up the cliff, and landed on the crest ahead of the line."[16] A Texan recorded that "for a moment, and a moment only, the Southern battle flag was planted on the summit."[17]

A private in the 48th Alabama told his mother that "I carried the colors in the fight for awhile."[18] A soldier in the 47th Alabama told of following the flag to the top, and tried to put what it meant into words:

Lieut. Col. Bulger, Capts. Johnston and Whitaker, and

Lieut. Adrian were killed just as the regiment gained the summit of the mountain. Would to God that I had a pen able as it is anxious to pay a fitting tribute to the memory of these and all other brave men who fell so nobly then and there! Let it, however, suffice for me only to say, they died as brave men love to die—for freedom, country, home; died at their posts unconquered.[19]

On the left flank of Longstreet's force the brigade led by Brig. Gen. William Barksdale tore into the Peach Orchard with the 21st Mississippi heading for the Federal artillery and infantry around the Trostle house. The smoke was so thick that it was hard to see. Some of the men in the nearby 141st Pennsylvania (Graham's brigade, Caldwell's division of the III Corps) saw a body of troops in their front and opened fire. Major Israel Spalding thought they were Federals, so he ordered his men to cease firing. Just then a slight breeze unfurled a Confederate battle flag. Pvt. George Forbes of the 141st quickly realized that they were enemy troops and yelled to Spalding, "They are rebels, major, I see their flag."[20] The 141st immediately opened up with a tremendous volley, and played a significant role in the defense of the Federal position. Not far away, Lt. Col. Adolfo Cavada, a member of Brigadier Andrew Humphreys' division staff watched the oncoming Rebel horde as it pierced the line and sent the Federals skedaddling:

On reaching the hollow I tried together with several other officers, to stop our men, and partially succeeded. Three Rebel battle flags at the head of the column were now within a few yards of me. Squads of our men dropping behind rocks and fallen trees kept up a spirited fire and just as I saw the head of the column of rebels hesitate. . . ."[21]

The Confederate attack proceeded on Longstreet's left with Lt. Gen. Hill's corps, led by the brigades commanded by Brig. Gen. Cadmus Wilcox and Brig. Gen. E. A. Perry (the latter now led by Col. David Lang). They moved from the fields east of Seminary Ridge *en echelon* up the Emmitsburg Road. A Federal captain in Sherfy's Peach Orchard spotted the "'stars and bars' of treason" above the clouds of dust and smoke, just before the flame of the Rebel guns erupted and their bullets begin hitting the Federal artillerymen in his front. Then the Rebel infantry burst forth into view, and "while the rebel standard-bearers waved their colors" their officers, swords in hand, charged at the retreating blue lines, now falling back.[22] A deadly fight pitting Wilcox's and Lang's men against Maj. Gen. Dan Sickles' III Corps followed along the road. The Union lines finally gave way and the men streamed back across the fields towards safety.

In this action occurred one of the few recorded examples of a battle flag being used in a specific tactical maneuver. The Confederates streamed across the Emmitsburg Road, chasing the retreating Yankees. "To follow them it became necessary to 'change direction to the left,'" remembered Col. Hilary A. Herbert of the 8th Alabama in Wilcox's brigade:

> The order was given. Holding the flag aloft, his manly form as erect as if on drill, the color bearer, Sergeant (L. P.) Ragsdale stepped forward in slow time, and the regiment aligning on him made a perfect half-wheel, and then the order was given to charge a double quick on the retreating foe. . . .[23]

The struggle in the triangle formed by the Wheatfield, Peach Orchard and Emmitsburg Road was deadly and chaotic. In the attack on the Wheatfield the 3rd South Carolina in Brig. Gen. J. B. Kershaw's brigade, McLaws' division, caught artillery fire from the left and right and rifle fire from the front, and lost four colorbearers, but not its flag. At one point an unidentified Confederate realized that the Federals were directing their fire at the 3rd's battle flag and hitting many men. He called out "lower the colors, down with the flag." In reply color sergeant William Lamb stepped to the front, where all could see him, and shouted out: "This flag never goes down until I am down."[24]

Another incident had occurred as Kershaw's brigade approached the battlefield:

> Orders had been issued not to display the colors as we were supposed to be in ambush, though a constant and continued fire of artillery had been made over our line at points in our rear, but doing us no harm. Before "attention" was called the enemy seemed to have discovered our position, and their shell became very destructive, doing far more damage to our reserves (Semmes' Brigade) and the battery of artillery than to Kershaw's Brigade. At this time Gen. Semmes was killed by a fragment of a shell severing the femoral artery as he stood but a few paces in rear of the left of the Seventh South Carolina Regiment.
>
> As we rose from our lying position behind the stone wall, preparatory to an advance, Sergt. Clarke, bearing the colors of the Seventh Regiment, unfurled them thoughtlessly, and in less than a minute thereafter a shell exploded in his front, killing three and wounding the rest of the color-guard. Nothing daunted[,]

we passed over the stone wall, ascending the slope of the clover field, not yet discovered as we thought by the enemy. When we reached the crest of the field, not more than forty yards from the stone wall, Lieut. Rutland was killed, shot through the head.[25]

Since 1861 the 8th South Carolina (also in Kershaw's brigade) had carried a state flag in addition to its battle flag. The Carolinians made it through the battle without losing either, and the state flag was retired shortly thereafter. They lost their battle flag two months later at Chickamauga, and years later a veteran remarked on the memories he carried of the flag and of the men who fought under it at Gettysburg:

We never saw our old flag again, but I would like to stand once more under its folds and let memory bring back some of the scenes when this same flag waved over so many victorious fields, while I can but remember that in its shadow I have seen some of my dearest friends yield up their noble lives for their country.[26]

In combat the private soldier in either army rarely knew what went on more than a few yards away from him. Journalists like to talk about the "fog of war," and the Civil War soldier knew what they meant, though he did not use that term. A Federal soldier who fought in the area near the Emmitsburg Road and was wounded there remembered what the battle was like that day. While he did not describe the role of the flag, he wrote an excellent description of the conditions under which the flag became of utmost importance for command and control:

A soldier who is in a battle can tell you about as little about the battle as anyone in the world. It's not what you think. It's all smoke and dust and noise. At first we could see the Confederates mob in around and putting up their guns. At that stage there is just occasional firing by the skirmishers and not enough smoke to hide anything. But later when the volleying began you might as well have been blind. The smoke lay over everything so that you were lucky to see the man next to you. Your ears couldn't distinguish shot from shot. It was all one roar, so that the hillside shook. You couldn't hear orders or guess them from seeing the man who gave them. You did just what the man ahead of you did, or the man next to you. When the officers gave orders, they would start one man going the way they wanted him to go, or doing the thing they wanted him to do. The rest would follow as well as they could.

121

After the first order to fire, everyone fired as often as they could. That part was alright, for you had something to keep your mind on. Load as fast as possible and shoot as often as you could see anything to shoot at.

When I first went into a battle, each battle, I would be scared and rattled and nervous, like all the rest. But after I had been fighting a little while, I would get control of myself again before I knew it. I would realize what was going on and see it and hear the noise. It had all been a kind of dazed feeling before. I could keep pretty calm while I was shooting away, but when I had to stand still and take fire—well, that tries the nerves.

But the battle as a whole leaves just an impression of being hot and sweaty and seeing people fall, and a jumble of smoke and dust and roar and now and then a glimpse of the hot sun, and being too busy to feel tired and feeling tired none the less. And then a bullet and then quiet and the rain, and not much more.[27]

The capture of a flag in the fighting along Emmitsburg Road underscores the chaotic nature of battle described by this soldier. The 26th Pennsylvania in Brig. Gen. Joseph H. Carr's brigade, Brig. Gen. Andrew Humphreys' division, held the right of the line that stretched from about 200 yards south of the Codori farm to the Wheatfield Road.

Lang's Florida Brigade on the left of Longstreet's attack charged into Carr's men.[28] The struggle quickly became desperate. Sgt. George W. Roosevelt, 26th Pennsylvania, came face-to-face with an unnamed Confederate colorbearer. Roosevelt got the drop on him and ordered him to surrender. The Reb handed Roosevelt the flag, and Roosevelt proceeded to turn around and march his prisoner toward the rear. But before they reached the safety of the rear, a bullet struck Roosevelt in the leg, knocking him to the ground. The Reb made his escape, and the leg was eventually amputated. Roosevelt received the Congressional Medal of Honor for capturing the flag.[29]

* * *

West of the slope of Cemetery Ridge the land falls away into the valley of Plum Run, a small creek that runs southeasterly from the Codori farm towards Devil's Den and Little Round Top. In the marshy area near the Run a brigade of Federal II Corps troops commanded by Brig. Gen. William Harrow had staked out a line, and the III Corps retreated through them. As this happened, another of Gettysburg's most famous incidents took place.

Maj. Gen. Winfield Scott Hancock, commander of the II Corps,

122

July 2

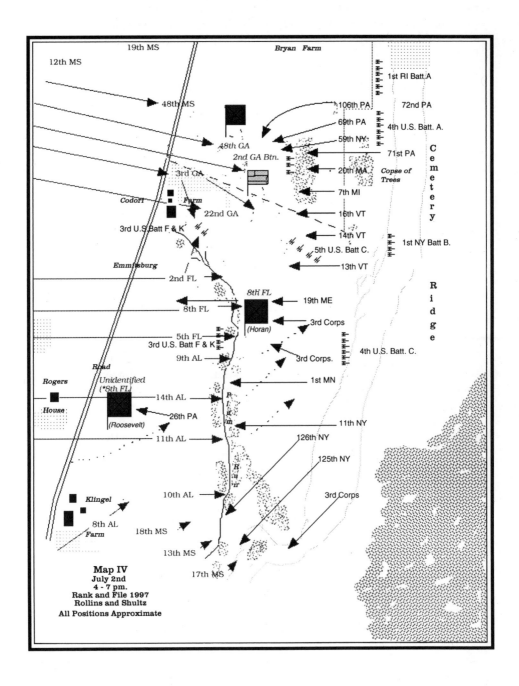

12th MS

19th MS

Bryan Farm

1st RI Batt. A

48th MS

106th PA   72nd PA

48th GA

69th PA   4th U.S. Batt. A.

2nd GA Btn.

59th NY

3rd GA

71st PA

20th MA   Copse of Trees

Codori   Farm

22nd GA

7th MI

3rd U.S. Batt F & K

16th VT

Emmitsburg

14th VT

1st NY Batt B.

5th U.S. Batt C.

2nd FL

13th VT

8th FL

8th FL

19th ME

C e m e t e r y

3rd Corps

(Horan)

5th FL

3rd U.S. Batt F & K

3rd Corps.

9th AL

R i d g e

4th U.S. Batt. C.

Road

1st MN

Rogers

Unidentified
(*8th FL)

14th AL

House

26th PA

(Roosevelt)

11th NY

11th AL

126th NY

125th NY

Klingel

10th AL

3rd Corps

8th AL

18th MS

Farm

13th MS

Map IV
July 2nd
4 - 7 pm.
Rank and File 1997
Rollins and Shultz
All Positions Approximate

17th MS

123

saw the break in the Union lines and frantically looked around for some help. A mere two regiments stood in the way of the Confederate charge: 1st Minnesota and 19th Maine of Harrow's brigade were in position to shore up the III Corps and stop the onrushing Confederates. (See Map IV)

Hancock rode along the line of the Maine regiment until he arrived at the far left flank. There he found Pvt. George Durgin, a short, heavyset man, and moved him to a spot a bit farther to the left. He yelled at Durgin, "Will you stay here?" Durgin looked up at Hancock, still on his horse, and replied, "I'll stay here, General, 'til Hell freezes over."[30]

Hancock smiled and told Col. Francis Heath to dress the 19th Maine's line on Durgin, then rode off to the left to see about finding more men to fill in the line. The closest troops were the 1st Minnesota, some 330 yards to the left, along Plum Run.[31] Hancock reached the Minnesotans, but time was almost gone. He was "confronted by a Confederate regiment with a color" and could see the flag of the 11th Alabama of Wilcox's brigade rushing toward him.[32] Hancock turned to Col. William Colvill of the 1st Minnesota and boomed out: "Advance, Colonel, do you see that flag? I want you to take it."[33]

What followed was some of the fiercest, and later most celebrated, fighting of the entire battle. The Westerners obeyed his command, taking 262 men into action. That evening only 47 responded to roll call.[34] They failed to take the flag.

The story of the 1st Minnesota is well known, having been told countless times in essays, books and by battlefield guides. However, the events that occurred at approximately the same time just a few hundred yards to their right are equally important, yet have rarely been recalled. Since they resulted in the capture of at least two flags, including at least one with some controversy surrounding it, the story is well worth telling in detail. The men of the 19th Maine watched from Cemetery Ridge as the battle developed, and then moved down the slope to Plum Run. There they lay with their faces down, hugging the ground as Sickles' line collapsed and Humphreys' division retreated, "stubbornly . . . contesting every foot of ground." Through the smoke they could "see the approach of the coming storm."[35]

Col. Francis Heath walked along the line, telling his men to lie still and let the disorganized mass cross over them. "These men were not particular where they stepped in walking over us, they only seemed intent upon getting to the rear and out of the reach of their relentless pursuers," complained one of the men.[36] Some of the retreating Federals yelled out: "Run boys, we're whipped, the day is lost." Yet others called out to "hang on, boys, and we will form in your rear." About one hundred men from New York's Excelsior Brigade attempted to re-form, but were soon swept away in the general panic. As the III Corps passed through them, Confederates immediately appeared, causing one of the Maine boys to note that the routed men had "good and sufficient reasons for being in a hurry." Heath gave the order to "rise and fire." Another soldier heard Heath yelling "'give it to them'" as the regiment sprang to its feet and sent "a sudden volley into the teeth of the advancing enemy, but a few rods distant, who must have thought that God had suddenly raised from the earth an army to oppose their march."

The 19th had about 400 men in line of battle when the regiment rose and delivered its deadly fire into the faces of the Confederates. The Rebels staggered, halted, then inched forward, "slowly, sullenly, but still onward." One Federal thought "Oh my God," would "they never stop! Their fire is making fearful havoc in our ranks." Were "our bullets punishing them as severely?" He could not tell. The 19th's left flank was badly exposed: "To remain longer in that position [would have been to invite] destruction."[37] Another remembered that "in this position of some thirty yards from their lines we fired about eight rounds each into their ranks."[38]

As the fighting continued, the left company of the 19th and an artillery battery to its left were drawn back to face left, and as they moved they could see and hear the charge of the 1st Minnesota off in the distance. Also during this action a colorbearer from Lang's Florida Brigade of three regiments (2nd, 5th, and 8th), "made himself conspicuous advancing to the front and waving his flag." Heath yelled out "drop that color-bearer," (or perhaps just "drop him"[39]); shots rang out, and down he went along with his flag.[40] The 8th Florida lost not only its colorbearer, but also its colorguard, consisting of two corporals.[41] Now Lang's men could be seen overlapping the 19th on the left and the right, so Heath ordered his men to fall back, which they did in good order. They moved back about 50 feet, then turned to face the enemy again. Sgt. Silas Adams of the 19th looked behind them:

> While the Nineteenth is engaged in loading and firing, it is observed that a small body of men had formed in our rear. They were waving their flags and appeared to be cheering us on in the work we had in hand. They showed no anxiety, however, to advance with us. We heard the ringing order of Colonel Heath to fix bayonets. Then the order to charge was given and the Regiment started forward and down across the plain, like a tornado let loose. The men made much noise in the way of cheering. The rebels fell back rapidly and our Regiment advanced nearly to the Emmitsburg road, capturing many prisoners, two stands of colors, three pieces of artillery and four caissons.[42]

The charge carried the 19th Maine to within 60 feet of the Emmitsburg Road on their right flank. There they stopped and resumed firing at the Confederates. As they charged again, they ran over the flag of the 8th Florida, lying on the ground where the color-bearer (or Sgt. Roosevelt) had dropped it. Heath walked "directly over the rebel flag . . . putting one of my feet on it, but not stopping to pick it up." A second Confederate flag had also fallen and passed under their feet. As they were ordered back their attention was grabbed by a loud cheer in their rear. It was "the men from New York who had followed us about one-third of the distance we had charged and had come up to the 8th Florida flag, lying upon the ground," said a Maine sergeant. "These New York men were waving that Rebel flag and cheering wildly. The other Rebel flag over which we had charged was also picked up and some of the cannon from which the Nineteenth had driven the Rebels were hauled back as trophies of the III Corps."[43] The second flag cannot be identified at this time.[44]

The trophies and honors were rapidly disappearing, carried away by men who had not fought but had followed the battle in relative safety behind the lines. Sgt. Thomas Horan of the 72nd New York, part of the Excelsior Brigade raised by Daniel Sickles in 1861, was given credit for capturing the flag of the 8th Florida and was awarded a Congressional Medal of Honor.[45] Sgt. Silas Adams of the 19th Maine stated that, "when Horan picked up the flag in question there was not a live Rebel soldier within half a mile of him, unless such Rebel soldier was a prisoner of war."[46]

* * *

As the evening sun set behind South Mountain and Seminary Ridge in the attackers' rear, its reddish glow shone directly into the faces of the Federals. Even more action occurred north of the right of the 19th Maine, where Brig. Gen. Ambrose Wright's brigade, on the far left of the Longstreet-Hill attack, crossed the Emmitsburg road. The line ran northeastward from near the Codori buildings almost to Cemetery Ridge, with the 48th Georgia on the left of the line. As they advanced, the guns of several batteries on the ridge raked their lines, and as they came up the slope they let out their ear-splitting and nerve-jangling Rebel yell. To it was added the individual and group cheers of "huzza!" by Federal soldiers. One historian noted that mere words or even pictures could not recapture "the fear, excitement, anger, and responsibility of those who were a part of the actual scene."[47] The bitter smoke from gunpowder that blanketed the area blurred and obscured features as men tried to see what was in front of them. The booming and barking from nearby artillery, combined with the duller thumping by the Confederate guns in the distance, added to the roar produced of thousands of muskets.

As Wright's Georgia Brigade ran up the slope toward the Federal positions along Seminary Ridge the colors of the 48th Georgia were shot down no fewer than seven times, and a brigade of blue infantry moved in against the regiment's unprotected left. The colorbearer and all five of the color guard of the 22nd Georgia were shot down, but the flag was saved by a sergeant.[48] Just to the right of the 48th a bullet killed Color Sergeant Langston of the 3rd Georgia, but the flag was grabbed simultaneously by Capt. Andrews and Adjutant Samuel Alexander. Alexander carried it up and over the stone wall. He planted the flag amidst several cannon captured by the brigade, and Wright's men remained there for 10 to 20 minutes, waiting for reinforcements. None came, but Federal reinforcements arrived in force. Alexander, badly wounded, leaned the 3rd's flag on a gun where it was taken by another man in the regiment and brought back down the slope.[49] In the fighting Sgt. James Wiley of the 59th New York, in Col. Norman Hall's brigade just south of the Copse of Trees (which would become famous on July 3rd), captured the flag of the 48th Georgia and was later awarded the Congressional Medal of Honor for his effort.[50] The 2nd Georgia Battalion, leading the brigade into the charge while deployed as skirmishers, suffered heavily and probably lost its flag. A Federal soldier, his name now lost, apparently picked up the First National flag.[51]

The Federal reinforcements forced Wright's Georgians to retire down the slope towards the Emmitsburg Road. Some of them sought shelter in the Codori buildings, along with their wounded colonel, and there many were captured.[52]

* * *

It was twilight by the time Wright's brigade retreated west toward the Emmitsburg Road, and about one mile off to the north the men of Maj. Gen. Edward "Old Allegheny" Johnson's division of Ewell's II Corps had been waiting for several hours, listening to the sounds of battle in the distance. They lay along Rock Creek on the east and south sides of Culp's Hill, the large, boulder-strewn and heavily wooded mass that rose some 120 feet above Rock Creek along its eastern base. The hill was located about 800 yards southeast of Cemetery Hill and connected to it by a sagging crest line that included a significant rise now known as Stevens' Knoll.

Culp's Hill is actually one ridge with two peaks, the lower one some 80 feet above the creek and 400 yards south of the taller summit, the two separated by another saddle that runs east-west. Culp's Hill's height and position made it a dominant feature, important in any military assessment of the area. Its dense woods and rough slopes made it a soldier's nightmare, and on its sides some of the most bitter fighting of the entire three days would occur. South of the hill the ground was marshy, with a natural spring, called Spangler's Spring, offering water to the thirsty men from both sides and draining into Rock Creek. A stone wall originated at Rock Creek on the southeast side of the lower peak and ran west and northwest up the hill to the saddle between the summits.

Since the previous evening the Confederates had listened to the sound of the industrious Yankees chopping down trees and building breastworks along the crest. As they listened, they knew that it meant certain death to many of those who would have to try to take those works. While they waited, two regiments held evangelical revival meetings; the preachers no doubt emphasized God's control of the destiny of the men about to make the charge and urged them to fight for their righteous cause.

Johnson had four brigades, about 5,000 men in line. The attack was led by Brig. Gen. John M. Jones' Virginia Brigade on the right flank (facing the highest peak), Col. J. M. Williams, leading Nicholls' Louisiana Brigade in the middle, and Steuart's brigade on the left. A second wave was scheduled to follow them up the hill, with Stonewall Jackson's old brigade, commanded by Brig. Gen. James A. Walker, anchored the left (south) of the line, facing the lower peak behind Steuart. O'Neal's Alabamans came behind Williams, and Daniel's North Carolinians followed Jones.[53]

Johnson's right flank attacked what may have been the strongest position in the entire Union line. The Federals had been digging for several hours, and were strongly ensconced in deep trenches with thick abatis in front that would slow down the Confederates and make them excellent targets.[54] One Confederate officer wrote later that "the hill in front of this position is, in my opinion, so strong that it could not have been carried by any force."[55] When the advance began about 7:00 p.m., the Federal line was defended only by the brigade of Brig. Gen. George Greene, with approximately 2,000 men in blue. By the end of the fight three hours later, Greene would be reinforced by parts of two additional brigades of the XII Corps, as well as elements of the I and XI Corps.

Walking or running in an attack up this steep hill, around trees and large boulders and through brush, was difficult at any time of the day. But it was now dark, and when the attack got underway the night obscured everything even more. Harry Pfanz, the principal historian of this action, notes that this charge would have been "a difficult thing to do in the daylight but a hellish feat at night."[56] As the charge began the flash of muskets could be seen, but it was not clear who was doing the firing, the enemy at the crest or the far end of the Confederate line. One of "Allegheny" Johnson's aides, Lt. Randolph McKim, saw a line of fire about 100 yards in front, "but owing to the thick foliage could not determine whether the musket flashes were up or down the hill." He concluded that it was the Union line, and fired back, only to have Major Parsley of the 3rd North Carolina in Brig. Gen. Steuart's brigade yell at them to stop firing at his men.[57]

The Louisiana brigade commanded by Col. J. M. Williams was in the center of Johnson's line and came up against the 78th New York of Greene's brigade. Sgt. Charles Clancy, carrying the flag of the 1st

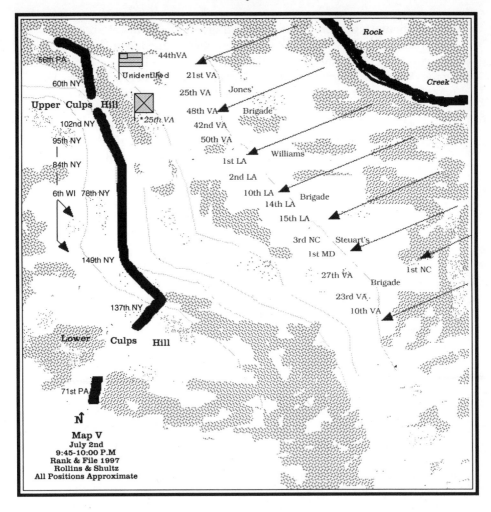

56th PA
44thVA
Unidentified   21st VA
60th NY
25th VA   Jones'
Upper Culps Hill
102nd NY   48th VA   Brigade
25th VA   42nd VA
95th NY   50th VA
84th NY   1st LA   Williams
2nd LA
6th WI 78th NY   10th LA   Brigade
14th LA
15th LA
149th NY   3rd NC   Steuart's
1st MD
1st NC
27th VA   Brigade
23rd VA
137th NY   10th VA

Lower   Culps   Hill

71st PA

N

Map V
July 2nd
9:45-10:00 P.M
Rank & File 1997
Rollins & Shultz
All Positions Approximate

Rock
Creek

Louisiana, got in among the Federal lines and realized he was about to be captured. In the inky blackness he removed the flag from its staff and wrapped it around himself underneath his shirt and jacket. He was captured, and held prisoner for six months, first at Ft. McHenry and then at Ft. Delaware. He kept the flag hidden beneath his clothes and when he was exchanged and returned to his regiment, he took the flag with him. The flag reportedly bore the marks of over 200 bullets.[58]

For about three hours the two sides traded fire, the Confederate line gradually moving uphill until they enveloped the Federals on both sides. One unidentified colorbearer reached within 20 paces of the breastworks held by the 60th New York on the left of Greene's brigade, and was killed. A member of Jones' brigade climbed to within 30 paces of the Federal breastworks before his comrades fell back to re-form. Another brigade got within 100 yards during their four charges. Still other troops managed to occupy one line of works before the attacks ceased about 10:00 p.m.[59] After repulsing a Confederate charge at the end of the fight the men of the 60th New York leaped over their works and captured 56 Confederates, along with a "Brigade battleflag" from Jones' Virginia Brigade, and one "regimental banner, which, as we learn from one of our prisoners, was a present from the ladies of the district in which the companies were organized." The brigade flag, a "stars and bars" First National, was found amid seven Confederate officers and the entire colorguard, all dead. The "regimental flag" probably belonged to the 25th Virginia.[60] The capture of the flags and prisoners showed how desperate was the Federal defense. The 60th New York's chaplain related that "the effects of our fire are so terrible that the flags were abandoned, and the prisoners were afraid to either advance or retreat." Both colorbearers were killed.[61]

The men of Greene's brigade, with some reinforcements, said their division commander, Brig. Gen. John W. Geary, behaved "with the most unflinching gallantry. . . They sustained their desperate position during an incessant attack of 2 1/2 hours by vastly superior numbers . . ." Geary reported that "the heaps of rebel dead and wounded in front of their lines afterward attested to their desperate determination."[62]

During the next five or six hours both sides continued to entrench, build breastworks and receive reinforcements. About 3:30 a.m. on July 3rd, the battle began again in earnest and for seven hours the fighting continued, with almost uncountable numbers of charges and counter-charges, flank movements and desperate, hand-to-hand combat as well as nearly continuous musketry and cannon fire. In one of these charges around 5:00 a.m., Col. Charles Candy's brigade of Federals carried a stone wall held by Walker's Stonewall Brigade. They charged ahead, according to Geary, "in handsome style, their firing causing heavy loss to the enemy, who then abandoned the entire line of the stone wall."[63] At some point during this action the colorbearer of the 14th Louisiana in Williams' Louisiana Brigade found himself cut off from the rest of the men. He was captured, but managed to remove the flag from its staff and secret it inside his jacket. He kept it there until he was exchanged the following winter, then returned it to the regiment.[64]

* * *

The sounds of Johnson's attack on the evening of the 2nd reached the ears of two brigades in Maj. Gen. Jubal Early's division—Col. Isaac Avery's North Carolinians and Brig. Gen. Harry T. Hays' Louisian-ians—deployed behind a low ridge just east of Cemetery Hill. Both brigades would attack up the east face of Cemetery Hill, with the North Carolinians beginning about 200 yards south of the Louisianians. (See Map V)

The Louisiana Tigers were among the most colorful soldiers, and among the most aggressive and hardest fighters, in the Army of

Northern Virginia. Men from the working-class districts along the wharves in New Orleans and French Acadians from the bayous, they had fought and drunk their way all along the route through the Valley with Jackson, in the Second Manassas, Sharpsburg, Fredericksburg and Chancellorsville campaigns, and then into Pennsylvania with Lee.

These were exuberant, voluble and excitable men, used to loud arguments and ribald jokes. Yet now they were "quiet and fearful," for they knew well the reception that lay in store for them. They too had listened for hours as the Yankees on the heights in their front felled trees, built breastworks and moved cannon into place. While they waited, 45 of their number were wounded by Federal fire. As the sun set and the sound of Johnson's attack grew, they knew their time had come, and they feared it. "I felt as if my doom was sealed," wrote an officer in the 9th Louisiana, "and it was with great reluctance that I started my skirmishers forward."[65]

Choking down their fear, and with their colorbearers leading them on, they started over the rise and then up into the face of the Yankee artillery. The guns on the hill "vomit[ed] forth a perfect storm of grape, canister, shrapnel, etc." But their commander shouted "forward!" and on they marched, "over fences, ditches, through marshy fields." After crossing the valley, the left flank of the Federal infantry behind a stone wall at the base of Cemetery Hill hit them with a sheet of flame and lead. Yet because of the darkness and the rolling nature of the terrain, their aim was high; most of the bullets shrieked overhead while the Louisiana Tigers kept going, up the hill and into the first line of rifle pits.

The fighting became hand to hand as both brigades climbed the slope. One Southerner remembered "with bayonets & clubbed guns we drove them back" out of the Federals' lines.[66] Seeing their forward lines break and the Rebels come screaming at them, the troops in the Federal second and third lines of rifle pits also broke and ran. With Hays' Tigers hot on their tails, the Federals retreated to the breastworks and emplacements around two batteries at the top of the hill, just below the entrance gate to Evergreen Cemetery. Along the way scores of Federals surrendered, but the Confederates refused to stop to take them prisoner officially, instead simply ordering them to the rear. It was pitch dark, but now the Louisianians and North Carolinians were in among the guns along the crest. Here the fighting became "desperate," recalled Capt. James F. Beall of the 21st North Carolina:

> but like an unbroken wave, our maddened column rushed on, facing a continual stream of fire. After charging almost to the enemy's [third] line, we were compelled to fall back, but only a short distance. The column reformed and charged again, but failed to dislodge the enemy. The brigade held its ground with

131

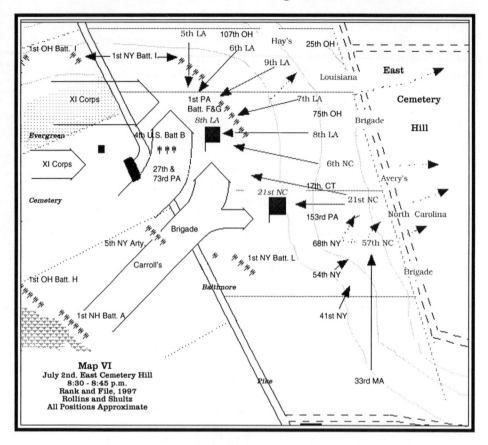

Map VI
July 2nd. East Cemetery Hill
8:30 - 8:45 p.m.
Rank and File, 1997
Rollins and Shultz
All Positions Approximate

unyielding determination—ever keeping afloat our flag
to battle and breeze.[67]

It was combat of the most vicious kind. A Louisiana officer
grabbed for the colors of one battery but was shot dead by its colorbearer, who in turn was quickly killed by a bullet that splintered his
flagstaff. Another Federal flag fell, and as a Confederate bent over to
pick it up he was hit in the head by a rock wielded by an angry Federal.

A Marylander commanding the division's Provost Guard, Major
Harry Gilmor decided to make the charge with Hays' brigade, and was
the only mounted officer in this section of the attack. He recalled that
the Confederates held the Federal works for some 15 or 20 minutes:

> While advancing on the main line of works, I saw one of
> our color-bearers jump on a gun and display his flag. He
> was instantly killed. But the flag was seized by an
> irishman, who, with a wild shout, sprang upon the gun,
> and he too was shot down. Then a little bit of a fellow,
> a captain, seized the staff and mounted the same gun;

132

but, as he raised the flag, a ball broke the arm which held it. He dropped his sword, and caught the staff with his right before it fell, waved it over his head with a cheer, indifferent to the pain of his shattered limb and the whizzing balls around him. His third cheer was just heard, when he tottered and fell, pierced through the lungs. The retreat had now begun. Some men picked him up with the flag, and carried them across to the parapet near where I sat on my horse. I had him placed before me, and holding on, guided my horse carefully along, and succeeded in safely reaching the town, though my horse was terribly wounded by a shell that exploded under him, cutting him in twenty places from shoulder to stifle. I met this hero some months afterward, nearly well; he had escaped from the hospital in Winchester. I regret that I have not preserved his name.[68]

The colorbearer of the 9th Louisiana planted their flag on the guns. The Federal artillerymen and soldiers of Brig. Gen. Adelbert Ames' division of the XI Corps made a stand "with a tenacity never before displayed by them, but with bayonet, clubbed musket, sword, and pistol, and rocks from the wall, we cleared the heights and silenced the guns."[69]

Hays' brigade got clear to the top of the hill, and in among the guns. At a lunette protecting the left section of Capt. Michael Wiedrich's battery they met the 107th Ohio, most of whom had retreated up the hill and through the guns.[70] Lt. Peter F. Young, the 107th's adjutant, saw the Rebels among the guns "yelling like demons at the supposed capture." He feared that the day was about to be lost, but spotted a Rebel colorbearer, possibly Capt. Charles Du Champ of the 8th Louisiana, waving a flag and urging his men onward. Young shouted for the Ohioans around him to fire at the Rebel flag, and the colorbearer fell to one knee, still holding the flag. Young, trying to urge his men to an even more "glorious effort," ran toward the flag, with his revolver shot the wounded colorbearer and grabbed for the "vile rag." Another Confederate, Cpl. Leon Gusman, grabbed it first and fell to the ground. The two wrestled over the flag, and Young came away with it. He got up and with the flag in one hand and his revolver in the other, turned back to his men to rally them again. He was immediately hit in the shoulder, but managed to stumble back to his regiment, where Sgt. Henry Brinker caught him and kept him from falling. A Confederate officer followed him with a sword in hand, intent upon taking the flag back, but an officer from Young's regiment struck the Rebel on the shoulder with his sword, stopping him in his tracks. Young had captured the flag of the 8th Louisiana in Hays' brigade.[71]

Over on the right of Avery's brigade the 6th North Carolina had fought its way up to the section of the wall defended by the 153rd Pennsylvania of Col. Leopold Von Gilsa's brigade. At least 75 Tarheels crossed the wall, fighting with clubs, knives, stones, fists and anything else a man could use to defend himself or attack the enemy. A Confederate colorbearer, probably from the 6th North Carolina, jumped up on the wall, pistol in one hand, flag in the other. He shouted out "surrender, you Yankees," but a Federal stuck his bayonet into him and pulled the trigger of his rifle, blowing a hole clear through the Confederate. The colorbearer fell backwards, his dead hand tightly wrapped around the flagstaff. A Federal soldier grabbed for it at the same moment that another Confederate grabbed the other end. The ensuing tug-of-war was won by the Rebel.[72] What was left of the 6th cleared the ridge and captured Federal guns, then retreated down the side of the hill to the stone wall, taking their battle flag with them.[73]

When the first colorbearer of the 21st North Carolina was killed while charging up the hill, the flag was picked up by Major Alexander Miller. When Miller went down, Pvt. J. W. Bennett picked it up, and was also shot. Four more men of the 21st North Carolina were killed carrying the flag, then Capt. James Beall picked it up. "The hour was one of horror," recalled Beall:

> Amid the incessant roar of cannon, the din of musketry, and the glare of bursting shells making the darkness intermittent—adding awfulness to the scene—the hoarse shouts of friend and foe, the piteous cries of wounded and dying, one could well imagine, (if it were proper to say it), that "war is hell. . . ." To remain was certain capture, to retreat was almost certain death. Few, except the wounded and dead, were left behind. Here, these brave North Carolinians 'stood, few and faint, but fearless still.'[74]

Like Wright's brigade on Cemetery Ridge, and Johnson's division on Culp's Hill, the Confederates could not hold East Cemetery Hill in the face of overwhelming Federal reinforcements. Two new brigades of Federal troops stunned the Confederates in the Federal works, their lines broke, and the remainder retreated back down the hill. At least one North Carolinian who got to the crest of the ridge with his men believed that the battle had been lost because reinforcements did not come. The 6th North Carolina's historian recalled:

> It was then after daylight had gone down, the smoke was very dense, and, although the moon was rising, we could not see what the enemy was doing, but we could hear him attempting to rally his men, and more than once he rallied close up to us. But our men had formed

behind a rock wall, and as he approached we fired a volley into him, which drove him back. This occurred at least twice. No one who has never been in a similar position can understand how anxiously we looked for re-inforcements. None came, however, and before long orders came for us to fall back to our original position.

By not supporting Hoke's Brigade of North Carolina and Hays' Brigade of Louisiana in the storming and capturing of Cemetery Hill the battle of Gettysburg was lost. I do not know whose fault it was, but I feel assured in saying that it was not the fault of the storming column. It did its whole duty and fell back only when orders came for it to do so.[75]

Capt. Beall carried the 21st North Carolina flag to a lower line of works, where he gave it to Cpl. Eli Wiley. A further retreat was ordered, and during it Wiley was killed, and the flag disappeared.[76] The next morning Capt. Oliver Rood of the 14th Indiana picked up the flag of the 21st North Carolina.[77]

So ended the action of East Cemetery Hill, and the second day of fighting at Gettysburg.

* * *

Early on the morning of July 4th a scouting party from the 7th Ohio moved down Culp's Hill under Cpl. John Pollock. According to their commander they "advanced over the entrenchments and captured the rebel flag belonging to the 4th Virginia Regiment Infantry, which, in compliance with orders received, was delivered to . . . headquarters."[78] A private who was involved in the action stated that they engaged in hand-to-hand combat and captured virtually all that was left of the 4th Virginia of the famed Stonewall Brigade, "but there was only about seventy of them left to surrender. We got their flag."[79]

At about the same time a squad from the 78th New York also went out to look at the grisly scene in the Confederate positions. They found an unidentified North Carolina flag, probably from the 1st or 3rd North Carolina of Steuart's brigade, surrounded by the remains of its men. Its mortally wounded bearer had torn it off its staff and buried it beside a large rock. "Eleven dead Confederates representing seven different regiments lay piled around the rock where it fell."[80]

Notes

[1] Alan K. Sumrall, *Battle Flags of Texans in the Confederacy* (Dallas: Eakin Press, 1994).

[2] Letter from George A. Branard, July 1, 1896, Museum of the

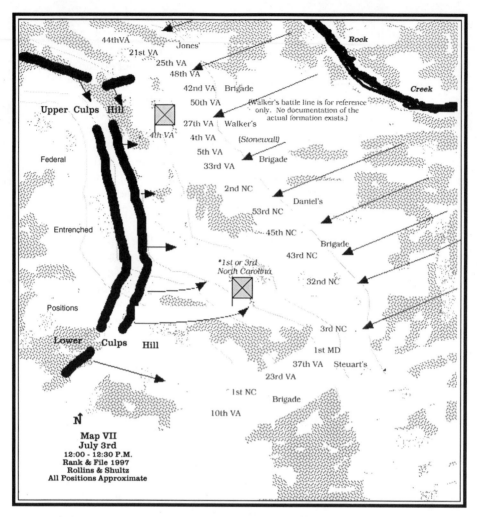

Map VII
July 3rd
12:00 - 12:30 P.M.
Rank & File 1997
Rollins & Shultz
All Positions Approximate

Confederacy. A diagram of this miniature flag may be found in Tom Jones, *Hood's Texas Brigade Sketchbook* (Hillsboro, TX: Hill College Press, 1988), n.p. Six young ladies in Houston had given it to him in December, 1862, and he carried it, along with the regimental colors, until Appomattox. "Recollections of A. C. Sims at the Battle of Gettysburg," Confederate Research Center, states that Branard carried the Texas flag, not the battle flag.

[3] *Hood's Texas Brigade*, 350.

[4] W. H. Berryman to Mother, Sister and Family, July 9, 1863, USAMHI.

[5] F. B. Chilton, *Unveiling and Dedication of Monument to Hood's Texas Brigade* (Houston: F. B. Chilton, 1911).

[6] Polley, *Soldier's Letters to Charming Nellie*, 135.

[7] *Hood's Texas Brigade*, 350. Many Texas regiments who

carried ANV pattern battle flags enlarged the center star to represent their state's "lone star," and that phrase was used in general to describe anything Texan.

[8] "Tout-Le-Monde," "Letter from the Army," July 7, 1863, *The Savannah Republican*, July 22, 1863.

[9] Report of Col. J. D. Waddell, 20th Georgia, July 27, 1863, *OR*, II, 425-7.

[10] Quoted in (Anonymous), "The Gettysburg Trip: The Lone Star Flag Over Devil's Den," undated manuscript, Texas file, GNMP.

[11] Report of Capt. George Hillyer, 9th Georgia, *OR*, II, 399-400.

[12] Diary of H. C. Reid, 8th Georgia, Alabama State Archives, photocopy, 8th Georgia file, GNMP.

[13] Report of Major J. C. Rogers, 5th Texas, July 8, 1863, *OR*, II, 413-414.

[14] Quoted in Marion G. Phillips and Valerie P. Parsegian, eds. *Richard and Rhoda: Letters From the Civil War* (Washington, D.C.: Legation Press, 1981), 30.

[15] William C. Oates, *The War Between the Union and the Confederacy. . . the History of the 15th Alabama Regiment* (New York: Neale Publishing Co., 1905), 219, 711, 756. Archibald had enlisted at age 48 and was seriously wounded at Sharpsburg and in the Wilderness. At Appomattox he saved the regiment's flag from surrender by putting it underneath his shirt. He told Oates he wanted to use it as a pillow in his coffin.

[16] W. F. Perry, "The Devil's Den," *CV*, 1901, 162.

[17] Harold B. Simpson, *Gaine's Mill to Appomattox: Waco & McLennan County in Hood's Texas Brigade* (Waco: Texian Press, 1963), 143.

[18] Henry L. Figures to Mother, July 8, 1863, 48th Alabama File, GNMP.

[19] Correspondence from "Soldier," July 7, 1863, published in the *Montgomery Daily Mail*, July 26, 1863.

[20] John D. Bloodgood, *Personal Reminiscences of the War* (New York: Hunt and Eaton, 1893), 140.

[21] "Adolfo Cavada Diary," Pennsylvania Historical Society.

[22] Capt. Henry Blake quoted in Richard Wheeler, ed., *Witness to Gettysburg* (New York: Harper and Row, 1987).

[23] Hilary A. Herbert, "History of the Eighth Alabama Regiment, CSA," edited by M. S. Fortin, McLaws Papers, University of North Carolina Archives. See also Hilary A. Herbert, "A Short History of the 8th Alabama Regiment," 8th Alabama File, GNMP, and Harry W. Pfanz, *Gettysburg: The Second Day* (Chapel Hill: The University of North Carolina Press, 1987), 374. Hereafter cited as Pfanz, *Second Day*.

[24] Quoted in C. Augustus Dickert, *History of Kershaw's Brigade* (Dayton: Morningside Press, 1976), 241.

[25] D. Wyatt Aiken, "The Gettysburg Reunion. What is Neces-

sary and Proper for the South to do. An Open Letter from Col. D. Wyatt Aiken to Gen. J. B. Kershaw," *Charleston News and Courier*, June 21, 1882. See also David Aiken to wife, July 11, 1863, 7th South Carolina File, GNMP.

[26] W. E. James, in John K. McIver Chapter, United Daughters of the Confederacy, *Treasured Reminiscences* (Columbia, S.C.: The State Co. Printers, 1911), 27.

[27] Account of Bernard Matthews, 108th New York in "Leg Taken Off by Gettysburg Shell," *The Louisville Evening Post* (July 3, 1913), in Gettysburg Newspaper Clippings, Vol. 6., 102, GNMP.

[28] John Heiser, "Action on the Emmitsburg Road," *GB*, 1(July 1989), 79-85.

[29] *Deeds of Valor*, 222. There is no trace of this flag after its capture. The flag of the 2nd will be captured on July 3rd. John Heiser's map and research indicate that the 26th fought against the 5th Florida. The 5th Florida returned the flag it carried at Gettysburg to the state in September, 1863 (see n. 44 below). In the 1880s and 90s Roosevelt conducted an extensive correspondence in an effort to receive the Medal of Honor. He never claimed to have taken the flag to his lines and did not turn one in. He failed to identify it or even describe it. (See his file in the National Archives, Record Group 93). I believe this flag was the 8th Florida flag overrun by the 19th Maine a few minutes later and claimed by the 72nd New York, but it impossible to be certain.

[30] John D. Smith, *The History of the Nineteenth Regiment of Maine Volunteer Infantry, 1862-1865* (Minneapolis: n.p., 1909), 70.

[31] Smith said they were "sixty rods" away.

[32] Quoted in Lt. Col. Charles Morgan to Bachelder, (no date, but probably April, 1876), *Bachelder Papers*, III, 1358. Hancock remembered his words as "Advance, Colonel, and take those colors!" Maj. Gen. Winfield S. Hancock to Bachelder, November 7, 1885, *Bachelder Papers*, II, 1135.

[33] Quoted in Pfanz, *Second Day*, 411.

[34] See John Imholte, *The First Volunteers: History of the First Minnesota Volunteer Regiment, 1861-1865* (Minneapolis: Ross and Haines, Inc., 1963); Return I. Holcombe, *History of the First Regiment Minnesota Volunteer Infantry* (Stillwater: Easton and Masterman, 1916); and Robert W. Meinhard, "The First Minnesota at Gettysburg," *GB*, 5(July 1991), 79-88.

[35] Testimony of Sgt. Silas Adams, in Smith, *Nineteenth Maine*, 71.

[36] *Ibid.*

[37] *Reunions of the Nineteenth Maine Regiment Association* . . . . (Augusta, ME: Sprague, Owen & Nash, 1878), 11.

[38] Testimony of Sgt. Silas Adams in Smith, *Nineteenth Maine*, 71.

[39] Francis Heath to John Bachelder, 12 October 1889, *Bachelder*

Papers, III, 1653.

[40] Testimony of Silas Adams, in Smith, *Nineteenth Maine*, 72.

[41] Report of Col. David Lang, 8th Florida, commanding Perry's Brigade, July 29, 1863, *OR*, II, 632. See also David Lang to Gen. E. A. Perry, July 19, 1863, printed in *SHSP*, 27(1889), 191.

[42] Testimony of Silas Adams, in Smith, *Nineteenth Maine,* 72.

[43] Heath to Bachelder, October 12, 1889, GNMP.

[44] This mysterious flag was apparently not from Lang's brigade. The 5th Florida's flag was not captured at Gettysburg, and was retired and sent to the state government in September of 1863. See Junius Taylor to Suradford, September 2, 1863, Pine Hill Plantation Papers, Special Collections, Florida State University. (I thank Bruce Gretz for this citation.) The 2nd Florida flag will be captured on July 3rd. It is possible that the mysterious flag came from Wilcox's brigade, or that it was a state flag carried in addition to the battle flag, and that it was kept permanently and not reported. It is also possible that it was recaptured by Confederates.

[45] Report of Asst. Adj. Gen. E. D. Townsend, July 29, 1863, *OR*, II, 282. Henry LeFavre Brown, *History of the Third Regiment Excelsior Brigade Seventy-Second New York Volunteers* (Jamestown, N.Y.: Journal Printing Co., 1902), 105, incorrectly states Horan captured the flag of the 2nd Florida. Report of Capt. John Darrow, 82nd New York, August 3, 1863, *OR*, I, 426, incorrectly states Horan was in his regiment, and also claims the capture for his regiment. "Record" # 73. It is now in the Florida Museum of History. Report of Col. John S. Austin, 72nd New York, August 15, 1863, *OR*, I, 566, mentions only the capture of the 8th Florida, and does not mention a second capture. Report of Col. William Brewster, *OR*, 1, 559, and Report of Brig. Gen. Andrew Humphreys, *OR*, 1, 533, incorrectly call the captor Thomas Hogan.

[46] Smith, *Nineteenth Maine*, 72. See also Report of Maj. Gen. A. A. Humphreys, (2nd Division, 2nd Corps), August 16, 1863, *OR*, I, 533; Report of Col. William R. Brewster, 73rd New York, commanding 2nd Brigade, August 15, 1863, *OR*, I, 559.

[47] Pfanz, *Second Day,* 416.

[48] Report of Capt. B. C. McCurry, 22nd Georgia, July 17, 1863, *OR*, II, 629.

[49] Capt. C. H. Andrews, "Another Account of General Wright's Brigade at Gettysburg," *Atlanta Journal*, March 9, 1901.

[50] *Confederate Military History* (Atlanta: Confederate Publishing Co., 1899), Vol. 6, 227-233; "Record" #38. Report of Maj. Gen. George Sykes, V Corps, July 31, 1863, *OR*, I, 593 does not cite the regimental number. It is now in the Georgia State Capitol, Atlanta. The 82nd New York also claimed to have captured the 48th's flag, but Wiley was given the medal and apparently had possession of it, since it was officially recorded by the War Department as having been turned in by him. See Report of Capt. John Darrow, 82nd New York, August 3rd, 1863 *OR*, I,

426; Francis Heath to Capt. A. H. Embler, July 21, 1863, and [Anonymous], "Report of Flags Captured in the Battles at Gettysburg, Pa., by the 2nd Army corps(sic). July 2nd and 3rd, 1863," National Archives. After the battle Major Sylvanus Curtis of the 7th Michigan in Hall's brigade reported that he observed reinforcements filing past his left flank where they picked up "two flags and one regimental banner" that the Rebs had left on the ground. Report of Major Sylvanus Curtis, 7th Michigan, *OR*, I, 448. See also Report of William McFadden, 59th New York, July 16, 1863, *OR*, I, 452.

[51] "Record" #59 and Howard Madaus to author, February 16, 1996. This is probably the flag Maj. Curtis called the "regimental flag" picked up by the 59th New York, cited in the above note. The area of combat limits the possibilities to Lang's and Wright's brigades. All of Lang's flags are accounted for. In Wright's brigade, the 3rd Georgia returned their Gettysburg flag to the state; the 22nd's flag was accounted for, and the 48th was captured on July 2nd. Only the 2nd Georgia Battalion flag is unaccounted for. The 2nd Battalion was transferred from Walker's division just before Fredericksburg, and apparently had not been issued ANV pattern flags. Thus it seems most likely that WD #59 was the 2nd Battalion's flag at Gettysburg.

[52] Report of Brig. Gen. A. R. Wright, September 28, 1863, *OR*, II, 623-5. See also Report of Capt. Charles Moffett, 2nd Georgia Battalion, July 18, 1863, *OR*, II, 630.

[53] For a clear presentation of this very confusing part of the battle, see Harry Pfanz, *Gettysburg: Culp's Hill and Cemetery Hill* (Chapel Hill: University of North Carolina Press, 1994), 111-113. Hereafter cited as Pfanz, *Culp's Hill*.

[54] Maj. Gen. Edward Johnson's Report, September 20, 1863, *OR*, II, 504.

[55] Report of Brig. Gen. Junius Daniel, August 20, 1863, *OR*, II, 568.

[56] Pfanz, *Culp's Hill*, 215-6.

[57] *SHSP*, V(1877), 293.

[58] Undated clipping from the *Richmond Examiner*, courtesy Howard Madaus and Don Troiani.

[59] Wayne E. Motts, "To Gain A Second Star: The Forgotten George S. Greene," *GB*, 1(July 1990), 65-76. 73.

[60] The "regimental" flag, WD #30, now in the Museum of the Confederacy, is a cotton flag, of the type issued in May, 1862. Only two regiments in Jones' brigade, the 25th and 44th Virginia, had been among the troops receiving those flags. Since the 25th was in front of the the 60th New York and the 44th some distance away, I conclude it was the 25th's flag. I thank Greg Biggs for this information. The "brigade flag," a First National, "Record" #22, is now in the Museum of the Confederacy.

[61] *Ibid*. Richard Eddy, *History of the Sixtieth Regiment New*

York State Volunteers (Philadelphia: Privately Printed, 1864), 261. See also Report of Col. Godard, July 4, 1863, *OR*, I, 861, for the timing of the capture.

[62] Report of Brig. Gen. John W. Geary, July 29, 1863, *OR*, I, 824. See also Report of Maj. Gen. Henry Slocum, *OR*, 1, 763.

[63] *Ibid.*

[64] "Memoir of W. P. Snakenberg," photocopy, 14th Louisiana File, GNMP.

[65] Quoted in Terry L. Jones, *The Louisiana Infantry in the Army of Northern Virginia* (Baton Rouge: Louisiana State University Press, 1987), 172.

[66] *Ibid.*

[67] James Beall, "Twenty-first Regiment," Clark, *Histories*, II, 137.

[68] Harry Gilmor, *Four Years in the Saddle* (New York: Harper & Brothers, 1866), 99.

[69] Report of Major Samuel Tate, 6th North Carolina, July 8, 1863, *OR*, II, 486. See also N. W. Ray, "Capture of Cemetery Hill: The Second Day at Gettysburg," Clark, ed., *Histories*, V, 608, and Richard Iobst, *The Bloody Sixth: The Sixth North Carolina Regiment Confederate States of America* (Gaithersburg, MD.: The Butternut Press, 1987).

[70] Frederick Smith, "Historical Sketch by Sergeant Frederick Smith at the Dedication of the Monument To Weidrich's First New York Light Artillery, May 20, 1889," *New York At Gettysburg*, V. III, 147.

[71] Young to Bachelder, 12 August 1887, Bachelder Papers, GNMP. See also A. J. Rider to Bachelder, August 20, 1885, *Bachelder Papers,* II, 1118-1119; Report of Capt. John Lutz, 107th Ohio, July 4, 1863, *OR*, I, 720; J. Warren Jackson to Lt. R. Stark Jackson, July 20, 1863, in Merle E. Reed, ed., "The Gettysburg Campaign—A Louisiana Lieutenant's Eye-Witness Account," *Pennsylvania History*, 189. The latter is the account of Lt. Joseph Warren Jackson, 8th Louisiana. It tells the same story but from the Louisiana point of view. Lt. Stark Jackson of the 8th said that the man with whom Young wrestled was named Willis. See his letter to his brother, July 20, 1863, 8th Louisiana File, GNMP. This was probably Private Holmes Willis of Company I. See Andrew Booth, comp., *Records of Louisiana Confederate Soldiers and Louisiana Confederate Commands* (New Orleans: n.p., 1920), Vol. III, Book 2. In a letter to the Editor of the *National Tribune*, July 15, 1909, a member of the 107th Ohio claimed Young killed the colorbearer with a saber thrust into his chest. The flag may have ended up in the Grand Army of the Republic post in Cayuga County, New York. On December 8, 1941, the Cayuga County Historical Society Secretary, Richard Drummond, wrote a letter to the Governor Sam Huston Jones of Louisiana, and described a flag that had been in the possession of the post when it was closed after the last veteran passed away. Drummond described the flag as having an oral tradition of being the flag captured

by the 107th on July 2nd and a white field with a red St. Andrews cross. The cross had 11 stars cut out of the red so that the white would show through: two stars on the upper and lower left, three each on the upper and lower right, and one in the middle. It also had the words "Louisiana Tigers" painted in blue letters. Drummond offered to return it to the governor, but no record of such a flag being returned has been found. I thank Ken Legendre for a photocopy of the *National Tribune* letter and the letter from Drummond to Gov. Jones. A photocopy of a photograph of this flag sent by Drummond to Frederick Tilberg, GNMP historian, in 1942, reveals that it was not an ANV flag, and thus probably not the flag captured at Gettysburg. See the photocopy and accompanying correspondence between Drummond and Tilberg in the 8th Louisiana file, GNMP.

[72] Pfanz, *Culp's Hill*, 262.

[73] Report of Samuel McD. Tate, July 8, 1863, OR, II, 486-7. See also Iobst, *The Bloody Sixth*, 137.

[74] Beall, in Clark, *Histories*, II, 138.

[75] Clark, *Histories*, II, 313-314.

[76] *Ibid.*, 137.

[77] G. T. Fleming, ed., *The Life and Letters of Alexander Hays* (Pittsburg: n.p., 1919), 463, 468, and Townsend, July 29, 1863, *OR*, II, 282. Statement of Lt. Col. Elijah H. C. Cavins (extract of Diary entry for July 3, 1863), *Bachelder Papers*, II, 977. Townsend mistakenly attributes it to the 20th Indiana, part of the III Corps. There is no trace of this flag after its capture.

[78] Report of Col. William R. Creighton to Lt. A. H. W. Creigh, A. A. A. Gen., 1st Brigade, 2nd Division, XII A.C., July 6, 1863, in Lawrence Wilson, ed., *Itinerary of the Seventh Ohio Infantry, 1861-1864* (New York: Neale Publ. Co., 1907), 256.

[79] "Excerpts from The Portage County Newspaper" letter from an unidentified soldier, July 5, 1863, 8th Ohio File, GNMP. Geary's Report, *OR*, I, 831. Willson, *Struggle,* 286, claimed that the flag of the 4th was captured on Cemetery Ridge on July 4th by the 126th New York. Report of Major Theodore Ellis, 14th Connecticut, July 6, 1863, *OR*, I, 467, claimed the 4th's flag as part of their victory on the 3rd. Both of these claims are erroneous, since the 4th was at Culp's Hill. Col. Charles Candy of the 66th Ohio, in his official report, July 6, 1863, *OR*, I, 837, stated that this flag was a blue Virginia state flag belonging to the 14th Virginia. The 14th was in Armistead's brigade and did not fight in this area. If true, this would be the only state flag captured at Gettysburg. I have been unable to find any confirmation of this identification or any trace of this flag after its capture, or to verify its design or color. I conclude that Candy never actually saw the flag but reported a rumor, and therefore I find Candy's report unconvincing and probably incorrect.

[80] Inscription on the flag now in the National Museum of

American History at the Smithsonian Institution, Washington. The identification as one of the two North Carolina regiments that fought in front of the 78th is by Howard Madaus, based on his curatorial assessment and the position of the troops. Howard Madaus to Author, April 1, 1996.

Chapter Seven

"Remember What You Are Fighting For! Your Homes, Your Firesides, and Your Sweethearts!"

July 3

The rising sun brought with it a clear and cloudless day, and the early morning heat showed that it would be a hot and humid afternoon. Much of the morning was consumed by a meeting of the high command of the Army of Northern Virginia. General Robert E. Lee met with two of his corps commanders, Longstreet and Hill, as well as many of their division commanders. As couriers came and went, they walked and rode along Seminary Ridge, discussing what would happen next. In the end Lee told Longstreet to organize a major attack on the center of the Union line on Cemetery Ridge, using troops from Longstreet's and Hill's Corps. It was to be preceded by an enormous artillery barrage, designed to demoralize the Federal infantry and crush the artillery along the center of the enemy line. As the Confederate infantry reached their objective, a small copse of Trees, Jeb Stuart's cavalry would appear in the rear of the Federal line and wreak havoc among the retreating troops.

By three o'clock in the afternoon, the incredible cannonade—the loudest noise ever heard on the North American continent—was over. It sounded like "the crash of Krakatoa and Pele in violent eruption blazing at once," recalled a surgeon with the 2nd Mississippi.[1] Death filled the air; men lay on the ground horribly wounded, while others had already died. All knew that in the next hour many more would die and many would be wounded.

A young private in the 11th Mississippi, Jeremiah Gage, was one of the first hit during the cannonade. He was a muscular, athletic man, with a deep tan and sun-bleached hair, his friends would remember him as the embodiment of the spirit and image of the Confederate soldier. A graduate of the University of Mississippi, he had been in the army since the beginning of the war, had fought at Manassas and Seven Pines and been severely wounded at Gaines Mill in 1862. One of his comrades recalled that "he did not know what fear was."[2]

During the cannonade, part of an exploding shell had ripped Gage's left arm between the shoulder and elbow, nearly tearing it off. One of his messmates carried him to a doctor, hoping something could be done. As the doctor examined the wounds, Gage told him it was nothing, then showed him his abdomen, or what was left of it after another shot had carried away the bladder, some intestine and part of the pelvis bone.

Despite his wounds Gage was still in control of his senses, composed and deferentially polite to the doctor, who told him he had but a few hours to live. Gage was given a strong dose of medicine and asked if he had any last messages. The young man asked to write to his mother. The doctor found paper, pencil and a knapsack to write on, then supported Gage's head and hand as he wrote.

At this moment the ideas and values that were most important to him dominated his thoughts. The letter summed up the soldier's sense of why he had come north with the army, why he followed the flag from Mississippi to Pennsylvania. It also crystallized most, though not all, of the motivations of the typical Confederate soldier in the summer of 1863: courage and personal honor, community and family, and the cause of Southern independence:

> Gettysburg, Penn.
> July Third
> My dear Mother
>
> This is the last you may ever hear from me. I have
> time to tell you that I died like a man. Bear my loss
> best you can. Remember that I am true to my country
> and my greatest regret at dying is that she is not free
> and that you and my sisters are robbed of my worth
> whatever that may be. I hope this will reach you and
> you must not regret that my body can not be obtained.
> It is a mere matter of form anyhow.
> This is for my sisters too as I can not write more. Send
> my dying release to Miss Mary . . . you know who.
> J.S. Gage
> Co. A, 11th Miss.

Gage was surrounded by his messmates and by members of Company A, some of whom were weeping silently and every one of whom would be killed or wounded in the next hour. A cup was handed to him and Gage made a last statement to his comrades in a feeble voice: "Come around, boys, and let us have a toast. I do not invite you to drink with me, but I drink the toast to you, and to the Southern Confederacy, and to victory!" He laid back down, and the surgeon continued on to other wounded. In a short time Jeremiah Gage was dead.[3]

The men in butternut and gray stood up in front of the woods on Seminary Ridge and dressed their line of battle, nearly a mile in length. Brig. Gen. Lewis A. Armistead walked up and down the line of his brigade, giving encouragement, helping his men get their stomach-turning fear under some control. Some of his men were already casualties, and the rest knew many of them would never return. Armistead spoke to these soldiers from the heart, his words chosen carefully to remind them why they were there, and the cause for which they would give their lives. In this moment of extreme stress and emotion only the truth, as they understood it, would be spoken and heard.

The 53rd Virginia served as the center guide regiment in Armistead's brigade, and the general called out to it to pay attention to his voice. Then Armistead approached the color guard with some words especially for them. To Color Sgt. Leander Blackburn, the general pointed toward the Union lines and asked if he would plant the colors there. Blackburn grimly replied, "Yes, sir, if God is willing." Armistead pulled out a small flask and offered a drink to Blackburn, who quickly downed it as Armistead turned to his troops, and implored them to follow their flag and remember the brave vow of the color guard. Then he shouted out, loud enough for all to hear, a command that he gave whenever going into battle: "Men, remember your wives, your mothers, your sisters and your sweethearts!"[4] He walked down the line to the men of the 57th Virginia, to whom he yelled: "Remember men, what you are fighting for. Remember your homes and your firesides, your mothers and wives and sisters and your sweethearts."[5] All was nearly ready now. He walked a bit farther down the line, and called out: "Men, remember what you were fighting for! Your homes, your firesides and your sweethearts! Follow me!"[6]

The Formation

Maj. General George E. Pickett's division was awakened about 3:00 a.m. and marched the final few miles, arriving about 8:00 a.m. and falling in line on the Spangler farm on the edge of Seminary Ridge. It formed the southernmost section of the Confederate line of attack, the men of Kemper's brigade filing into line with the 24th Virginia leading the way and anchoring the extreme right of the division. The 11th Virginia, followed by the 1st, 7th, and 3rd Virginia, formed on the left of the 24th. Then came Brig. Gen. Richard Garnett's brigade, the 8th Virginia on the right, followed by the 18th, 19th, 28th and 56th Virginia regiments. Armistead's brigade formed behind Garnett, with the 14th Virginia on the right. Then came the 9th, 53rd, 57th and 38th Virginia, the last anchoring the left of Pickett's division.[7]

In the fields about 200 to 250 yards east of the woods along Seminary Ridge, slightly ahead of Kemper's brigade and seemingly disconnected from the main line, lay two brigades from Maj. Gen. Richard Anderson's division of Hill's Corps. On the left of Anderson's short line waited Perry's Florida Brigade, under the command of Col. David Lang: the 2nd, 5th, and 8th Florida. On Lang's immediate right were Brig. Gen. Cadmus M. Wilcox's Alabamians, the 8th, 9th, 10th, 11th, and 14th Alabama regiments. Some of Wilcox's men were skeptical of the feasibility of the charge they were about to make. They had lost 50% of their numbers on July 2nd and believed their commander was bent on losing the rest today. Grumbling accompanied ominous shakes of the head. Wilcox, one said, was determined to sacrifice "the whole caboodle."[8]

North of Pickett's division, packed in behind Seminary Ridge, rested the troops of several brigades. Maj. Gen. Henry Heth had been wounded and his division would go into battle under Brig. Gen. James Johnston Pettigrew. They formed with Archer's brigade, now commanded by Col. Birkett D. Fry of the 13th Alabama, on its right. Not much remained of this brigade after the struggle on July 1st. With Fry and his regiment were the remnants of the 5th Alabama Battalion and the 1st, 7th, and 14th Tennessee. Next up the line waited the brigade previously commanded by Pettigrew, now led by Col. J. K. Marshall, including the 11th, 26th, 47th and 52nd North Carolina. To their left stood the men of Brig. Gen. Joseph R. Davis' Mississippi Brigade, including the 11th, 2nd and 42nd Mississippi and the 55th North Carolina. On the far left of the line, just south of the McMillan farm, was Col. John Brockenbrough's brigade, the 40th, 47th, and 55th Virginia regiments and the 22nd Virginia Battalion.

Further north, behind the brigades of Fry and Pettigrew, were two brigades from Pender's division of Hill's Corps, now commanded by Maj. Gen. Isaac Trimble. Brig. Gen. Alfred Scales' brigade, now commanded by Col. Lee J. Lowrance, included the 13th, 16th, 22nd, 34th and 38th North Carolina regiments. Finally, north of them lay the men of Brig. Gen. James Lane's brigade, the 7th, 18th, 28th, 33rd and 37th North Carolina.

All through the morning the Confederates lounged about, drinking coffee and preparing themselves for the ordeal they knew was in store for them. In the Union lines a mile and a half away men strained to see what the Rebs were doing, but most could only pick out the numerous artillery pieces being lined up along Seminary Ridge in the woods or in front of them. While the guns were being positioned, Lt. Frank Haskell of Brig. Gen. John Gibbon's staff spotted some Confederate flags on the far right of the enemy line near the Peach Orchard: "Above the top, and behind a small crest of a ridge, there seemed to be two or three of them, and they move too fast to be carried on foot."[9] This may well have been Maj. James Dearing, commander of an artillery battalion in Pickett's division. At about this time he was observed mounting his horse and galloping, flag in hand, trailed by his staff, from gun to gun in front of his men.[10]

The Confederates looked out at the mile of open valley they would cross, and the blue infantry dug in on the heights, supported by long lines of artillery. It was an awesome, unnerving sight. "My heart almost failed me," recalled a soldier who had walked out to the high ground near the Emmitsburg Road, where he could get a good look at the Federal works. "This is going to be a heller!" he said to the man next to him. "Prepare for the worst."[11]

The Captured Battle Flags
Color Photographs of 41 Confederate Battle Flags
Captured During the Gettysburg Campaign
(All numbers correspond to tables)

1. 13th Virginia Cavalry
Courtesy of the Museum of the Confederacy
Photograph by Katherine Wetzel

2. 2nd Mississippi
Courtesy of the Mississippi Deptartment of Archives and History

4. 23rd North Carolina
Courtesy of the North Carolina Museum of History
Photograph by Eric Blevins

8. *2nd Georgia Battalion (WD 59)
Courtesy of the Museum of the Confederacy
Photograph by Katherine Wetzel

9. 8th Florida
Courtesy of the Museum of Florida History

10. 48th Georgia
Courtesy of the Georgia Secretary of State's Office
Photograph by Bill Murphy

11. *25th Virginia (Jones' Brigade, WD 30)
Courtesy of the Museum of the Confederacy
Photograph by Katherine Wetzel

12. Unidentified (Regimental) Flag (WD 22)
Courtesy of the Museum of the Confederacy
Photograph by Katherine Wetzel

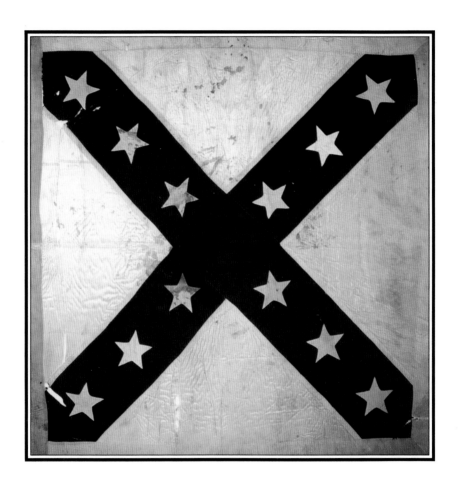

16. *1st or 3rd North Carolina
Courtesy of the Smithsonian Museum of American History

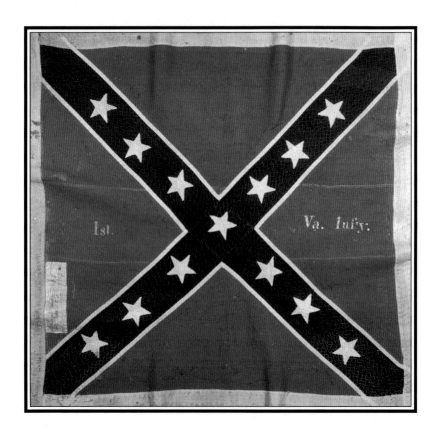

17. 1st Virginia
Courtesy of the Museum of the Confederacy
Photograph by Katherine Wetzel

18. 7th Virginia
Courtesy of the Museum of the Confederacy
Photograph by Katherine Wetzel

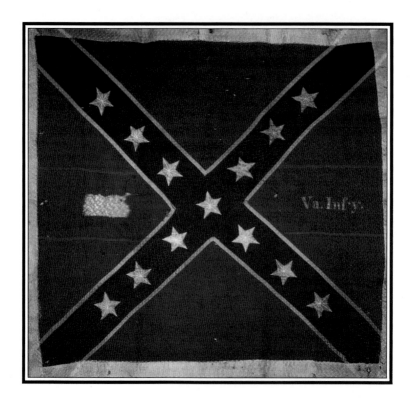

19. 19th Virginia
Courtesy of the Museum of the Confederacy
Photograph by Katherine Wetzel

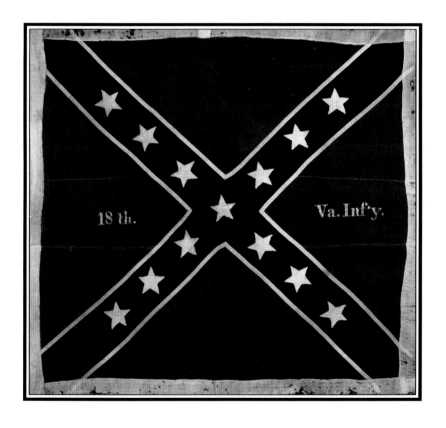

22. 18th Virginia
Courtesy of the Museum of the Confederacy
Photograph by Katherine Wetzel

23. 28th Virginia
Courtesy of the Minnesota Historical Society
Photograph by Thomas G. Shaw

25. 3rd Virginia
Courtesy of the Museum of the Confederacy
Photograph by Katherine Wetzel

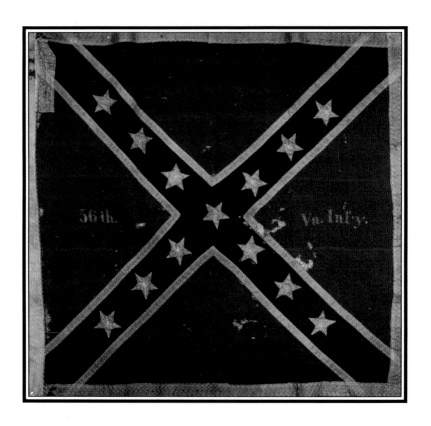

26. 56th Virginia
Courtesy of the Museum of the Confederacy
Photograph by Katherine Wetzel

27. 9th Virginia
Courtesy of the Museum of the Confederacy
Photograph by Katherine Wetzel

28. 14th Virginia
Private Collection: Photograph Courtesy of Howard M. Madaus

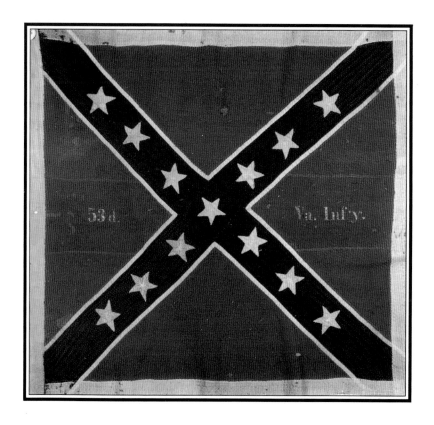

29. 53rd Virginia
Courtesy of the Museum of the Confederacy
Photograph by Katherine Wetzel

30. 57th Virginia
Courtesy of the Museum of the Confederacy
Photograph by Katherine Wetzel

32. 8th Virginia
Courtesy of the Museum of the Confederacy
Photograph by Katherine Wetzel

34. 1st Tennessee
Courtesy of the Tennessee State Museum

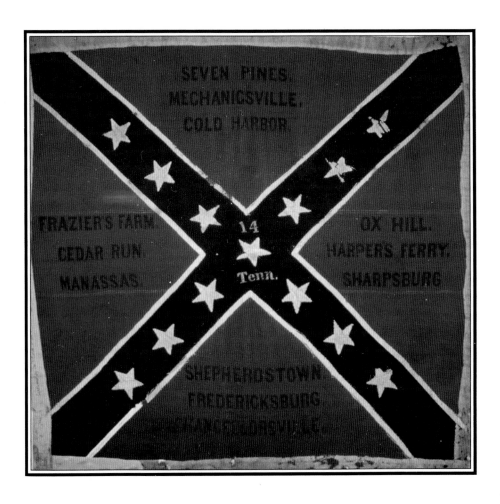

35. 14th Tennessee
Courtesy of the Tennessee State Museum

36. 11th Mississippi
Courtesy of the Museum of the Confederacy
Photograph by Katherine Wetzel

38 . *55th North Carolina (WD 75)
Courtesy of the Museum of the Confederacy
Photograph by Katherine Wetzel

39. 52nd North Carolina
Courtesy of the North Carolina Museum of History
Photograph by Eric Blevins

40. 16th North Carolina
Courtesy of the North Carolina Museum of History
Photograph by Eric Blevins

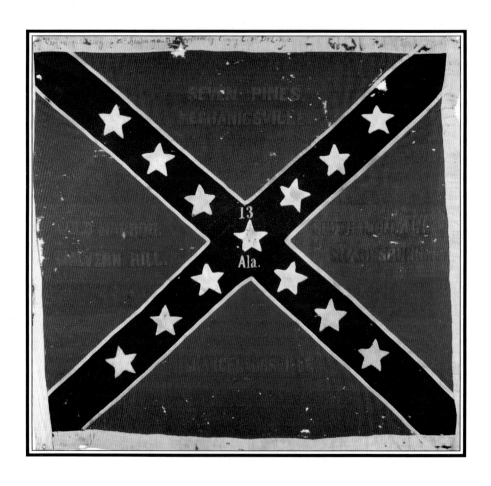

43. 13th Alabama
Courtesy of the Alabama Department of Archives and History

44. 7th North Carolina
Courtesy of the North Carolina Museum of History
Photograph by Eric Blevins

45. 5th Alabama Battalion
Courtesy of the Alabama Department of Archives and History

46. 22nd North Carolina
Courtesy of the North Carolina Museum of History
Photograph by Eric Blevins

47. *47th North Carolina (WD 68)
Courtesy of the Museum of the Confederacy
Photograph by Katherine Wetzel

48. *26th North Carolina (WD 62)
Courtesy of the Museum of the Confederacy
Photograph by Katherine Wetzel

49. 28th North Carolina
Courtesy of the Museum of the Confederacy
Photograph by Katherine Wetzel

51. *38th North Carolina (WD 63)
Courtesy of the Museum of the Confederacy
Photograph by Katherine Wetzel

52. 34th North Carolina
Courtesy of the North Carolina Museum of History
Photograph by Eric Blevins

53. 38th Virginia
Courtesy of the Museum of the Confederacy
Photograph by Katherine Wetzel

55. 15th Georgia
Courtesy of the Georgia Secretary of State's Office
Photograph by Bill Murphy

57. 55th Virginia
Courtesy of the Museum of the Confederacy
Photograph by Katherine Wetzel

58. 40th Virginia
Courtesy of the Museum of the Confederacy
Photograph by Katherine Wetzel

59. 47th Virginia
Courtesy of the Museum of the Confederacy
Photograph by Katherine Wetzel

Many of them took the opportunity to pray. Some prayed loudly, for they believed their time had come. "Yes, great big, stout-hearted men prayed, too, and they were in earnest," recalled a private in the 7th Virginia, "for if men ever had need of the care and protection of our heavenly father, it was now."[12]

The men in Fry's brigade learned that they would be the center of the line: both Pickett's and Pettigrew's divisions would align on them.[13] The colorbearer of the 13th Alabama took care to affix a "formidable looking lance head" to the flagstaff he carried.[14] Another soldier called it a spear.[15] A line officer in the 14th Tennessee asked himself: "June Kimble, were you going to do your duty to-day?" His audible answer was: "I'll do it, so help me God."[16]

* * *

During the cannonade that had just ended Col. Joseph Mayo of the 3rd Virginia had moved to the center of his regiment, "in front of the flag," and sat down, but the heat soon drove him back into the trees.[17] As the shells exploded and round shot crashed among the trees, the men waited, mostly in silence. "It seemed that death was in every foot of space, . . . a fire like that, . . . must be experienced," remembered one soldier, "it can not be told in words. For a few moments all was quiet again. Then was to come the work of death."[18] "One thing was especially noticeable," wrote one private, "from being unusually merry and hilarious they on a sudden had become as still and thoughtful as Quakers at a love feast."[19] The men of the 7th Virginia were "grave and thoughtful."

Yet a supreme confidence pervaded the Army of Northern Virginia, as one Virginian recalled, "from the commanding general down to the shakiest private in the ranks."[20] This was not mere wishful thinking, nor braggadocio, nor sincere but irrational illusion. It was instead the collective sense of skilled veterans, of men who had been through much combat and had a firm grasp of what it took to charge an enemy's works successfully. All felt that an extraordinarily significant moment was at hand.

After two days of bloody struggle, the most important moment of the war had arrived. Perhaps the end of the war was just over those hills in front. An officer in Armistead's brigade recalled that "they knew that many, very many, would go down under the storm of shot and shell . . . but it never occurred to them that disaster would come after they once placed their tattered banners upon the crest of" Cemetery Ridge.[21] Said Col. Eppa Hunton of the 8th Virginia, "All appreciated the danger and felt it was probably the last charge for most of them. All seemed willing to die to achieve a victory there, which it was believed would be the crowning victory and the end of the war."[22] As the 11th Mississippi lined up for the charge, Lt. William Peel noticed that "the ashen hue that lingered upon every cheek, showed the a[c]curacy with which the magnitude of the task before us was esti- mated, while the firm grasp that fixed itself upon every musket, & the look of steady determination that lurked in every eye, bespoke an un- flinching resolution to 'do or die.'"[23]   Some in the 28th Virginia called out "good-bye, boys, good bye" in anticipation of certain death.[24] A young soldier in the 9th Virginia thought hard about why he was there and what Pickett's Charge was all about:

> All knew that victory won or defeat suffered, was to be at a fearful cost—that the best blood of the land was to flow copiously as a priceless oblation to the god of battle. The intelligent soldiers of the South knew and profoundly felt that the hours were potential—that on them possibly hung the success of their cause—the peace and independence of the Confederacy. They knew that victory meant so much more to them than to the enemy. It meant to us uninvaded and peaceful homes under our own rule and under our own nationality. With us it was only to be let alone. With this end in view, all felt that victory was to be won at any cost. All were willing to die, if only their country could thereby triumph.   The sense of the importance of the issue, and the responsibility of fully doing duty equal to the grand occasion, impressed on us all a deep solemnity and a seriousness of thought that left no play for gay moods or for sympathy with nature's smiling aspect, however gracious.[25]

General Pickett rode along the line of his division and called out to his men. One officer recalled that he said "Remember Old Virginia" as he passed his regiment.[26] A bit farther down the line another re- membered that he said more: "Up, men, and to your posts! Don't forget today that you were from old Virginia."[27] The effect of his words was "electrical."[28]

At times it seemed that the Confederate battle flag was every- where. Col. Hilary Hebert, commanding the 8th Alabama, described an incident involving Col. E. P. Alexander, temporarily in command of Longstreet's artillery. At this moment of emotional tension, Hebert saw what seemed like an allegorical vision of the South at its apotheo- sis; the embodiment of its spirit, both past and future, and of its de- feat. The Confederate battle flag was a part of it:

> There is one scene particularly that I wish I could paint and hand down so that posterity might see it as I saw it. You know the hero of the picture but I do not. In

fact I never heard his name. It was on the ever memorable 3rd July 1863 at Gettysburg. One hundred and twenty pieces of Confederate artillery drawn up in line belched forth their forked lightening and more than that number of Federal pieces replied. The summer sun poured down his red hot rays upon the combatants. The very air seemed as if about to take fire. The earth shook and the air resounded with the roar of artillery. Just behind your Battalion lay Wilcox's Brigade of Ala. infty(sic) in support. We were not fifty yards off but such was the smoke of battle that we could with difficulty and only now & then distinguish the forms of the artillerists as a breath of air blew aside the smoke to let in the yellow sunlight or the lurid glow of the burning powder lighted up the scene. Viewed from our stand point(sic) the artillerists seemed like weird specters of the dammed(sic) in the place of departed spirits plying the hellish work of destruction. Shells were screeching & bursting over our heads, round shot were whizzing through the air which seemed peopled with the missiles of destruction. Now and then appeared an officer, most probably yourself, upon the scene calmly riding among his men. Close by you rode what appeared to me to be a mere boy. The buttons on his new gray jacked now and then glittered in the sunlight. Lithe and straight as an arrow he sat upon his horse — a young iron grey with glossy coat, clean limbs, and a step that indicated the pride and spirit of the horse to be equal to that of his master. In his hand the boy carried a small and beautiful Southern Cross whose stars glittered in the light of battle & whose red folds danced in the glancing sun beams.

When the roar of battle had ceased & the smoke had cleared away, I saw no more of the boy. I never learned his fate or his name but I shall never forget him as I saw him that day.[29]

As the gray line stood up to prepare for the charge, some were shocked to see many men still on the ground, face down. Some were wounded or killed in the cannonade, others were immobilized by sunstroke. Across town at Gettysburg College Professor Michael Jacobs would record a temperature of 87 degrees at 2:00 o'clock, and it was very humid.[30] Yet others were still lying down, their fear having overcome all efforts to rise and get in line.[31] Those who stood were silent, dressing lines and checking weapons, preparing themselves internally as well as externally.

* * *

Federal soldiers across the valley recalled that as soon as the cannon ceased firing "all eyes were turned upon the front to catch the first sight of the advancing foe. Slowly it emerged from the woods, and such a column!"[32] There appeared to some to be three lines, extending a mile or more. "It was magnificent," wrote Maj. Theodore Ellis of the 14th Connecticut, and another soldier in his regiment wrote that "as far as the eye could reach could be seen the advancing troops, their gay war flags fluttering in the gentle summer breeze, while their sabers and bayonets flashed and glistened in the midday sun."[33] Still another of their regiment wrote home of the Rebels advancing "with battle lines a mile long. . . in beautiful style with their beautiful battle flags flying open to the breeze it was a splendid sight to see but alas how many there were of those brave men that were launched into eternity during that terrible struggle onward they came cheering. . ."[34] Capt. Andrew Cowan pulled his guns into place near the Copse of Trees. "Then at a glance over yonder," he said, "I saw the enemy's skirmish line advancing from the trees with colors flying."[35]

A Pennsylvanian saw the Confederates forming a line in front of the trees as soon as the cannonade stopped: "over the fields beyond Emmitsburg road the gray brigades . . . with flaunting red battle flags and the sunlight sparkling on their polished rifle-barrels, were in full view, the lines extending to the right and left as far as could be seen."[36] A New York soldier in Col. George Willard's brigade (commanded by Col. Eliakim Sherrill) lay in waiting behind the stone wall near the Bryan barn, where his view was memorable. "Oh! What a splendid sight," he wrote, "you can't imagine how beautiful it looked to see them stretching away across the field in three columns in good line and banners flying."[37]

* * *

Kemper's Brigade

3 VA 7 VA 1 Va 11 VA 24 VA

The 1st Virginia, with only about 200 men in line, formed the center of Kemper's line. When the order came to prepare to start forward, the colorbearer, Sgt. William M. Lawson, stepped four paces in front of the center of his line. He had carried the colors since May, 1862, and was not about to give them up today. He was surrounded by Sgt. Pat Woods, Pvt. Theodore Martin, Sgt. John Figg and Pvt. Willie

Mitchell, his color guard on this day. When the line moved, they stayed in front the entire way across the valley, and as each man was shot, the next grabbed the flag and kept ahead of the line.[38]

Colorbearer David Johnston of the 7th Virginia had been struck in the back by an exploding shell, and was lying in the shade on Seminary Ridge, where he would be left and taken prisoner on July 4th. Color Sgt. G. W. Watson stepped up to the front and took the flag.[39] Nearby Capt. Thomas Gordon Pollock shouted out, as they began to move, "Boys, I trust you will all behave like Southern Soldiers."[40]

Kemper's brigade had already lost about 15% of its men in the cannonade.[41] The 3rd Virginia's colorbearer, Pvt. Joshua Murden, had been killed. His right hand still grasped the staff of the "beautiful new flag which to-day for the first and last time had braved the battle and the breeze." Murden would be remembered by his colonel as "fine a type of true soldiership as ever stepped beneath the folds of the spotless stars and bars, now lying there stark and stiff, a hideous hole sheer through his stalwart body."[42]

A skirmisher out in front of the first line looked back over his shoulder and described the scene unfolding behind him:

> Presently behind the hill a stentorian voice is heard giving the command— 'Forward!—Guide on the Right— March!' Gen. Pickett appears on the crest among the artillery and sends his brother, Charlie, to bid us keep about 120 yards in advance of the division. Now we hear the murmer[sic] and jingle of a large corps in motion. Colonels on horseback ride slowly over the brow of the ridge; followed by a glittering forest of bright bayonets. The whole column is now within sight, coming down the slope with steady step and superb alignment. The rustle of thousands of feet amid the stubble stirs a cloud of dust, like the dash of spray at the prow of a vessel. The flags flutter and snap—the sunlight flashes from the officer's sword—low words of command are heard—and thus in perfect order, this gallant array of gallant men marches straight down into the valley of Death![43]

Garnett's Brigade

| 56 VA | 28 VA | 19 VA | 18 VA | 8 VA |

In Garnett's brigade, Maj. Nathaniel C. Wilson took his place in front of the 28th Virginia and called out to his men: "Now, boys, put your trust in God, and follow me!"[44] Just before stepping off he pulled a small diary out and made an entry: "July 3. In line of battle, expecting to move forward every minute. With our trust in God, we fear not an earthly enemy. God be with us!"[45]

Adjutant James Crocker watched as an artillery battery stepped aside to let the troops pass through. Even amid the oppressive heat and humidity he felt a rush of excitement: "with their flags proudly held aloft, waving in the air, with polished muskets and swords gleaming and flashing in the sunlight, they presented an inexpressibly grand and inspiring sight."[46]

A few hundred yards north of Pickett's left flank Brig. Gen. James Johnston Pettigrew commanded what remained of Heth's division. When the cannonade ceased they emerged onto the ridge. Pettigrew, his face lit up in expectation of battle, turned to Col. J. K. Marshall and gave him the command to go: "Now, Colonel, for the honor of the good Old North State, forward."[47] An officer recalled the splendor of the moment: "their bright guns gleaming in the noonday sun and their unnumerable battle flags flying in the breeze, making as fine a pageant as was ever seen on any field of battle."[48]

Col. Birkett D. Fry's brigade formed the right of Pettigrew's line. When the 14th Tennessee moved out, one private looked down the line and saw the infantry, "clad in somber homespun with nothing bright about them but thier(sic) bloodied Battle flags and the glittering sheen of cold steel" moving out "to that death charge as if on Parade. . ."[49]

Lane's and Lowrance's brigades, the second line of the advance, emerged from the trees and followed Pettigrew's men, trailing by about 150 yards. As they moved out a staff officer rode by and cautioned them not to fire into the troops ahead of them. "Don't pass them," he yelled, unless they waver. "The men in front never waver," he added.[50]

* * *

The Federal soldiers on Cemetery Ridge watched as the long gray line took shape. What they saw was a sight they would remember for the rest of their lives, whether they lived an hour or half a century: twelve thousand or more men, stretching over a mile, with red flags waving and the sun glinting off their bayonets. And the Confederates began marching straight toward them.

One of the observers on Cemetery Ridge was Lt. Frank Haskell. "More than half a mile their front extends . . . man touching man, rank pressing rank, and line supporting line," he recalled. "Their red flags wave; their horsemen gallop up and down . . . right on they move, as with one soul, in perfect order." Each time he glanced at the gray ranks "treason's flaunting rag" caught his eye, floating above their gray lines. Across the valley came the Rebels, making no noise amid the thunder of the Northern guns, "but the courage of these silent men amid our shot seems not to need the stimulus of other noise."[51]

The right wing of the Confederate line moved out before the left, and it had further to travel. Thus as the entire line, a little over a mile long in two distinct wings, moved out from Seminary Ridge and toward the Emmitsburg Road, it was shaped like a lopsided arrowhead, its point being the men of Garnett's brigade, with the right wing in front of the left.

There was almost no flat ground on the field traversed by Pickett's Charge. It was rolling land, with swales as much as 40 feet below the crest of the small ridges, and this had a significant effect on the ability of men and officers to see the units down the line from them. Often, they could see nothing at all on their flanks. The troops more than a hundred or so yards away seemed to disappear, causing many of the men who survived to believe they went into the crucial stages of the assault unsupported.

The color guard of the 1st Virginia moved out in front of the line, Lt. Lawson holding the flag up high. They covered the first 300 yards quickly, but in silence. Then the stilled cannon across the way began to open up on the massed lines, and ragged holes immediately appeared, which were closed up by the men. About halfway across, Pvt. Willie Mitchell was wounded, but refused to go back and continued to march forward. He was about 16 years old, and had joined the army the previous December, after returning from studying at the University of Paris. About 100 yards farther he was hit again and killed.[52]

A captain in the 11th Virginia saw his regiment's colors knocked down several times as they crossed the fields. Twice the colorbearer staggered and the man next to him "seize[d] the staff and [went] ahead." When the flag struck the ground a third time they were still on the west side of the high ground near Emmitsburg Road. H. V. Harris, the adjutant of the regiment, grabbed the flag and carried it across the road and up the slope toward Cemetery Ridge.[53]

The 8th Virginia, anchoring the right of Garnett's brigade, started off in hopes of making contact with the 3rd Virginia on Kemper's left. The regiment suffered little until it approached the Emmitsburg Road, where it began receiving fire from the skirmishers of the 106th Pennsylvania. About 100 yards before reaching the Codori house Col. Eppa Hunton was hit in the leg, and knocked off his horse. The 8th split around the Codori house, then began receiving withering fire from artillery on their right (commanded by Lt. Col. Freeman McGilvery) that increased in deadliness as they moved up the slope.

One third of the distance across the valley, Maj. Nathaniel Willson of the 28th Virginia was mortally wounded, pierced by a piece of shrapnel. Carried back to the division hospital behind Seminary Ridge, he faded fast. With his final effort he told the chaplain, "Tell my mother I died a true soldier, and I hope a true Christian."[54]

Garnett's men, with their objective off to their left, made an oblique maneuver, forcing the units on the right to walk almost parallel to the Federal line. The 8th Virginia, on the right, endured a heavy pounding from the Federal cannon on their right and suffered severe casualties. They entered a swale providing some protection from the fire, then realigned to face forward.

A soldier on the left of the Federal line watched as "great gaps were made every second in their ranks, but the gray soldiers closed up to the center and the colorbearers jumped to the front shaking and waving 'the stars and bars'. . ."[55]

Armistead's Brigade

Now Armistead's men were marching hard and coming up just 40 yards behind Garnett's line. Capt. James E. Poindexter of the 38th Virginia remembered them "moving on like waves of the sea," their battle flags whipping in the breeze and "marching in perfect order, with disciplined tread . . . and bayonets and guns reflecting the bright sunlight."[56] Being near the center of the line, Armistead's men suffered greatly from the artillery on the ridge. Company K of the 57th Virginia lost 14 men to one shell, and great holes appeared in the lines all across the valley. As one soldier remembered, "over us, in front of us, behind us, in our midst and through our ranks poured solid shot and bursting shell dealing out death on every hand. . . . Nearly every minute the cry of mortal agony was heard above the rumble of guns. At almost every moment of time guns, swords, haversacks, human flesh and bones [were] flying and dangling in the air."[57]

When the 53rd Virginia reached the Emmitsburg Road, the men bunched up at the openings, trying to crowd through, and large numbers of them were hit. Finally the remnant got through and paused to get back in line, while men continued to fall. "Great gaps were made in their ranks as they moved on but they were closed up as deliberately and promptly as if on the parade ground," Lt. Col. Rawley Martin said, "the touch of the elbows was always to the centre, the men keeping constantly in view the little emblem which was their beacon light to guide them to glory and to death."[58]

Approaching the Emmitsburg Road, Armistead's men obliqued left for almost 300 yards, then realigned and continued to close with Pettigrew's right flank. They continued forward, all the while watching Garnett's and Kemper's brigades on their right melt away.[59]

As they continued forward under the incredible fire of canister, cannons and musketry, a lieutenant in the 9th Virginia murmured to himself:

> My God! It was magnificent—this march of our men. What was the inspiration that gave them this stout courage—this gallant bearing—this fearlessness—this steadiness—this collective and individual heroism? It was home and country. It was the fervor of patriotism— the high sense of individual duty. It was blood and pride of state—the inherited quality of a brave and honorable ancestry.[60]

Brockenbrough's Brigade

55 VA 47 VA 40 VA 22 VA Btn

Pride swelled in Confederate breasts as the left wing of the attacking force emerged from the woods south of the McMillan house and formed its line of battle. Adjutant S. A. Ashe in Pettigrew's division said "they moved in quick time and with admirable precision, as if on some gala day parade. It was a glorious spectacle, evoking admiration from foe and friend alike, and being the theme of unstinted praise from every one who witnessed it."[61]

Across the way a Federal officer saw the line move forward and remembered its visual impact:

> As far as the eye could reach could be seen the advancing troops, their gay war flags fluttering in the gentle summer breeze, while their sabers and bayonets flashed and glistened in the midday sun. Step by step they came, the music and rhythm of their tread resounding upon rockribbed earth. Every movement expressed determination and resolute defiance, the line moving forward like a victorious giant, confident of power and victory . . . There is no swaying of the line, no faltering of the step. The advance seems as resistless as the incoming tide. It was the last throw of the dice in this supreme moment of the great game of war.[62]

The 8th Ohio was stationed west of the Emmitsburg Road and north of the Bliss barn, in a swale so they could not see the left wing of the Confederate line emerge from the trees. But they heard a distant murmur and then the artillery opened up again:

> All at once the murmur increased into a prolonged yell,
> and we saw the enemy colors flying advancing in
> columns in mass, to the left of where the barn had been
> burnt in the morning. I had often read of battles and
> of charges; had been in not a few myself; but until this
> moment I had not gazed upon so grand a sight as was
> presented by that beautiful mass of gray, with its small,
> square colors, it came on in serried array, cheering their
> peculiar cheer, right towards the crest of the hill which
> we and our batteries were to defend.[63]

The Confederate skirmish line, still ahead of the main body, stood
and fired directly into the 8th, which returned their fire; "a few seconds . . . a cheer rises to the west of us—(that was, directly in *front*).
Now [the Rebel] line, with colors flying, issues from the trees that cover
the crest of the low [hills] . . ."[64]

As the first line moved toward the 8th Ohio "it looked as if their
line of march would sweep our position, but as they advanced their
direction lay considerably to our left, but soon a strong line, with flags,
directed its march immediately upon us."[65] One man remembered "our
blood was up, and the men loaded and fired and yelled and howled at
the passing column. . . The rebels came so close they expected to be
trampled into the earth. . . Our little band, some down under cover,
some kneeling some standing, were pouring their steady fire into this
moving almost solid mass."[66] Another member of the same company
recalled that "as they came sweeping towards us the left of their line
came opposite Company H's position on the skirmish line, it was a
magnificent sight, their well-dressed lines and colors flying."[67]

At the north end of the stone wall along Cemetery Ridge, approximately 185 yards east of the Emmitsburg Road, stood a small
clapboard barn rented by a African-American family named Bryan.[68]
It anchored the Federal line, and would mark the northern most point
of penetration by the Confederates.

Most of Col. John M. Brockenbrough's brigade (under the command of Col. Robert Mayo), on the extreme left of the Confederate line,
did not make it across the Emmitsburg Road. Instead, as soon as the
8th Ohio opened up on the Confederate line, Mayo's Rebels jumped
into Long Lane, a sunken road near the Bliss farm and remained there
while the rest of the line moved forward.[69] Only a few managed to
move forward with the rest of the line. Among them were a small
group from the 47th Virginia. Now Gen. Joe Davis' brigade formed the
left flank, with the 11th Mississippi anchoring it on the left. They took
fire from two directions: the muskets in front, and a line of infantry on
the left inclg some Massachusetts sharpshooters and the 8th Ohio.

Alfred Waud, "Longstreet's Assault"
(Courtesy of the Library of Congress)

To the Wall

As each Confederate brigade crossed the Emmitsburg Road, its organization dissolved. As they ran up the slope to the wall, men moved individually or in small groups, often clustered around their regimental colors. To the Federals behind the wall, it appeared as if they were a mob, 15 to 30 men deep, with banners waving overhead.

On the slope and in front of the stone wall, three of the color guard of the 1st Virginia in Kemper's brigade, Theodore Martin, Pat Woods, and John Figg were shot down. A man in this regiment said he saw half the flags in Pickett's division shot down in the first volley from the wall, "but quickly they were raised by the survivors and borne forward." Soon two-thirds of his regiment were *hors du combat*. He was "stunned, dazed, bewildered," but managed to shake it off, pick up a discarded musket and resume firing. He watched a soldier from another regiment lying on the ground about 15 feet from the wall tear a flag from its pole and conceal it in his jacket.[70] Near the stone wall, Colorbearer Lawson was hit in the shoulder, his arm torn off. Pvt. J. R. Polak grabbed the flag and tried to hold it up, but was also wounded. The men could go no farther. What was left of them fell back, leaving the flag behind.[71] It was picked up south of the Copse of Trees by Sgt. Martin McHugh of Co. D, 82nd New York.[72]

Three men of the 3rd Virginia, Col. William "Old Buck" Terry, and brothers George and Val Harris, reached the wall "between the

colors of the 11th and 24th Virginia regiments," near where the monument to the 15th Massachusetts now stands.[73] The 24th's flag was
carried by Pvt. Henry Taylor, who held it high as elements of the 24th
and 11th faced south to fire directly into the oncoming men of Stannard's
flank attack.[74] When the 3rd's colorbearer, Sgt. William Gray, was
shot down, Sgt. Robert A. Hutchins picked up the banner and carried
it to within 20 yards of the stone wall, where he was severely wounded.[75]

One of the men of the 7th Virginia recalled Kemper's charge up
the slope:

> To those who have ever faced artillery fire it was
> marvellous[sic] and unexplainable how human beings
> could have advanced under the terrific fire of a hundred
> cannon, every inch of air being laden with the missiles
> of death; but in splendid formation they still came
> bravely on till within range of the musketry. . . .[76]

Color Sgt. G. W. Watson, who started out as the colorbearer, had
been hit, as well as the next six men who picked up the 7th Virginia's
flag as the regiment crossed the valley.[77] Cpl. Jesse B. Young finally
picked up the flag and carried it up the slope, but a bullet smashed
into him within a few feet of the wall. He fell and with him went the
flag. A Federal officer behind the wall stood up and took aim at him
with a revolver. Young instinctively threw up his hands to protect himself, the officer fired, and Young was hit again, this time in the right
elbow.[78] Pvt. John N. Tolbert, described by one of his mates as "a mere
boy of ours," snatched the flag from him and took it to the wall. He was
the ninth man to carry the flag since it left Seminary Ridge.[79] The
7th's ranks were thinned at every step, and its officers rapidly cut down.
In the desperate, face-to-face struggle, Tolbert was shot in the head;
his assailant grabbed for the flag as Tolbert fell across the wall. Capt.
Alphonso Jones, in the regiment's post-battle report, noted that "the
colors of the regiment were gallantly borne and were only relinquished
when death took the power from its bearers to protect them longer."[80]
The flag was placed on the "breastworks," where it was captured. Pvt.
Hugh Carey, 82nd New York, grabbed the flag and ran to the rear with
it.[81]

As Kemper's men passed the Codori farm and came up the slope,
Col. Wheelock Veazey, commanding a regiment in Brig. Gen. George
Stannard's Vermont Brigade on the left flank of the Federal line, thought
the Confederates were heading right for him. The Vermonters watched
in awe as the Rebel charge crossed Emmitsburg Road and came up the
slope:

> No such sight in all the history of battles had ever been
> seen. On they came regardless of the carnage among

them, nearer and nearer until horse and rider, officer and private, standards and banners waving in the lead were plainly seen, and almost within musket range, the right wing now face to face with Stannard's brigade.[82]

Stannard ordered the 13th and 16th Vermont to swing out of line along the ridge and wheel right, coming into line directly on the flank of Kemper's brigade:

Forming in the open meadow in front of our lines, the Thirteenth changed front forward on the first company; the Sixteenth, after deploying, performed the same, and formed on the left of the Thirteenth, at right angles to the main line of our army, bringing them in line of battle upon the flank of the charging divisions of the enemy, and opened a destructive fire at short range, which the enemy sustained but a very few moments before the larger portion of them surrendered and marched in— not as conquerers[sic], but as captives.[83]

Kemper's men drifted north, melding into Garnett's line and overlapping them. Elements of the brigade approached the wall in front of Harrow's and Hall's brigades, while others reached it near the Copse of Trees. Others turned to face south, toward the Vermonters, and attempted to stop them with musketry.

What was left of the 1st Minnesota after its valiant charge on July 2nd stood with Brig. Gen. William Harrow's brigade in line behind the stone wall just south of the Copse of Trees. These men had marched and fought hard, and they looked it:

The men worn with the fatigue of three days' fighting and with torn and bloody uniforms, dust begrimed and smoke blackened faces, looked toward the enemy and charged repeatedly at the word of command.[84]

They watched as Federal cannon tore savage gaps in the Rebel line without causing any pause, and, as one Federal remembered, "we could not repress feelings and expressions of admiration at the steady, resolute style in which they came on, breasting that storm of shell and grape, which was plainly thinning their ranks." When the entire brigade opened fire, "the slaughter was very great," but the Confederates kept coming toward them, running at full speed.[85]

The 11th Virginia was devastated by musketry fire as it came up the slope. The colorguard, Sgt. Martin Hickok and Cpl. Charles Simpson, were both wounded. Their colorbearer was knocked down again and the flag finally fell to the ground.[86] East of the Emmitsburg Road near the rough ground north and slightly east of the Codori house, Pvt. George "Big Foot" Walker, a courier for Kemper, found the general already bleeding from a wound, and informed him that so many were down that reinforcements were needed if the line was to carry the works.

Kemper ordered him to go to Longstreet and request support. Walker rode off, found the corps commander, delivered the request, then returned to the brigade. There he found everyone around the 11th Virginia flag already wounded and the colors on the ground. He dismounted, grabbed the flag, climbed back on his horse and started toward the stone wall. His horse was soon killed, but Walker carried the flag to the works and planted it on the wall.[87]

A volley raked the line, and as it hit, the men of the 11th screamed the Rebel yell and charged toward the wall. Thirty yards from it they stopped and delivered a volley into the blue ranks, then dashed ahead. About 300 reached the wall south of the Copse of Trees, at a point where the stones were gone but a small breastwork jutted out toward the ravine in front of the lines. They crossed the wall, overran the lines, and pushed the Federals back behind an artillery battery.

A Federal soldier in line against Kemper watched them come "up to the rifle pits, across them, over the barricades—the momentum of the charge swept over them." The thin Federal line could fight, "but it had not weight enough to resist this momentum. It was pushed behind the guns. Right on came the enemy. They were upon the guns— were bayoneting the gunners—were waving their flags above our pieces."[88] Haskell watched as the Federal infantry, now just behind the guns, let loose a ragged fire, driving back the Rebs. He recalled that "a regiment threw down its arms and with colors at its head, rushed over and surrendered."[89]

The 11th had crossed the wall at a point originally guarded by the 15th Massachusetts and 1st Minnesota. Behind the lines stood two guns in Battery B, 1st New York artillery. Capt. Rorty and Lt. Sheldon, the first two commanding officers, had gone down, and the battery was commanded by Lt. Robert Rogers. The gunners were frantically loading and firing double rounds of canister. "These rapid, deadly discharges opened great gaps in the advancing host," said one Federal, "only to be filled up again." The Confederates surged over the wall and through the infantry, and, for the first time in the battery's history, succeeded in capturing one of the guns. Hand to hand fighting raged; as one Federal sergeant fired his revolver, a Confederate officer "planted his colors on a gun, exclaiming 'This is ours!'" The sergeant retorted "You lie!" and grabbed a trail hand spike, struck the officer in the forehead, killing him on the spot, then he too fell dead, riddled by several bullets. Col. Norman Hall, in command of a brigade of infantry in this area, said that "colors were captured with clubbed muskets, and many men of both our own and the enemy had their clothes blown off for a large space around their wounds by the close discharge."[90] Capt. John Holmes Smith, now in command of the 11th, looked back for reinforcements. He saw none, but sent a courier hustling back to find and guide the troops he expected to be coming up. Meanwhile, the 11th huddled in the Federal lines along the wall.[91] But the Federal lines closed around the guns and the Rebels and cut off their retreat. "A few minutes more, and all who were not dead were prisoners."[92] The flag of the 11th Virginia disappeared.

The oncoming mass of men in gray split, some going south against the Vermonters, the rest obliquing off to the north. As soon as the Confederates passed Harrow's brigade, the Federals "ran to the right for the threatened point, passing in rear of Hall's brigade, which, as soon as uncovered, wheeled to the right to strike the enemy's flank." The Confederates crossed in front of the 1st Minnesota "diagonally, under our fire and that of Hall's brigade to our right" and charged into the area held by Brig. Gen. Alexander Webb's brigade.[93]

Webb commanded the Philadelphia Brigade, made up of the 69th, 71st, 72nd and 106th Pennsylvania. Primarily raised from the city's firefighting organizations, they occupied the area behind the rock wall from the Angle to a spot in front of the Copse of Trees, approximately 100 yards south of the Angle. Behind them sat the guns of Battery A, 4th U. S. Artillery, commanded by Lt. Alonzo Cushing. After the cannonade Cushing had wheeled his left section(2 guns) of his 3-inch Ordnance Rifles down to the wall, roughly half way between the Angle and the trees. This would be the scene of fierce fighting. The middle section was left about 40 yards east of the wall and midway between the Copse of Trees and the Angle, while one gun of the right section was pulled down to the wall a few feet south of the Angle.

The 19th Massachusetts, of Hall's brigade, had been stationed behind the 15th Massachusetts south of the Copse of Trees. They watched as Kemper's men came up to the wall, then veered toward the trees. The 19th's colonel, Arthur F. Devereux, heard Maj. Gen. Winfield Scott Hancock come up behind him, and ran over to him. "See, General, their colors, they have broken through," he cried. "The colors are coming over the stone wall! Let me go in there!" "Go in there pretty God-damned quick!" Hancock shouted back, and, along with most of the rest of Hall's line, ran to the right to reinforce the men in the Copse of Trees and Angle, where the fighting was hand-to-hand.[94]

It was nearly impossible to hear shouted commands over the roar of cannon and musketry and the screams of men, so most of themen took action on their own. As they ran north they continued to load and fire their rifles. It was a vast, macabre, deadly recapitulation of a ritual many of them had no doubt practiced in their youths at home when the circus came to town, following the parade from one point to the next. Each man shot his rifle at the Confederates moving parallel to them just west of the wall, then stopped, reloaded his gun, ran up a few more yards and popped another shot at the Rebs.

Maj. Edmund Rice
(Courtesy of Richard Carlile)

Several men in Hall's brigade witnessed bizarre incidents close to the rock wall. Pvt. John Robinson of the 19th Massachusetts captured a flag, only to have an officer take it from him.[95] The officer would later be named as Maj. Edmund Rice of the 19th.[96] Cpl. William Deming, Co. F, 7th Michigan, came face to face with a Confederate colorbearer at the wall. Deming shot the man and took the flag from him. As Deming stood, loading his rifle with the flag by his side, an unidentified colonel rode up to him, waved his sword and screamed at Deming to give him the flag, threatening to cut him down if he refused. Deming complied, and the flag disappeared.[97]

By the time Garnett's brigade reached the wall it was 50 to 60 yards in front of Kemper's left flank. All organization was gone; its officers and most of its men were down. The survivors halted about 20 yards in front of the wall, then elements of all three of Pickett's brigades rushed the wall together. On Garnett's right the 8th Virginia became intermingled with the 3rd Virginia from Kemper's brigade. The 8th's flag, originally born by Pvt. William Thomas, fell four times in four minutes after crossing the road.[98] All of the color guard were down, but others, now nameless, picked up the flag and continued toward the wall, "carrying down a life each time. New men picked it up and carried it on at a full run."[99] About 20 or 30 paces from of the Copse of Trees, the flag went down again, but a Southern soldier picked it up, tore it from its staff, and concealed it in his coat.[100]

Two colorbearers in the 18th Virginia were among those who were shot down during Garnett's advance. As the regiment ran up the slope, they heard a voice (probably Garnett's but no one knew for sure) shout out: "Boys, you see that battery? I want you to take those guns! Remember, you are Virginians!"[101] One writer described the struggle here succinctly:

> Men fire into each other's faces not five feet apart. There were bayonet thrusts, sabre strokes, pistol shots, cool, deliberate movements on the part of some; hot, passionate, desperate efforts on the part of others; recklessness of life, tenacity of purpose, fiery determination, oaths, yells, curses, hurrahs, shoutings.[102]

Lt. Col. Henry A. Carrington, commanding the 18th, picked up the colors and carried them up to the Federal line.[103] He was shot down in front of the stone wall, and the colors were captured by Lt. Charles F. Hunt, 59th New York.[104]

Part of the 18th reached the wall in front of Capt. Andrew Cowan's battery. When the Rebs fell back, two artillerymen from this unit raced across the wall and picked up two battle flags as well as a flagstaff that lay on the ground on the west side of the wall. A staff officer demanded the flags from them and carried them off, leaving the flagstaff behind. A piece of material remained tied to it, on which was stenciled the name of the 18th Virginia.[105]

Capt. Walter A. Van Rensselaer of the 80th New York (20th New York State Militia) was in this part of the Federal line, watching the fight develop. Near a slash of timber he discovered:

> A Rebel flag behind the fence in the hands of an officer— I demanded its surrender—he replied, 'not by a d—d sight!' and fired at me with his revolver, wounding me in the small of the back. I lunged at him with my sabre when he fired again, the ball striking my sabre scabbard—five or six of my boys came to the rescue and he surrendered, followed by his whole regiment— they came over the fence like a flock of sheep. . . .[106]

Back on Seminary Ridge, Brig. Gen. Ambrose Wright watched through his field glasses as the charge went up the slope. He saw the troops go over the wall and "our battle flag waving in the enemy's bat

Captain Walter Van Rensselaer
(Courtesy of Richard Davis)

teries, where but a moment since the Yankee colors floated in the breeze."[107]

The veneer of culture is useless in the intense frenzy of combat. Men communicate with each other in sharp, direct statements, speaking only of things that are of the utmost, immediate importance, of essential matters of life and death. During Pickett's Charge no dissertations on social or political theory, on history or economics, were made or heard and none was needed.

Just before Kemper's and Garnett's brigades reached the wall, Lt. Charles Phillips of the 14th Virginia screamed out a brief statement that was intended to remind the men of the most important reason why they were risking their lives in that terrible place. He sought to incite them to even greater bravery, to motivate them in the most emotional manner possible. His words sketched an image of their past and their future, where they had come from and where they were going. For Phillips, and for the men who heard him, memory and dreams were fused into one powerful ideal. He put into words what the Confederate battle flag was all about: "Home, home, boys! Remember, home is over beyond those hills!"[108]

The 69th Pennsylvania of Webb's brigade waited behind the stone wall. When the Confederates got to within 20 or 30 yards the command to fire was given. A devastating volley poured directly into the faces of the Southerners. It staggered and disordered them but they kept coming. Men used their rifles as clubs and fought with their fists over the wall. The fight was "desperate and destructive." To the 69th's right Armistead and his men were over the wall, and some of Garnett's and Kemper's men crossed the wall through their ranks.[109] Gradually the right companies of the 69th bent back, ending up at a 90-degree angle to the stone wall, facing north.

One Federal recalled that at this point:

> Not a man ran, or seemed to feel like running, but they fell back slowly, loading as they did so, and firing, while the flags of the enemy, which are small red affairs, with a white cross diagonal on them, got up to the stone wall, and some crossed the line of the rail fence. . . ."[110]

But as the 69th was forced back, Harrow's and Hall's men suddenly appeared behind them. They had been ordered to his support at double quick;

> We ran in all in a huddle and took a position immediately to the left of the copse of trees, and opened fire as best we could, the enemy was safely layed[sic] down behind the wall, having planted their flags in the stones and poured a deadly fire into us from behind it, while our shots affected them little more than to *prevent their advance farther.* We stood their fire perhaps *five minutes, possibly more* and lost fearfully, when a *private soldier* named *George H. Cunningham* of Co. "B" of the 15th Mass. Regt (Harow's[sic] Brigade) cried out *'For God's sake let us charge, they'll kill us all if we stand here,'* and we did charge towards the wall, all in a mass, and the enemy jumped up to run and several attempted to take their *flag* off the wall, but as soon as they started we stopped and gave them a volley and nearly all lay down again and cried out to us to stop firing and let them come in, which we did and while a few was coming over the wall, the rest again started on the run towards the Emmitsburg road, when we again opened fire and kept it up until they got out of range. We was obliged to fire through those who were ready to come in and many was killed coming tords[sic] us but nearly all lay down untill[sic] we ceased firing.[111]

One man in or near the 69th watched as "their red flags were waving, as it seemed to me, in triumph already, though Hall was all right, and his men were steady on our left."[112]

The 19th Virginia had been shattered during the approach. Cpl. John Harvey started out with the flag, but was wounded, and the flag was carried to the wall by Cpl. William Black. The few who had survived the advance came within 20 paces of the wall, then their line recoiled under "the terrific fire that poured into our ranks from both their batteries and from their sheltered infantry." At this moment some of Kemper's men appeared on their right and some of Armistead's in their rear. The action at the wall would be recalled by their major, Charles Peyton, one of only a handful of field officers in the division to make it through the charge unhurt. The three lines joined together and "rushed forward with unyielding determination and an apparent spirit of laudable rivalry to plant the Southern banner on the walls of the enemy," he remembered. "His strongest and last line was instantly gained; the Confederate battle flag waved over his defenses, and the fighting over the wall became hand to hand."[113]

As the 19th Virginia reached the south end of the Copse of Trees, Pvt. Benjamin Falls of the 19th Massachusetts spotted a Confederate battle flag flying above the wall. The clash of bodies in the trees was audible; fierce hand-to-hand combat raged.[114] The flag seemed to be standing by itself, planted in the rocks. He reached for the flag, but could not pull it out of the rocks. Peering over the wall he saw a man from the 19th Virginia lying on the ground, still holding the staff. Falls raised his rifle, bayonet poised to thrust into the Confederate's head, and said "Hut, Tut! Let alone of that or I'll run ye through." The soldier took his advice, surrendering himself and the flag. Falls received the Medal of Honor for his work.[115]

In the Copse of Trees Maj. Edmund Rice of the 19th Massachusetts saw Garnett's and Kemper's men crossing the wall, carrying their flags high, and shouted for his men to follow him as he ran in that direction. "One battle-flag after another, supported by Pickett's infantry, appeared along the edge of the trees, until the whole copse seemed literally crammed with men," he wrote. As the 19th and 42nd [New York] passed along the brigade line, "on our left, we could see the men prone in their places, unshaken, and firing steadily to their front, beating back the enemy. I saw one leader try several times to jump his horse over the line. He was shot by some of the men near me."[116]

At about the same time another man in the 19th recalled the scene in the Angle, probably at Cushing's middle section some 40 yards east of the wall:

> The remainder of Hall's Brigade rushes toward the
> left[sic]. For twenty minutes, at this point, ball, steel

Pvt. Benjamin Falls
(Courtesy of Richard Davis)

and clubbed muskets plied their awful work. A Confederate color bearer rushed upon Cushing's Battery, planted his color against one of the guns, and died instantly. Another rushed out to recover the color and he, too, fell dead. Subsequently several rushed to the gun. They all fell about the piece, but the Confederate color still waved over the Union gun. Two more Confederate colors were planted upon this gun.[117]

Behind the Federal line in the Angle Lt. Haskell worked to get more men to the point of combat. He glanced up and saw that the Confederates were at the wall and over it, as "the damned red flags of the rebellion . . . thicken and flaunt . . . and one is already waving over one of the guns of the dead Cushing." Little could be seen of the enemy through the smoke, "except the flash of his muskets, and his waving flags." "Those red flags were accumulating at the wall every moment," Haskell noted. The red in them "maddens us as the same color does the bull." Now the men of Brig. Gen. Alexander Webb's brigade were nearly overpowered, "with more than a dozen flags to Webb's three. . . Webb's line blaze[d] red with [Confederate] battle flags."[118]

Garnett, still on his horse in front of the wall, screamed out to the 28th Virginia, "Faster men, faster, we're almost there." The Rebels hit the wall, jumped up and over it, their line in complete disorder. Color Sgt. John Eakin of the 28th Virginia had the colors in front of the wall, but was hit three times and knocked down. The rest of the colorguard, Cpls. Dexter Britts, Lindsey Creasey and James Hamilton, had apparently been hit.[119] The flag was grabbed by a private, who was immediately shot.[120] Col. Robert Allen picked up the flag, was immediately struck down and mortally wounded.[121] Somehow he managed to hand it to Lt. John A. Lee, who leapt on the wall and stood defiantly waving it in the face of withering fire. A shot hit the flagstaff, knocking it out of his hands and back over the wall. Lee retrieved it, climbed back over the wall, and fell wounded, yet still waved the flag until a "burly german" took him prisoner. The Federals retreated 25 or 30 yards, and men from the 28th, 19th, 53rd Virginia and other regiments were in the Angle, near Cushing's middle section.

Capt. Michael Spessard of the 28th, his dying son now far behind him, was confronted by a group of Federals who demanded his saber and tried to wrench it from his hands. He continued to fight, throwing rocks from the wall at them.[122] Others fought with bayonets, rocks and revolvers. For Col. Allen, the flag was nowhere to be seen. He suffered a severe head wound, sat down beside Maj. Dearing and asked, "whar[sic] was the colors?" He put his hat back on his head and promptly died, the flag being in his last thoughts.[123]

Near Cushing's middle section Pvt. Marshall Sherman of Company C, 1st Minnesota, stood loading and firing his rifle. His company had been on provost guard duty on July 2nd and thus had missed the Minnesotans' desperate defense of Plum Run. Brig. Gen. John Gibbon had ordered the division's Provost Guard into line, and it had moved north with the rest of William Harrow's brigade.[124] There was no soldier in his regiment more "ragged and blackened" than Sherman. His frock coat was torn and soiled, as were his blue trousers, and he was completely without shoes. They had fallen apart on July 2nd, and during the night he had decided to try to find a dead Rebel and get some new ones, but had not yet succeeded. Despite his cut and bleeding feet he had run up from the position south of the Copse of Trees with the rest of the regiment. The men around him fired a volley into the Confederates and knocked down a large number, including a color-bearer. Through the smoke Sherman saw a Rebel lieutenant run to the flag and pick it up, turn and yell to the men behind him, then turn again and start toward the Federals. The Confederate quickly found himself alone, waving his flag and shouting like mad, but Sherman could not hear his words over the din of battle.

Sherman thought that "there would be an opportunity of depriving the Rebs of the stimulus of their colors." He did not stop to assess the possibility of danger. Carrying his rifle and bayonet in both hands, he ran straight for the officer with the flag. When Sherman reached the flag, he placed the tip of his bayonet a few inches from the chest of its bearer. "Throw down that flag, or I'll run you through," he shouted. The lieutenant could not hear Sherman over the din and appeared to reach for a weapon. Sherman shouted again and thrust his bayonet even closer. The lieutenant dropped the flag and raised his hands. Sherman picked up the flag and the Federal troops near him shouted a great "hurrah!" The private then proceeded to march his prisoner to

Pvt. Marshall Sherman and the Flag of the 28th Virginia
(Courtesy of the Minnesota Historical Society)

the rear, waving the captured banner of the 28th Virginia over his head. The Federals opened up to let him through amid their shouts of con gratulations and victory. When Sherman got to the rear he tore the flag from its staff and stuffed it in his coat for safekeeping, but later turned it in.[125]

The colorbearer in Sherman's regiment was holding its flag when a shot splintered the staff. He picked up the staff of a Confederate flag, spliced it onto the end of his flagstaff, and kept fighting. The Federal flag was carried throughout the remainder of the war with this union of flagstaffs, and is currently in a museum in St. Paul.[126]

Another private in the 1st Minnesota, Daniel Bond, had his heart and mind set on capturing a flag. As it turned out, Sherman got there first. Bond watched as Confederates planted two flags on Cushing's middle section:

> There they seemed to mass on that point and we had[?] them with a thin semicircle. They could never lift their colors from these guns so deadly was our fire. Every man fighting on his own hook. . . . I soon after passed by [a friend] . . . I saw a spot of blood on his pants leg and asked him if he was wounded he said not. I told him I guessed he was and rushed on towards the enemy's flags two of which I was very anxious to secure a specimen to shake in Lt. Ball's face. But I was not to be so highly favored. When I approached within a few steps of their flags I saw our old friend H. J. W. Brown firing as if his whole soul were bound up in the destruction of the rebel army. Close by was Jackson of Co. G, covered with dust and dirt and blacked with powder fighting like he might have been a descendant of the *Hero* of the same name. My own gun had become so heated that I could hardly hold it in fact I had a bullet part way down but could not push it on. Jackson yelled "why don't you shoot?" This was sound advice but I was too much interested in securing a flag to heed it. I pushed on and reached the wall just a little to the left of where the flag was. Directly[?] behind there was twenty rebels jumped up without their guns. Holloring[sic] don't shoot. Do not take this to [be] that I mean to say that twenty men surrendered to me. (I am not that kind of hero and God forbid that I ever should be.) But I was on this occasion the first one to the wall and the rebels knew when I appeared that our men would not fire on them should they spring up and surrender. We never attempted to guard them to the rear, but just told them to run back leaving the duty of the collecting for the provost guards. But to the right of the flags the rebels were still fighting and I saw one loading his gun with his eye fixed on the particular flag which was nearest to me. And I stopped put my ramrod against the stone wall and pushed the bullet home capped my gun and raised my eyes. The rebels

to the right of the flag were all passing through our lines minus their guns. And Marshall Sherman of Co. C had my prize. The rest of the flags were gobbled up by other soldiers so that out of the 28 stands which were taken by our corps I did not get a rag.[127]

From their first position east of the Copse of Trees the 72nd Pennsylvania of Webb's brigade moved toward the wall, passing through Cushing's middle section on the way, where they joined in the fierce individual combat. Pvt. George Moore of the 71st Pennsylvania, fighting near the wall, captured a flag with no number or identification.[128] Nearby occurred struggles over two other flags. Capt. Alexander McCuen of the 71st fought with the colorbearer of the 3rd Virginia from Kemper's brigade, and wrestled the flag away from him.[129] One of his comrades remembered that:

> We had quite a little dispute before we came to the stone wall; we fought hand to hand and clubbed guns, any way at all; each man picked out his man, that lasted a very short time and they fell back, what was left of them. I saw Captain McCuen directly on my right when he captured the colors; that took place at the angle near the wall, I may say at the wall. I think he had a little argument with the colorbearer, in other words he cut his head off with a sabre and took the colors with him. I saw Captain McBride; didn't see him take the colors.[130]

The McBride referred to was Capt. Robert McBride, who captured a flag and colorbearer. "The engagement in the Bloody Angle was a fight, a bloody one, not a surrender," he recalled. "I saw Captain McCuen; I saw the colors he captured; I saw him when he took them; that was at the stone wall, to the right of me; he took them—he struggled for them. The colors I took I struggled for."

McBride grabbed the flag of the 56th Virginia from the colorbearer, Cpl. Alexander L. P. Williams, who stood defiantly waving it 15 feet east of the stone wall. Williams was hit by a bullet in the thigh, and McBride grabbed Williams and the flag, then sent Williams to the rear as a prisoner.[131] McBride put his name on the flagstaff and sent it to Webb's headquarters.[132]

What was left of the 9th Virginia—virtually all their officers were down by now—followed Armistead across the wall and another thirty to fifty paces inside it. There they were halted by fire from in front and both flanks. The struggle was desperate, and nearly all the men were killed or wounded, "but even its remnants bore its colors to the very stronghold of the Enemy and fell with them, overpowered but still victorious, beaten by numbers but proud & defiant in Spirit. . . ."[133] They held on for as long as they could, then turned and walked back toward Seminary Ridge, stopping to pick up their wounded commander on the slope of Cemetery Ridge. Pvt. John Clopp of the 71st Pennsylvania captured the colorbearer and flag of the 9th Virginia.[134]

Advancing up the slope, Sgt. Dennis Easley of the 14th Virginia dove "through a little gap in the company to our right, and ran to the front looking back, but my company seemed to have disappeared. . . ." He ran into a squad of Yankees who were surrendering, but ran by them, over the wall, and saw Armistead mortally wounded by a volley. "I glanced to the right and left but the wall was vacant with the exception of the two squads, and my recollection was they huddled around the colors, and they seemed to have given us a little more breathing room to our right. . . I struck the wall with two . . . guns to my right, and two to my left pointing over the wall." He continued fighting for some time, and recalled seeing the flag of a regiment in Garnett's brigade within 10 feet of the 14th's flag.[135]

There were at least three, and possibly as many as eight Confederate battle flags around Cushing's middle section, including the 14th Virginia's. An unidentified flag was planted on the guns, its bearer immediately shot down. Another man came on to grab it and was shot, then a small group rushed to retrieve the flag. All were shot down, and the flag remained by itself against the guns.

Color Corporal Joseph De Castro of the 19th Massachusetts had run to this area from his place in line south of the Copse of Trees with the rest of Hall's and Harrow's brigades. He knocked the Confederate colorbearer down with the staff of his flag, and took possession of the flag of the 14th Virginia.[136] De Castro received the Medal of Honor for his "extraordinary gallant conduct."[137]

In the Angle the adjutant of the 14th Virginia, Lt. John Summerfield Jenkins, fell near his regiment's flag. Four decades after the war, a friend eulogized him and recalled how he felt about the flag:

> He fell among the bravest, sealed his devotion to his country by his warm young blood, in the flush of early vigorous manhood when his life was full of hope and promise. *He gave up home which was particularly dear and sweet to him, when he knew that hereafter his only home would be under the flag of his regiment, where it might lead, whether on the march, in the camp or on the battlefield.* His life was beautiful and manly—his death was heroic and glorious, and his name was of the imperishable ones of Pickett's charge.[138]

Color Sgt. Leander Blackburn of the 53rd Virginia was not able to plant his flag on the enemy's works, as he told Armistead he would, for he was cut down by an artillery shell during the march across the valley.[139] He had gone barely 50 yards when a piece of shell cut off the end of the flagstaff and went completely through him.[140] Walking next to him, Cpl. James T. Carter grabbed the colors, but was hit in the left shoulder. In an instant Cpl. John Scott snatched the flagstaff and ran about 15 feet out in front of the brigade, waving the flag aloft. The flag of the 53rd Virginia "flashed like a meteor in the van," recalled another Confederate.[141]

"As we got within forty yards of the stone wall," recalled Lt. Wyatt Whitehead of the 53rd,

> there came all along the line the order to charge, and charge we did. From behind the fence the Yankee infantry rose and poured into our ranks a murderous fire. Garnett's brigade and Kemper's men had almost entirely disappeared; their brave commanders and their gallant officers were stretched on the field, and it remained for Armistead's men to do the work. After a desperate fight the Yankees began to give way; and as they fell back our men rushed forward to the stone wall with unfaltering steps, Armistead leading the charge.[142]

The tenth and last of the color guard, Pvt. Robert Tyler Jones, grandson of former President John Tyler, ran forward and picked up the flag after Cpl. Scott fell:

> I shook its folds in the air. Still onwards we went, amid storms of shot and death until, just as we made our dash and raised the "rebel yell," Armistead, who had kept ahead of his line all the way, said to me: 'Run ahead, Bob, and cheer them up!' I obeyed and passed him, and shook the flag over my head. Then the 'wild charge' began. In the excitement of the hour I only knew that I had reached the fortifications, when, faint from the loss of blood due to a shot in the head, I fell. [143]

Jones had leaped upon the wall, waved the flag triumphantly, but had been shot again, and fell forward over the wall, where the flag lay on the ground.[144] The air was filled with an unimaginable cacophony of gunfire, shouts, curses, the sound of men being clubbed and stabbed; screams and hurrahs. Dead and severely wounded soldiers covered the ground and lay in heaps.[145]

As he reached the stone wall, Brig. Gen. Lewis Armistead turned to Lt. Col. Rawley Martin (who had picked up the 53d's flag) and shouted: "Colonel, we cannot stay here." Martin responded by yelling: "Forward the colors!" Over the wall they went, "now eye to eye with the enemy" and Armistead called out, "Follow me boys; give them the cold steel." The intrepid Martin fell, severely wounded and maimed for life, with 42 dead and wounded men from his regiment around him.[146] Lt. H. L. Carter grabbed the colors and ran forward, planting them among Cushing's middle section.[147] Carter found himself alone at Cushing's guns, and surrendered himself and the flag. The flag of the 53rd Virginia was credited to Pvt. Isaac Tibbins of the 71st Pennsylvania.[148]

The flag of the 57th Virginia was probably the fourth to be planted on Cushing's middle section and the eighth inside the Angle. Sgt. John D. Hutcherson of Company G had been the colorbearer since the men were mustered in and had carried the regiment's flag for more than a year, despite being wounded at Malvern Hill. As he approached the stone wall with the flag, he was shot and killed.[149] Someone else, now unknown, picked up the flag and carried it forward.

Cpl. Benjamin Jellison of the 19th Massachusetts had picked up his regiment's colors during the fighting on July 2nd not far from the same area. He had been promoted to sergeant on the spot. On July 3rd he lay behind the wall until the commander of an artillery battery had come to Jellison's company and said, "For god's sake, men, volunteer to work these guns; don't let this battery be silent." Jellison had jumped up and carried ammunition to one of the guns, only to be told by his colonel to get back into line and take charge of the colors again. As the 19th Massachusetts, led by Maj. Edmund Rice, ran over from the area south of the Copse of Trees Jellison carried both the national and state colors in his hands. As they arrived at the grove of oaks, the first Confederates broke over the wall and into the trees. The two lines stood just 15 feet apart, firing at each other at point-blank range. When some Confederates threw down their arms in surrender and others retreated down the slope, Sgt. Jellison got in the Angle between the trees and Cushing's guns. Jellison swung his flagstaff and knocked down the colorbearer of the 57th Virginia, then grabbed the flag.[150]

Maj. Gen. Hancock was wounded, but his description of the action in the Angle reveals the importance of the battle flag. "The fight here became very close and deadly," he wrote. "The enemy's battle flags were soon seen waving on the stone wall." A few minutes later

> the colors of the different [Federal] regiments were now advanced, waving in defiance of the long line of battle-flags presented by the enemy. The men pressed firmly after them, under the energetic commands and example of their officers, and after a few moments of desperate fighting the enemy's troops were repulsed, threw down their arms and sought safety in flight or by throwing themselves on the ground to escape our fire. The battle-flags were ours and the victory was won.[151]

Sgt. John and Pvt. Robert Hutcherson
(Courtesy of J. Francis Amos)

The 38th Virginia in Armistead's brigade was also in or near the Angle, and the color guard, Corporals John R. Bullington and Joseph Singleton, fought for several minutes, then decided to save the flag and headed back toward the Emmitsburg Road.[152]

Meanwhile, on the Federal left the Vermonters continued to fire into the flank of Kemper's brigade, but suddenly they saw a new line of about 1,500 Confederates coming up the slope to their left and rear. These were the brigades of Brig. Gen. Cadmus Wilcox and Col. David Lang, which had finally moved out from Seminary Ridge and now were in a position to do some real damage to the left flank of the Federal line. The men of these two brigades had remained in waiting until Pickett's division was beyond the Emmitsburg Road before starting out across the valley. They were perplexed, and could not understand what they were supposed to do. "What the devil does this mean?" asked one. It was not long before Federal artillery found the range and began sending shot into their lines. They could not see the ridge through

177

the smoke, so they careened off to the right of Pickett's men, who were already streaming back toward the woods behind them.[153]

Col. Wheelock Veazey of the 16th Vermont recognized a danger and an opportunity when he saw one. This new line was heading not towards his men, but toward the ridge in his rear, and if he could change front to the left oblique and attack, he could hit their flank.[154] Veazey quickly got his regiment straightened out, reformed and changed front in the middle of a raging fury of shot and shell. "I stepped to the front," Veazey recalled, "and called upon the men to follow." They fixed bayonets and "with a mighty shout the rush forward was made, and, before the enemy could change his front, we had struck his flank, and swept down the line, and again captured a great number of prisoners."[155]

The men they ran into were in Lang's Florida Brigade marching on the left of Wilcox's Alabama Brigade. Ostensibly support for Kemper's right, they had started off some 20 to 30 minutes later and now found themselves in a tight spot. The noise of the artillery and infantry fire was so deafening that the men could not hear the shouted commands.[156] Capt. Patrick Hart, commanding the 15th New York Independent Light Artillery, saw these two brigades as they came within easy range of his guns. They seemed to be headed directly for his guns, and he unloaded on them with shell, then canister, and finally with double canister. "I continued this dreadful fire until there was not a man of them to be seen," he recalled.[157] Hart claimed that he shot down two Confederate flags, and watched as they were picked up by Federal infantry.[158]

As the artillery fire took its effect, the Floridians became scattered in the bushes and among the rocks in the fields, and Lang found it impossible to maneuver his men to respond to the fire:

> To remain in this position, unsupported by either infantry or artillery, with infantry on both flanks and in front and artillery playing upon us with grape and canister, was certain annihilation. To advance was only to hasten that result, and, therefore, I ordered a retreat, which, however, was not in time to save a large number of the Second Florida Infantry, together with their colors, from being cut off and captured by the flanking force on the left.[159]

Capt. Charles Brink of the 16th Vermont captured the 2nd Florida flag.[160] It was described as "a beautiful silk flag bearing a rising sun with the inscription 'Williamsburgh' and 'Seven Pines.'"[161] Three men, probably in Wilcox's brigade, were seen "running back over the fields with a stand of colors, and the men in admiration of their heroism, refrained from molesting them."[162]

Pvt. Piam Haines of the 16th Vermont captured the flag of the

8th Virginia, probably taken from the body of the soldier who had torn it from its staff and concealed it while running back toward Seminary Ridge.[163] A third flag was captured by a soldier from the 16th Vermont who was subsequently shot; the banner was reportedly picked up by someone from another regiment and not turned in.[164]

* * *

Fry's Brigade

| 5 AL Bn | 7 TN | 14 TN | 13 AL | 1 TN |

Just before this disaster occurred on the Confederate right, the left flank of the Confederate line approached the Emmitsburg Road, where the division led by Brig. Gen. Pettigrew merged with Armistead and Garnett on Pickett's left. They crossed it together, then moved up the slope. Col. Birkett Fry's brigade formed the division's right flank, with the 1st Tennessee on the right, the 13th Alabama on its left, followed by the 14th Tennessee, 7th Tennessee, and 5th Alabama Battalion on the brigade's left.[165] As they crossed the Road, a Tennessean jumped out in front of the brigade and looked up and down the entire line. He was "an eyewitness of the most vivid and stupendous battle scene doubtless that ever fell to mortal" man.[166]

Brig. Gen. Alexander Hays, commanding the division behind the stone wall north of the Angle, had his men ready. As the charge began, Hays ordered his men to stand and run through the manual of arms, practicing their handling of their weapons in preparation for this moment. Now Hays ordered them to fire, and "four lines rose from behind our stone wall, and before the smoke of our first volley had cleared away, the enemy in dismay and consternation, were seeking safety in flight."[167]

One of Hays' soldiers behind the wall remembered the Rebels crossing the Road with the colorbearers conspicuously in front:

> When the charging columns reached the road our infantry opened with all the vigor that they could use, adding still further to the enemy's confusion, and by the time the second fence and the one nearest to us was crossed, about one hundred and fifty yards away, there was no semblance of formation remaining, only a great mass of desperate men pushing on, the colorbearers keeping well to the front. There was no rebel yell—their usual charging shout was lacking.[168]

179

Hays' statement about the effectiveness of his men's fire was exaggerated, for the Southerners did not turn tail and run. Those who were not hit continued up the slope between the road and the wall, while "withering volleys of musketry, grape, double-charged canister, shot and shell shattered and mutilated as fine a body of Southern heroes as ever trod a battlefield."[169] In fact, remembered one Southerner, "the waving battle flags seemed to be the special mark as soon as we came in range of the small arms."[170]

In the 14th Tennessee, Thomas Davidson carried the flag and was shot down just after crossing the Emmitsburg Road. He turned to the man next to him, Sgt. Robert Mockbee, and said "Bob, take the flag, I am shot." Mockbee had the flag for only a few steps when Pvt. Columbus Horn said to him, "Bob, give me the colors, they belong to Company G." Fifty feet farther on Horn went down and Mockbee again picked up the flag. Then Cpl. George B. Powell of Company C, a member of the regimental color guard, took the flag, crossed the Emmitsburg Road and met his fate. Finally Boney Smith picked up the flag and took it to a spot just short of the stone fence, where it was captured.[171] As they ran up the slope, the Confederate line on each side of them seemed to dissolve. One man said, "The line both right and left, as far as I could observe, seemed to melt away until there was but little left."[172]

By the time the Pettigrew-Trimble line got near the section of the wall held by Hays' division, their right flank had entered the Angle, while the middle was in front of the 14th Connecticut. Pettigrew's adjutant described the action: "His strongest and last line was instantly gained, the Confederate battle flag waved over his defenses and the fighting over the wall became hand-to-hand and of the most desperate character, but more than half having already fallen, our line was found too weak to rout the enemy."[173]

In the center of the Confederate assault Col. Fry heard Garnett call out to him, "I am dressing on you." A few seconds later Garnett was dead, and Fry was shot down. As he fell, Fry yelled: "Go on, it will not last five minutes longer!" His men rushed up the slope into a thick cloud of smoke from the Federal guns.[174] The colorbearer of the 13th Alabama used the lance head on his staff to stab and slash at the enemy, leaving a gaping wound in the shoulder of at least one Federal, and probably others.[175] All five of the brigade's colors reached the Federal line, "and many of my men and officers [were] killed or wounded after passing over it,"[176] recalled Fry. Soon all his men were shot down, but the Federals continued to fire into the smoke where only dead and wounded lay.

The 1st and 7th Tennessee in Fry's brigade were the first of Pettigrew's men to reach the Federal works. The 1st Tennessee had three colorbearers shot down, the last of whom managed to plant the colors "at the works," and there it was captured.[177] The 7th Tennessee lost three colorbearers in front of the wall, then Capt. Archibald D. Norris tore the flag from its staff, stuffed it in his jacket, and ran back to the Confederate lines.[178] With a fragment of his company Norris retreated "under a fire so destructive that his escape seemed miraculous."[179] Lt. Col. Sam Shepard, who succeeded Fry in command of the brigade, said, "Every flag in [Fry's] brigade except one was captured at or within the works of the enemy."[180] The men later remembered that Fry's brigade "remained at the works fighting as long as any other troops either on their right or left, so far as I could observe."[181] "For five, perhaps ten, minutes we held our ground and looked back for and prayed for support."[182]

The colorbearer of the 5th Alabama Battalion carried its flag near the wall before he was shot down. Pvt. Bullock grabbed it and raised it high, but he was quickly shot. Pvt. Manning picked it up and held it aloft, and was immediately shot. Pvt. Gilbert was next to seize the flag and carried it back down the slope, safe for the moment.[183]

Behind the stone wall the men of the 14th Connecticut watched as "the great line" moved forward up the slope. They rose and fired, cutting big gaps in the Tennesseans. The Rebels were so close that "no longer could the measured tread be heard, no longer were the orders of the commanding officers audible for the shrieks of the wounded and groans of the dying filled the air, but on they came, meeting with the same fate as their comrades." The Federals watched as:

> the color-bearers now advanced, apparently in obedience to previous orders, and, attended by their color guards, planted their battle flags in the ground much nearer. Then the firing being too hot for them, lay down, waiting for their men to advance and rally around them. One of them in particular was in advance of the others and planted his flag not more than ten rods distant from and in front of the center of the Fourteenth.[184]

At least two companies of the 14th Connecticut were armed with Sharps breechloaders, capable of firing far more quickly than regulation rifle muskets. Some of the Connecticut men made partners with each other and worked with two Sharps; as one fired, the other loaded. Their barrels soon grew so hot they had to use water from their canteens to cool them. Fry's men closed upon the battery on the Connecticut left, so Maj. Theodore Ellis yelled an order for his men to fire left oblique to halt the advance. As a "daring and audacious Confederate" jumped on the cannon that had been left about 30 feet in front of the wall, then waved his hat for the men to come with him, he was riddled with bullets.[185] A soldier on the right of the Federal line also saw this happen, but remembered that the Confederate waved a flag, not his hat. The Rebel gave a cheer, then "a gunner brained him with a sponge staff, or rammer."[186]

One of the flags by the wall belonged to the 14th Tennessee in Fry's brigade. The regiment had lost several colorbearers on the march across the valley, and finally planted the flag about 20 yards from the wall. By now there were no Confederates standing near it; all were lying down, firing and waiting for reinforcements.[187] Maj. Ellis of the 14th Connecticut yelled for volunteers to take it, and immediately Sgt.-Maj. William B. Hincks and two other men leaped the wall and began running "straight and swift for the color. . . ." The other two were shot down. Hincks ran to the flag, swung his saber over the Confederates and uttered a terrific yell. All the Connecticut men watched as he seized the flag and hastily returned to the line, amid a hail of bullets. As he jumped on the wall, trophy in hand, "the regiment to a man wildly cheered the gallant fellow."[188]

Marshall's Brigade

The North Carolinians in Col. J. K. Marshall's (Pettigrew's) brigade had suffered relatively little on the march across the valley, but as the Confederates approached Emmitsburg Road they began to take fire, and great holes were ripped in their ranks every five or ten yards. Crossing the road their ranks were thinned at every step by volleys of musketry. A private in the 47th North Carolina, hit in the shoulder, spoke to his captain and said: "They have wounded me, but I want to lead Company H." He was hit again and fell on the fence near the rock wall. Close to him the regimental colorbearer passed over this fence and fell mortally wounded about ten steps from the rock wall, and the flag disappeared.[189]

To their right the 52nd North Carolina, heads down into the storm of lead, came up close to the wall. The found themselves in front of "an overpowering force and almost impregnable position" and "were forced back, and then the slaughter was terrific."[190]

The 26th North Carolina, starting with only about 200 men in line, reached the Emmitsburg Road in good fashion, its lines intact. There they were hit by the first volley and responded by charging up the slope. A severely wounded Capt. W. T. Magruder shouted out, "Men, remember your mothers, wives, and sisters at home, and do not halt here."[191] All the way between the road and the wall they bunched together, continuously "closing on the colors," and maintaining their organization. As they came up the slope they drifted left, approaching the wall in front of the 12th New Jersey.[192] One of the men waiting for them behind the wall counted the flags he could see and described to his wife the sight of 18 battle flags coming at him. "Approaching our front they made a splendid appearance with their colors flying in the breeze," he said.[193]

Gaston Burroughs, commanding a company in the 26th North Carolina, remembered that "we crossed the road and went to the enemy's works, where we continued firing until most of the regiment were captured, the enemy closing in on us from our rear." By the time the regiment reached the area just below the wall but past the Angle, it had been reduced to the size of a skirmish line. The regimental commander, Maj. Jones, recalled:

> On we pushed and were now right on the enemy's works, when we received a murderous fire upon our left flank. I looked to see where it came from and lo! we were completely flanked upon our left not only by infantry, but artillery. One of our brigades had given way. The enemy had seized upon the gap and now poured a galling fire into our troops, forcing them to give way in succession to the right."[194]

Yet they marched, then ran up toward the Federals behind the wall, and men fell at every step, "but still they kept closing on the colours," recalled Lt. T. J. Cureton.[195] Sgt. W. H. Smith carried the flag over the Emmitsburg Road and up the slope, but was hit and killed. Pvt. Tom Cozort of Company F carried the battle flag to within a few feet of the stone wall, and was killed there.[196] Capt. S. W. Brewer picked up the flag but was immediately knocked down. Another colorbearer of the 26th North Carolina came close to the wall and heard a Federal yell out to him, "Come over to this side of the Lord!"[197] The Rebel was shot down while attempting to plant the flag on the wall.[198] Pvt. Daniel Thomas picked up the flag and carried it to the wall and there Pvt. James M. Brooks helped him plant the flag "on the works" and left it there.[199]

"It was the color company, and the flag that it bore was a target for the guns and rifles of the enemy," recalled the regimental historian of the 11th North Carolina:

> By the time they got near the wall all eight of the 11th North Carolina's colorbearers were down, and its flag was picked up by Capt. Francis W. Bird. The staff was hit twice while he carried it, but he managed to take it back to Seminary Ridge.[200]

Brockenbrough's Brigade   Davis' Brigade

55 VA 47 VA 40 VA 22 VA Btn	11 MS 2 MS 42 MS 55 NC

On the left of the attacking line most of Brockenbrough's brigade had halted in Long Lane, so Gen. Joe Davis' brigade took fire from the Federal troops lined up on their its flank. As the Confederates crossed the road, Lt. Egan's artillery section pulled into line a few yards west of the Bryan barn and began firing canister directly into them at nearly point-blank range. Then the men in Hays' division, lined up behind the stone wall, rose up and let loose a devastating volley at them.

The 11th Mississippi fired back, but kept moving, loading and firing as it came up the slope. A few yards in advance of the line "Thirteen of our Reg't had concentrated upon the colors, as if to constitute ourselves its guard," remembered one lieutenant.[201] They pressed steadily on: "Charging with a yell the few undaunted survivors impetuously rushed through the 'hell of fire' of all arms to and near the wall, continuing the battle there at close quarters for a short time." Capt. John Moore of Company A commanded the regiment, all other officers having been shot down. He stood about 20 yards south of the Bryan barn with his back to the wall, trying to fill the gaps that kept opening in the lines. Lt. A. J. Baker yelled to him: "For God's sake, John, give the command to charge." Moore turned to him and said he would not take the responsibility, so Baker gave the command himself and "a few surviving comrades" rushed to within 10 feet of the wall, "as individuals rather than as an organization," and there Baker was killed, 20 feet north of the Bryan barn. At least one man from Company A crossed the wall, was wounded, and came back across it.[202] Half a dozen men from other companies also crossed the wall; some were captured, others wounded or killed.[203]

Ten feet from the wall the third colorbearer of the 11th Mississippi, Cpl. Billy O'Brien, fell wounded at the feet of Pvt. James Griffin, who had just loaded his rifle. Griffin bent down to pick up the flag, but Joseph Smith grabbed it first and raised it aloft. Smith and Griffin were both shot down, so Pvt. William P. Marion picked up the flag, stepped a bit closer, and was killed. The flagstaff was shot in two. Pvt. Joseph Marable raised the colors and planted them on the wall, falling against it when he was stunned, knocked down, and the flag captured by Sgt. Ferninando Maggi of the 39th New York.[204] Cpl. Francisco Navarreto of the 39th New York came away with a second, unidentified flag, probably from the 42nd Mississippi.[205]

The 2nd Mississippi carried a new Army of Northern Virginia

pattern flag on July 3rd, replacing the one they had lost on July 1st in the railroad cut. On this day Sgt. Luke Byrn carried the flag almost to the wall, where he was wounded, and the flag went down with him. Byrn lay on the battlefield all night with the flag wrapped around his body. He somehow managed to get back to his regiment with the flag.[206]

The 55th North Carolina, so small after its losses on July 1st that it was commanded by a captain, had some companies commanded by non-commissioned officers. Federal artillery fire had cut down what was left of their number "to a mere skirmish line," but they got to within ten yards of the wall. Their colorbearer came within a few feet of the wall, but was shot and the flag momentarily disappeared.[207]

In the second line behind the stone wall south of the Bryan barn waited the men of Col. George Willard's old New York Brigade, now commanded by Col. Eliakim Sherrill. They had looked forward to a moment like this since September, 1862, when they were humiliated by their surrender at Harper's Ferry. The 39th, 111th and 125th New York regiments were lined up behind Col. Thomas Smyth's brigade, but the 126th was to their right, on the first line, north of the Bryan barn.[208] When the Mississippians and North Carolinians crossed Emmitsburg Road and came within musket range, the men of Willard's brigade made a left wheel down to a lane that ran between the Bryan house and Emmitsburg Road, coming in just west of Lt. John Egan's section of Lt. George Woodruff's Battery I, 1st U. S. Artillery on the flank of the battling Confederates. It was the last straw. They poured an enfilading fire into the Confederates, shattering the line and forced it to its right, then charged directly on its flank.[209]

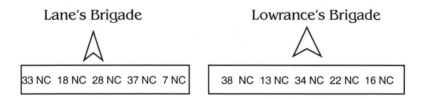

Lane's Brigade

33 NC 18 NC 28 NC 37 NC 7 NC

Lowrance's Brigade

38 NC 13 NC 34 NC 22 NC 16 NC

The demi-division commanded by Maj. Gen. Isaac Trimble, made up of just two brigades, Col. Lee J. Lowrance commanding Scale's brigade and Brig. Gen. James H. Lane's brigade, started out about 150 yards behind Pettigrew's men, but had drawn much closer after crossing Emmitsburg Road. As the brigades advanced up the slope, they were marching at a left oblique, with Lowrance's right near the wall at the outer Angle. Lane's men did not get as near the wall as the first lines and were soon headed back down the slope toward the road. The two left regiments in Lane's line, the 18th and 33rd North Carolina, appeared to be the last troops to break and head for the rear.[210]

The right flank of Lane's brigade crossed Emmitsburg Road behind Fry's brigade. Maj. J. McLeod Turner of the 7th North Carolina, leading his regiment, climbed both fences on either side of the road to advance toward the stone wall. Some of his men, along with other elements of the brigade, reached the wall and "planted their battle flags upon the enemy's breastworks."[211] All members of the color guard of the 7th North Carolina were killed or severely wounded. General Isaac Trimble rode in front of the 7th's flag bearer where he was wounded and knocked from his horse about 25 to 50 yards short of the wall.[212]

The Retreat

As the Rebel tide reached its zenith and then ebbed back down the slope of Cemetery Ridge, Lt. Frank Haskell watched the retreat. He was exultant, even euphoric over the apparent victory: *"The crest is safe!"*

Federal artillery and infantry continued to fire as the men in gray moved reluctantly and slowly down the slope. Capt. June Kimble of the 14th Tennessee remembered that "among others, I refused to yield, and made a break for my liberty in the face of their guns . . . for about one hundred yards I broke the lightening speed record. . . Suddenly I realized I was a good target for those yelling Yankees, and, having a horror of being shot in the back, I faced about and backed out of range, and all without so much as a scratch."[213]

In Davis's brigade Capt. E. Fletcher Satterfield and Sgt. J. Augustus Whitley of the 55th North Carolina had reached the area near the Bryan barn before turning around to look for support. When they saw that most of the regiment was gone, and that no support seemed to be coming, they began to walk back down the slope. Within a few feet Satterfield picked up the regimental flag, but just then a shell from a Confederate battery fell in front of him "and literally tore him to pieces."[214] The flag was probably picked up after the battle and turned in to the War Department.[215]

As Fry's brigade faded back toward the Emmitsburg Road, the men of the 14th Connecticut stood and fired into the retreating troops as long as they remained within range. Many of the Tennesseans lay down behind hillocks, stones and even bodies to avoid this fire. When they pulled out handkerchiefs and other bits of white cloth to signal surrender, the Connecticut men crossed the wall and moved down the slope, collecting prisoners as they neared the road. In their lead Cpl. Christopher Flynn picked up an abandoned flag from the 52nd North Carolina regiment, described as "new, without number or inscription," and Cpl. Elijah W. Bacon found the flag of the 16th North Carolina.[216] A flag thought to belong to the 4th Virginia (a regiment facing Culp's Hill in Ewell's Corps), was captured by a soldier, but the Provost Guard took it from him when it collected prisoners. Some of the men claimed that another, a beautiful silk flag, was picked up but kept by the sol-

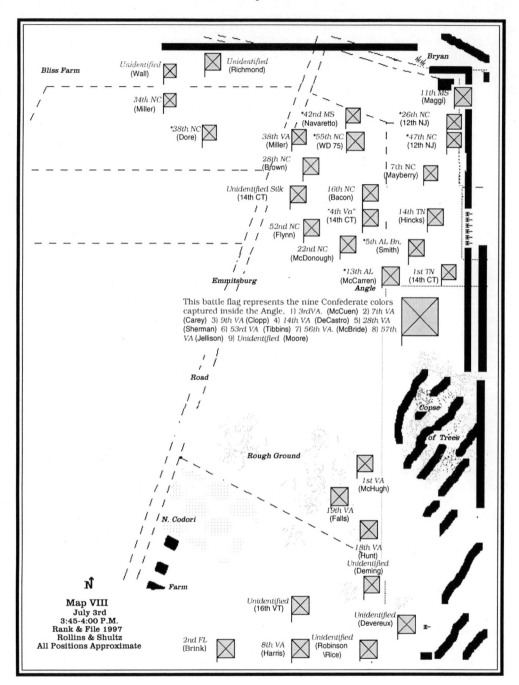

This battle flag represents the nine Confederate colors
captured inside the Angle. 1) 3rd VA. (McCuen) 2) 7th VA
(Carey) 3) 9th VA (Clopp) 4) 14th VA (DeCastro) 5) 28th VA
(Sherman) 6) 53rd VA (Tibbins) 7) 56th VA. (McBride) 8) 57th
VA (Jellison) 9) Unidentified (Moore)

Map VIII
July 3rd
3:45-4:00 P.M.
Rank & File 1997
Rollins & Shultz
All Positions Approximate

dier who found it and not turned in as part of the official tally.[217] In his diary a soldier recorded that this silk flag was "torn off the staff by the finder and concealed under his coat until he got a chance to send it home."[218]

A sergeant in the 1st Minnesota looked out over the field west of Cemetery Ridge after the charge had been repulsed. He watched the Confederates retreating down the slope, and believed that they deliberately left some of their flags behind: "The flags of the rebels were about the same (together in a corner of the wall), and when the assault was finally repulsed, they laid them on the ground in front of us, for anybody to get who chose," he recalled. He then went on to ridicule the men of Webb's brigade who walked out and picked them up:

> as might be expected, the brave men of the Second brigade were on hand to pick them up when there was no danger, and claim all the honor. They were welcome, though, to all they can get for among those who knew them and saw them in a fight, they will have to show something besides flags to establish their bravery on that field.[219]

Even before the charge was completely over, men of both sides treated the Confederate flags still in the area as trophies of war, the Federals eagerly picking them up instead of capturing prisoners:

> The men of the Third Division individually ran out when the assault was seen to have failed and were picking up the enemy's colors on the ground, passing the streams of the enemy coming in to surrender, paying no attention to them. The enemy were careful to drop their colors and took no chances of being shot with them in their hands, and our men brought in these colors as spoils of victory justly won, for those who had but a few minutes before waved them in our faces were now a retreating mob or prisoners of war in our midst.[220]

Confederate battle flags lay all over the ground in front of the wall just south of the Bryan barn. A private in the 69th Pennsylvania estimated that 10 flags were picked up along the stone wall between the Angle and the gate just south of his position.[221] A soldier in the 12th New Jersey jumped over the wall and picked up the flag of the 47th North Carolina lying just ten steps west of the wall.[222] Another man in the 12th New Jersey took the flag of the 26th North Carolina, apparently from on the wall itself.[223]

The enfilading fire of the 126th New York hit the left flank of Lane's brigade as it retreated halfway between the road and the wall.

A few minutes later the 126th New York moved out on the field, picking up four flags. Capt. Morris Brown found the 28th North Carolina's on which were written several battle honors: Sheppardstown, Malvern Hill, Manassas Junction, Sharpsburg, Harper's Ferry, Manassas, Cedar Run, Mechanicsville, Hanover, Ox Hill, Cold Harbor, Frazer's Farm.[224] Pvt. Jerry Wall picked up an unidentified flag.[225] Pvt. George Dore of the 126th New York watched as an artillery shell knocked down a flag and its bearer, probably in Lane's brigade, then rushed out into the field between the stone wall and Emmitsburg Road, seized it, exposing himself to fire from both sides.[226]

The 8th Ohio moved out from their position north of the charge. One soldier observed that the Confederates "threw away everything—cartridge boxes, waistbelts, and haversacks—in their stampede. We dashed in among them, taking prisoners by droves. One man of my company, a corporal, took fifteen prisoners including two officers as well as a stand of colors. As far as the eye could reach, the ground was covered with flying Confederates."[227] One of the flags credited to Sgt. Daniel Miller belonged to 34th North Carolina.[228]

The 8th Ohio also captured about 1000 prisoners:

> We had no trouble with them—they took kindly to the situation. There were squads, however, trying to save their flags, and we organized counter squads. One party under Sergeant Miller, Co. G, ran down and captured two flags, with their color guard, and another "volunteer party" captured a third flag, thus scoring three captured flags for the old Eighth as trophies of the day.[229]

The 47th Virginia in Brockenbrough's brigade still had their flag, but as the rest of the left wing of the charge retreated toward Seminary Ridge, the flag was shot down.[230]

The flag of the 38th Virginia was the only one from Armistead's brigade to have survived the charge uncaptured, but as the colorbearer retreated, Miller's company of the 8th Ohio emerged from the woods on the northern edge of the field. When the Federals reached the Emmitsburg Road they beheld an awful sight. "Many of the wounded had been carried back to it during the fight. . . . It was full of pools of blood, and the grass for some distance in front was saturated with blood."[231] Near the Emmitsburg Road they surrounded the colorbearer of the 38th Virginia and cut off his line of retreat. The flag, stained with the blood of its defenders, was credited to Sgt. Daniel Miller, for which he received a Congressional Medal of Honor.[232] A third flag was picked up by Pvt. James Richmond of Company F.[233]

Near the Copse of Trees some elements of Gibbon's division rushed over the wall and followed the Confederates down the slope to Emmitsburg Road, firing as they moved. A sergeant in the 19th Massachusetts was one of them. He came back to the lines behind the wall, a Confederate flag draped over his shoulder. "You will have to turn that flag in, sergeant. We must send it to the war department in Washington," said an officer. "Well, there are lots of them over behind the wall. Go and get one; I did," he replied.[234]

Four flags had already been claimed by the 19th Massachusetts, and now a fifth flag, not identified, was handed to Col. Devereux by a sergeant in his regiment. After the battle Brig. Gen. Alexander Webb sent a courier to Devereux, claiming that Webb had handed the flag to the sergeant during the battle for safekeeping, and requested its return. Devereux sent it back to Webb.[235]

Devereux would later comment on the nature of the Confederate infantry in combat. He was asked if the capture of flags indicated that his troops had been in close combat. "Well," he answered, "men like them don't give up their colors unless you are pretty close to them."[236]

Pvt. Andrew McDermott of the 69th Pennsylvania claimed, quite incorrectly, that "no flags were captured until the fighting had ceased." He stated that the ground between their refused line on the north side of the clump of trees and the Angle was covered with dead and wounded. He noted that "a large rebel flag" stood up against the wall and as he moved toward it he had to send prisoners back to the rear. When he got within six or eight feet of the flag "a soldier ran past me seized the flag and ran back I suppose to his regiment." McDermott spoke to him and belittled his act. He noted that the man had a 42 on his cap. "I could have had that flag without any trouble, and if I thought acts like that would have brought a medal, its more likely I would have preferred the flag to the gathering up of prisoners. In a similar way the other flags were gathered up."[237] Pvt. Michael McDonough of the 42nd New York in Hall's brigade had picked up the flag of the 22nd North Carolina.[238]

Gray prisoners were rounded up, and with them, noted Lt. Haskell, were taken "these red cloths that our men toss about in derision, the 'fiery red crosses,' thrice ardent, the battle-flags of the rebellion, that waved defiance at the wall." Haskell described the scene, the prisoners and the flags taken as trophies:

> Our men are still 'gathering them in.' Some hold up their hands, or a handkerchief, in sign of submission; some have hugged the ground to escape our bullets, and so are taken; few made resistance after the first moment of our crossing the wall; some yield submissively with good grace; some with grim, dogged aspect, showing that but for the other alternative, they could not submit to this. Colonels, and all less grades of officers, in the usual proportions, are among them, and all are being stripped of their arms. Such of them

as escaped wounds and capture, are fleeing routed and panic-stricken, and disappearing in the woods. Small arms, more thousands than we can count, are in our hands, scattered over the field. And those defiant battleflags, some inscribed with; 'First Manassas, 'South Mountain,' 'Sharpsburg,' . . . 'Fredericksburg,' 'Chancellorsville,' and many more names, our men have, and are showing about, *over thirty of them.*[239]

With victory in hand, the men of the Army of the Potomac engaged in a ritualistic celebration of their triumph, one that seemed to sum up how they felt about themselves, their enemies, and especially about the symbol of the enemy army, the Confederate battle flag. This was such an extraordinary event that several accounts were recorded, and deserve to be presented here. To Brig. Gen. Alexander Hays and the men of his division, these captured flags were despised symbols of rebellion and treason. He and his soldiers could conceive of no better celebration of their victory and the superiority of their cause than to underscore their hatred and triumph by riding on their horses, dragging a Confederate battle flag in the dust as evidence of their hatred for the Rebel cause.

A newspaper writer from Buffalo described the scene:

> Then enters Alexander Hays, brigadier general, United States Volunteers, the brave American soldier. Six feet or more in height, erect and smiling, lightly holding in hand his horse—the third within an hour—a noble animal, his flanks bespattered with blood, tied to his streaming tail a Rebel flag that drags ignominiously in the mud, he dashes along our lines, now rushing out into the open field, a mark for a hundred sharpshooters, but never touched, now quietly cantering back to our lines to be welcomed by a storm of cheers. I reckon him the grandest view of my life. I bar not Niagara. It was the arch-spirit of glorious victory triumphing wildly over the fallen foe.[240]

A soldier in the 126th New York remembered that the flag Hays grabbed and trailed in the dust was the one captured by their Capt. Morris Brown, the flag of the 28th North Carolina.[241] He recalled the scene:

> General Hays took a Rebel flag captured by a captain of the 126th New York Volunteers, on which was inscribed 'Harper's Ferry,' and the names of ten battles, and two of his staff, each with a captured flag, rode

Brig. Gen. Alexander Hays' Ride
(Courtesy of the Gettysburg National Military Park)

down in front of his command, and in the rear, trailing the Rebel colors in the dust, and amid the deafening shouts and cheers of the men who for a moment forgot the terrible battle scenes and thought only of the glory of their victory.[242]

Lt. David Shields, Hays' aide, rode with him and vividly remembered the moment:

Flushed with the glory of our victory, in the exuberance of that great joy that comes from such a victory, looking upon the trophies of war, *the most valuable trophies that can be taken from an enemy, their standards—while still in the hands of their captors*—when the enemy were retreating in disorder and confusion, the general exclaimed, "Boys, give me a flag." The Rebel color was handed to him. He then commanded his adjutant general, Capt. George P. Corts, and myself saying, "Get a flag, Corts; get a flag, 'Dave,' and come on." We each took a flag and the general immediately dropped his flag behind his horse and trailed it in the dust and blood of the battlefield. Capt. Corts and I did likewise, and we started on the grandest ride men ever took. Over the ground which the enemy had so proudly charged but a few moments before there were here and there companies, squads and groups, scarcely any having with them regimental colors, yet keeping up a brisk and ineffectual fire upon their triumphant adversaries, their artillery also dropping shells upon our position to cover their retreat.

We rode in the rear of our division line to the right flank of the 111th New York, then down the whole front of the division, turning at the left of the 14th Connecticut and then to the place of beginning, the men of the Third Division throwing their caps high in air as we rode along, cheering lustily in their exuberance, showing their admiration for their glorious division commander, some men dancing in their delirium of their joy, others hugging their comrades in close embrace, wild with the exultation of victory.

There were times when we had to weave in and out in our course to avoid riding over wounded Rebels and even prisoners still coming in and going to our rear. *These men, enemies at that, could but admire so intrepid a commander as General Hays, though at the time feeling most keenly the insult to their colors.* All the time of this most exhilarating ride the bullets of the sullen and defiant enemy came sputtering about us and overhead. These were the only moments in action I never felt fear. My horse seemed to be off the ground traveling through the air. I felt though a shot as large as a barrel should hit me in the back it would be with no more effect than shooting into a fog bank.

To General Hays and the men of his division these captured flags were but the emblems of disunion. He and the men under him could conceive of no better fate than to trample them under foot and trail them in the dust as evidence of utter disdain, both for the flags themselves and for the cause they represented.[243]

Across the valley, General Robert E. Lee, sadly greeting the men who managed to make it back to Seminary Ridge, heard the commotion over Hays' ride and wondered what it signified. Afraid the Federals were massing for a counterattack and suspecting that it may have already begun, he asked an aide, Capt. F. M. Colston, to "ride forward and see what that cheering means." Colston rode up and returned to Lee with a report. "I found out that it was a Union general galloping down his line, and so reported to Gen. Lee, who thanked me and said to Col. Alexander, as I backed my horse off: 'I can understand what they have to cheer for, but I thought it might be our own people.'"[244]

As soon as the charge of the enemy was broken, the men of the 1st Delaware sprang over the wall. They "gave them a countercharge, capturing many prisoners and five battle-flags." They were apparently west of the wall while Gen. Hays made his dramatic ride. The regimental colorbearer of the moment, Lt. John Brady, spotted a Confederate battle flag standing by itself in the "southwest corner of the meadow," apparently near the outer Angle and the fence running north from it. Brady handed the regimental banner to another, and called to Lt. William Smith to go and capture it. The two of them ran towards the flag, but ran into Hays as he was riding with a flag trailing upon the ground. While Brady stopped to talk to Hays, Smith continued on to the flag. Smith grabbed the flag and "wrested" it from its staff, then ran back to where Hays and Brady were talking. Smith showed them the flag and then set off to Brigade headquarters to turn it in. Before he got there he was hit and instantly killed, and later found with his sword in one hand and a captured Rebel flag in the other.[245] Smith had picked up the flag of the 5th Alabama Battalion.[246] Pvt. John Mayberry collected the flag of the 7th North Carolina.[247] Pvts. William Williams picked up another flag, and Pvt. Bernard McCarren probably picked up the 13th Alabama flag, dripping with blood from wounds inflicted by the spear on the top of the flagstaff.[248]

After his ride, Hays sat down by the Bryan barn, just behind the lines. Col. Clinton D. MacDougall of the 111th New York happened to walk by, his arm in a sling as a result of a Rebel bullet. Hays called out to him and MacDougall sat down for an enthusiastic discussion of the day's events, including the casualty list and the capture of prisoners and flags. Beside Hays' quarters lay a large pile of colors. Hays asked MacDougall to count them, and he added up 21, "large and small." Six southern brigades had fought in front of Hays' line, and left flags behind to mark their path of progress. MacDougall told the story of what happened next:

> Soon a staff officer appeared and said General Webb presents his compliments and asks that General Hays send him some battle flags he has, which were captured by him[Webb]. General Hays replied with a good deal of warmth, 'How in h-ll did I get them if he captured them?' and calling to his aide, Lt. Shields, 'Oh, "Dave!" pick out half a dozen flags and send them to General Webb as a present, with my compliments; we have so many here we don't know what to do with them and Webb needs them.'[249]

The 11th Virginia lost as many men in the retreat back to Seminary Ridge as it did in the charge. Federal artillery, now without the infantry attack or Confederate artillery shelling to hinder it, unleashed its fury on the backs of the Rebels. Men were killed, wounded and dazed by the heat and fighting. Many lost direction, wandering into Confederate lines with no sense of where their regiment might be. In shocked little groups, they asked about friends, looked for water and for officers to direct them. Some angrily inquired why they were not reinforced when they were on Cemetery Ridge.[250]

Pickett rode among them, as did Lee. Longstreet was nowhere to be seen. Lee told Pickett, "Come, General Pickett, this has been my fight and upon my shoulders rests the blame. The men and officers of your command have written the name of Virginia as high today as it has ever been written before." Pickett was told to put his division in order to receive an expected counterattack. Pickett replied, with tears rolling down his cheeks, "General Lee, I have no division now." Of the 4,500 men of Pickett's division who started across the valley, only 300 to 400 now huddled behind Seminary Ridge.[251]

Evening

The fighting on July 3rd was not quite over. Down near the foot of Houck's Ridge, just north of Devil's Den, the 15th Georgia waited behind a stone wall. An order had gone out for them to go back to the crest of the ridge, but they had not yet received it. Instead the skirmishers manned the wall, while the rest of the regiment relaxed behind the lines. The rest of their brigade had received the order, and had left the 15th with both its flanks "in the air," with no connection to the lines on either side of it.

All day long the Federals of Brig. Gen. Sam Crawford's division of the V Corps had lain in wait near the stone wall in the wheat field where the fighting had ended on July 2nd. They heard the cannonade and saw the Confederate charge across the valley and its repulse. About 6:00 p.m. they received orders from General Meade to strengthen the army's left flank by cleaning out the woods in front of them, full of men from Texas and Georgia. They crossed the wall and dressed their lines deliberately, skirmishers in their front and on both flanks. They moved across the Wheatfield to the southwest, through the woods, then half-wheeled to the right and through another woods and back up a ridge, where it struck the left flank of the 15th Georgia and attempted to drive them out toward the Peach Orchard. Suddenly the Federals were enfiladed from the left and rear; they changed front to meet this fire, then charged forward again. Their fight took them down through the low land and then up through the woods east of the Rose house, where they saw a low stone wall, with rails and logs added to make it a bit higher.

They could see rifles sticking up behind the wall with a Confederate battle flag above them. To the Federals, it looked as if they were facing an entire brigade. To Col. D. M. DuBose, commanding the 15th Georgia, it seemed that the Yankees had nearly surrounded his position.[252]

With the 1st and 2nd Pennsylvania Reserves in the lead, the Federals charged the wall, pressing hard in front. The rest of the 15th Georgia was up at the wall, along with a few men from the 2nd, 17th, and 20th Georgia, but the Federals were now enveloping both flanks. With the enemy within 20 feet of the wall, the colors of the 15th were shot down not once, but several times. Nine colorbearers in a row grabbed the flag and were shot down. A Federal battery on one flank opened up with a murderous enfilade, and the Confederate line broke, falling back even further. A soldier in the 15th recalled that the colors were left on the ground "as it was certain death to pick them up."[253] DuBose ordered a retreat, and what was left of the regiment fell back to the line it was supposed to have gone back to much earlier. Two hundred Confederates surrendered and Sgt. James Benjamin of the 1st Pennsylvania Rifles grabbed the flag of the 15th Georgia.[254] That evening the adjutant of the 2nd Pennsylvania recorded in his diary the capture of "many prisoners and . . . the 15th Georgia flag."[255]

* * *

Back on Cemetery Ridge the cleaning up of the bodies and wreckage of the two armies had already begun, with a II Corps burial party in the Angle. A soldier described the extraordinary scene near the Angle:

> Just as the sun was setting I went to the crest of the hill and took a look at the field. No words can depict the ghastly picture. The track of the great charge was marked by bodies of men in all possible positions, wounded, bleeding, dying and dead. Near the line where the final struggle occurred, the men lay in heaps, the wounded wriggling and groaning under the weight of the dead among whom they were entangled. In my weak and exhausted condition I could not long endure the gory, ghastly spectacle. I found my head reeling, the tears flowing and my stomach sick at the sight. For months the specter haunted my dreams, and even after forty-seven years it comes back as the most horrible vision I have ever conceived.[256]

A burial party found, a "young and comely Southern girl—who made that charge of Pickett's—lying dead in a Confederate private's uniform." Her name, status and indeed her story, were not known.[257] As one historian wrote "legend has it that her husband was a color sergeant, shot down at the crest of the charge—that she raised the fallen colors for one lightning swift moment, then died riddled beside him."[258]

About ten o'clock that night on Seminary Ridge a drum roll summoned the men of the 1st Virginia, and as they took their place in line, Pvt. Jacob Polak emerged with a new flag, retrieved from an ordnance wagon. This flag had been left in their possession by another regiment the previous summer, at Second Manassas. Polak lifted it up above his head and waved it in the night air. Although he had his hand in a sling from a wound, and with blood still on his face, he called for a new color guard to form, since all those who started out the day before were dead or wounded. No one came forward, and the flag was returned to the wagon.[259]

Notes

[1] Quoted in Maud Morrow Brown, *The University Greys: Company A, Eleventh Mississippi Regiment Army of Northern Virginia* (Richmond: Garrett and Massie, 1940), 40.

[2] *Ibid.*, 41.

[3] *Ibid.,* 40-41.

[4] James T. Carter, quoted in "Flag of the Fifty-third Va. Regiment," *CV*, 10(1902), 263.

[5] Quoted in Charles W. Sublett, *57th Virginia* (Lynchburg: H. E. Howard, 1985).

[6] Robert Tyler Jones, quoted in CV, 2(1894), 271.

[7] Kathleen Georg-Harrison and John Busey, *Nothing But Glory: Pickett's Division at Gettysburg* (Gettysburg: Thomas Publications, 1994), 66-85.

[8] George Clark, "Wilcox's Alabama Brigade at Gettysburg," *CV*, 17(1909), 230.

[9] Haskell.

[10] Letter from Capt. R. M. Stribling, April, 1889, *CV*, 29(1901), 215. See also John Holmes Smith, "John Holmes Smith's Account," *SHSP*, 32(1904), 194.

[11] Quoted in James I. Robertson, *18th Virginia Infantry* (Lynchburg: H. E. Howard, 1984), 21.

[12] David Johnston, *The Story of a Confederate Boy in the Civil War* Reprint of 1914 Edition (Raford, Va.: Commonwealth Press, 1980), 207.

[13] B. D. Fry, "Pickett's Charge at Gettysburg," *SHSP*, VII(1879), 92.

[14] *Ibid.*, 93

[15] I. T. Miller, *CV*, 2(1895), 281.

[16] June Kimble, "Tennesseans at Gettysburg—The Retreat," *CV*, 18(1910), 461.

[17] Col. Joseph Mayo, "Pickett's Charge at Gettysburg," *SHSP*, XXXIV(1906), 327.

[18] John H. Lewis, *Recollections from 1860 to 1865* (Portsmouth, VA., 1893).

[19] David Johnston, *Four Years a Soldier* (Princeton, W. VA: Privately Printed, 1887), 250.

[20] Johnston, *Confederate Boy*, 204-205.

[21] Rawley Martin and John Holmes Smith, "The Battle of Gettysburg, and the Charge of Pickett's Division," *SHSP,* XXXIX(1914), 184-185.

[22] Hunton to Daniel, July 15, 1904, John W. Daniel Papers, University of Virginia Library.

[23] "Diary of William Peel," Mississippi State Archives.

[24] Quoted in Frank S. Fields, Jr., *28th Virginia Infantry* (Lynchburg: H. E. Howard, 1985), 26.

[25] J. F. Crocker, *Gettysburg-Pickett's Charge and Other War Addresses* (Portsmouth, Va.: n.p., 1915), 37-38.

[26] Mayo, "Pickett's' Charge at Gettysburg," 331.

[27] R. A. Bright, "Pickett's Charge at Gettysburg," *CV*, 31(July 1903), 264. See also David F. Riggs, *Seventh Virginia Infantry* (Lynchburg, Va.: H. E. Howard, 1982), 25.

[28] Johnston, *Confederate Boy*, 208.

[29] H. A. Hilary to E. P. Alexander, August 8, 1869, McLaws Papers, University of North Carolina Archives.

[30] Michael Jacobs, *Notes on the Rebel Invasion of Maryland and Pennsylvania on the Battle of Gettysburg, July 1, 2, and 3, 1863, Accompanied by an Explanatory Map* (Philadelphia: J. B. Lippincott, 1864).

[31] Robert T. Bell, *Eleventh Virginia Infantry* (Charlottesville: H. E. Howard, 1985), 40.

[32] Charles D. Page, *History of the Fourteenth Regiment, Connecticut Volunteer Infantry* (Meridian, Conn.: The Horton Printing Co., 1906), 151.

[33] *Ibid.*

[34] Lora Goodrich to friends, July 17, 1863, 14th Connecticut File, GNMP.

[35] Andrew Cowan, "Address By Colonel Andrew Cowan," in New York State Monument Commission, *In Memoriam Alexander Stewart Webb[,] 1835-1911* (Albany: J. B. Lyon Company, 1916), 65.

[36] Vautier, *88th Pa*, 112.

[37] Lt. George Yost, quoted in Eric Campbell, "'Remember Harper's Ferry!' The Degradation, Humiliation, and Redemption of Col. George L. Willard's Brigade Part Two" *GB*, 8(January, 1993), 105.

[38] Charles T. Loehr, "The 'Old First' at Gettysburg," *SHSP*, XXXII(1904), 36. All ranks of men in Pickett's division are given as listed in Harrison and Busey, *Glory*. Other documents list various ranks, including many that were effective later in the war.

[39] Quoted in Harrison and Busey, *Glory*, 74

[40] Quoted in *Ibid.*, 105.

[41] Wallace, *3rd Virginia*, 37.

[42] Mayo, "Pickett's Charge," 331.

[43] *Ibid.*

[44] Walker, *Memorial, VMI*, 538-539, 82.

[45] *Ibid.*

[46] Crocker, *Gettysburg*, 42. James F. Crocker, "My Personal Experiences in Taking Up Arms and in the Battle of Malvern Hill. Gettysburg — Pickett's Charge," *SHSP*, XXXIII(1905), 128-134.

[47] Quoted in George C. Underwood, "Twenty-Sixth Regiment," in Clark, *Histories*, II, 365.

[48] Capt. S. A. Ashe, A. A. G., "The Pettigrew-Pickett Charge," *Ibid.,* I, 141

[49] Robert Theodore Mockbee, "Historical Sketch of the 14th Tenn. Regt of Infantry C.S.A. 1861-1865," [1912], Eleanor S. Brockenbrough Library, The Museum of the Confederacy. I thank John Coski for this citation.

[50] Quoted in James S. Harris, *Historical Sketches, Seventh Regiment North Carolina Troops* (Mooresville, N.C.: N.p., 1893), 36.

[51] Haskell.

[52] Loehr, "The Old First."

[53] Martin and Smith, "The Battle of Gettysburg," 191-2.

[54] Quoted in Fields, *28th Virginia*, 26.

[55] Thomas W. Hyde, "Recollections of the Battle of Gettysburg," *War Papers* (Portland, Maine: The Thurston Print, 1898), Vol. I, 202.

[56] Rev. James E. Poindexter, "Address on the Life an Services of Gen. Lewis A. Armistead, delivered . . . before R. E. Lee Camp, No. 1, Confederate Veterans," (Richmond: January 29, 1909), 3.

[57] Quoted in Sublett, *57th Virginia*, 33.

[58] "Rawley Martin's Account," *SHSP*, XXXIX(1911), 184-184.

[59] Gregory, *38th Virginia*, 40.

[60] Crocker, *Gettysburg*, 43.

[61] Ashe, "The Pettigrew-Pickett Charge," 141.

[62] Report of Maj. Theodore Ellis, *OR*, II, 151.

[63] Thomas Francis Galway, *The Valiant Hours* (Harrisburg, Pa.: The Stackpole Company, 1961), 115.

[64] Quoted in James Warner Bellah, *Soldier's Battle: Gettysburg* (New York: David McKay Co., Inc., 1962).

[65] Franklin Sawyer, *A Military History of the Eighth Regiment Ohio Vol. Inf'y: Its Battles, Marches and Army Movements* (Cleveland: n.p., 1881), 130.

[66] G. H. Dugout, "Glimpses of the Nation's Struggle," MOLLUS, 360. Photocopy in 8th Ohio file, GNMP.

[67] T. S. Potter, "The Battle of Gettysburg," *National Tribune*, August 5, 1882, photocopy in 8th Ohio file, GNMP.

[68] This name is sometimes spelled Brian.

[69] Letter of [?] Sullivan, 13th Alabama file, GNMP.

[70] Randolph Shotwell, "Virginia and North Carolina in the Battle of Gettysburg," *Our Living and Our Dead* IV(1876), 93.

[71] Loehr, "The 'Old First'," 32-40. See also Report of Capt. John Darrow, 82nd New York, August 3, 1863, *OR*, I, 426, and "Record" #37.

[72] Loehr, "Old First," 40. See also Lee A. Wallace, *First Virginia Infantry* (Lynchburg, Va.: H. E. Howard, 1984), 43, and "Record" #37. The identification of Sergt. Martin McHugh appears only in (Anonymous), "Report of Flags Captured in the Battles at Gettysburg, Pa. by the 2nd Army Corps, July 2nd and 3rd 1863," National Archives, RG 93. I thank T. L. Murphy for this citation.

[73] Mayo, "Pickett's Charge," 334.

[74] Harrison and Busey, *Glory*, 240.

[75] Wallace, *3rd Virginia*, 38.

[76] Johnston, *Confederate Boy*, 209.

[77] *Ibid.*, 215.

[78] Johnston, *Four Years A Soldier*, 263.

[79] Riggs, *Seventh Virginia,* 25-26. See also A. N. Jones to Col. W. T. Fry, 5 July 1863, 13th Alabama File, GNMP; Report of Capt. John Darrow, 82nd New York, August 3, 1863, *OR*, I, 426.

[80] Report of Capt. A. N. Jones, 7 July 1863, George Edward Pickett Papers, Perkins Library, Duke University.

[81] Darrow's Report, *OR,* I, 426; "Record" #36.

[82] R. O. Sturtevant, *Pictorial History of the 13th Regiment Vermont Volunteers* (Burlington: The Self-Appointed Committee of Three, 1911), 259-284.

[83] Report of Brig. Gen. George Stannard, *OR,* I, 259.

[84] *St. Paul Pioneer Press*, July 21, 1895. I thank Steve Osman of the Minnesota Historical Society for this quote and the one from the same source cited below. The 1st Minnesota had fought on July 2nd, but not on July 1st.

[85] William Lochran, "Narrative of the First Regiment" in *Minnesota in the Civil and Indian Wars* (n. p: n.d.), 37-38.

[86] Martin and Smith, "Gettysburg," 191-2.

[87] Johnston, *Four Years A Soldier*, 257-258.

[88] Haskell. Haskell did not identify the regiment.

[89] *Ibid.* I have not located any record of a regiment surrendering that would coincide with this observation.

[90] Report of Col. Norman Hall, July 17, 1863, *OR*, I, 437-441.

[91] Johnston, *Four Years A Soldier*, 25. Johnston estimated that they stayed east of the wall for 20 minutes.

[92] W. O. Beauchamp, "Monument Dedication to Pettit's Battery," in N.Y. Monument Commission, *Final Report on the Battlefield of Gettysburg* Vol. 2, First Regiment, Battery B., ed. William Fox (Albany: J. B. Lyons and Company, 1912), 1184.

[93] Lochran, "Narrative," 37-38. See also Report of Capt. Henry C. Coates, 1st Minnesota, August 3, 1863, *OR*, I, 425.

[94] Hugh Devereux Purcell, *The Nineteenth Massachusetts at Gettysburg* (Salem, Mass: Essex Institute Historical Collections, 1963), 285. See also [Capt. John Reynolds], "The Nineteenth Massachusetts At Gettysburg, July 2, 3, 4," 19th Massachusetts File, GNMP.

[95] Report of Col. Arthur Devereux, July 7, 1863, *OR*, I, 444. See also Meade's statement of Oct. 17, 1864, *OR*, Series III, Vol. 3, 816.

[96] *Ibid.*

[97] Report of Maj. Sylvanus Curtis, 7th Michigan, August 6, 1863, *OR,* I, 449-450. Brigade commander Norman Hall, August 3, 1863, *OR*, I, 441, called this man William Dunning. *Record of Service of*

Michigan Volunteers in the Civil War(Kalamazoo: Ihling Brothers, no date), 31, lists him as Deming.

[98] Harrison and Busey, *Glory*, 240.

[99] Shotwell, *Three Years in Battle*, 14.

[100] John E. Divine, *Eighth Virginia Infantry* (Lynchburg: H. E. Howard, 1983), 24-25.

[101] Quoted in Robertson, *18th Virginia*, 21.

[102] *Ibid.*, 23.

[103] Edmund Berkeley to Daniels, 26 September [no year], Daniels Papers, University of Virginia. See also Report of Col. Charles Candy, July 6, 1863, *OR,* I, 836.

[104] This flag, a square ANV pattern, is now (October 1995) on display at the Gettysburg Visitor Center. The "Record" incorrectly records this as WD #49. That flag bears remnants of the original citation handed in with the flag indicating that it was captured at "Logan's Field," aka the battle of Logan's Cross Roads in Kentucky in 1862. A mixup apparently occurred when the first numbers were stenciled on the flags in December of 1863. The 18th Virginia flag captured on July 3rd is WD #56. Howard Madaus to author, February 16, 1996, and also my own conclusion.

[105] Andrew Cowan to John P. Nicholson, 27 July 1913, Cowan Papers, Yale University. This may have been the flag of the 57th Virginia, not the 18th.

[106] Diary of Walter A. Van Rensselaer, photocopy, 80th New York File, GNMP. Note that Van Rensselaer does not claim the capture of this flag. Two unidentified flags were reportedly dropped in front of the stone wall in this area and were picked up by men from the 80th New York, Theodore Gates to Bachelder, 30 January 1864, *Bachelder Papers*, I, 85.

[107] [Ambrose Wright], "From Wright's Brigade," *Augusta Daily Constitutionalist*, July 23, 1863.

[108] Quoted in William H. Stewart, *A Pair of Blankets: War-Time History in Letters to the Young People of the South,* ed. Benjamin H. Trask (Wilmington, N.C.: Broadfoot Publishing, 1990), 111.

[109] A. W. McDermott and John E. Reilly, *History of the 69th Regt., Pennsylvania Veteran Volunteers* (Philadelphia: D. J. Gallagher Co., 1886).

[110] Anonymous letter, dated July 23, 1863, printed in the *Cincinnati Daily Commercial*, August 11, 1863.

[111] A. C. Plaisted to Bachelder, 11 June 1870, *Bachelder Papers*, I, 393.

[112] Anonymous letter, dated July 23, 1863, printed in the *Cincinnati Daily Commercial*, August 11, 1863.

[113] Report of Maj. Charles S. Peyton, 19th Virginia Infantry, commanding Garnett's brigade, *OR*, II, 386.

[114] *Deeds of Valor*, 235.

[115] Ernest Linden Waitt, *History of the Nineteenth Massachusetts Volunteer Infantry, 1861-1865* (Salem, Mass: The Salem Press Co., 1906), 246. The regimental number had been torn out of this flag. See also A. F. Devereux to E. D. Townsend, May 1, 1878, National Archives, RG 94, photocopy in 19th Massachusetts file, GNMP. "Record" #71 lists this as unidentified. The Museum of the Confederacy has identified it as the 19th Virginia flag captured by the 19th Massachusetts. See also Devereux's Report, *OR*, 1, 444; Hall's Report, *OR*, 1, 441, and Meade's statement, Oct. 17, 1864, *OR*, Series III, Vol. 3, 816.

[116] Edmund Rice, "Repelling Lee's Last Blow At Gettysburg," *Battles and Leaders of the Civil War* (Seacaucus, N.J.: Castle, 1888), Vol. III, 387-90. See also "Captured Four Regimental Flags," *Deeds of Valor*, 235.

[117] [Reynolds], *"Nineteenth Massachusetts,"* 9.

[118] Haskell.

[119] *Ibid.*

[120] This may have been Lindsey Creasey, see Harrison and Busey, *Glory*, 357.

[121] Ida Lee Johnson, "Over the Stone Wall at Gettysburg," *CV*, 31(1923), 249.

[122] Fields, *28th Virginia*, 26.

[123] Quoted in *Ibid.*, 27.

[124] Lochran, "Narrative," 37-38. See also Coates' Report, 1st Minnesota, *OR*, I, 425.

[125] *St. Paul Pioneer Press*, July 21, 1895. This flag is in the Minnesota Historical Society. See also "Narrative," 37-38; Coates' Report, *OR*, I, 425, and William Colvill to Bachelder, 9 June 1866, *Bachelder Papers*, I, 258. Adjutant Townsend incorrectly lists this as the flag of the 58th Virginia, *OR*, II, 282; the same is true for Maj. Gen. George Meade, statement, Oct. 17, 1864, *OR*, Series III, Vol. 3, 815. "Record" #58.

[126] Lochran, "Narrative," 38. See also *Rebellion Record*, IV(1863), 177, and *Papers*, 614.

[127] Daniel Bond, "Bonds Recollection," Minnesota Historical Society.

[128] Diary of Joseph P. Elliott, 71st Pennsylvania File, GNMP. Col. R. Penn Smith thought this was the flag of the 17th Virginia, a unit not at Gettysburg: R. Penn Smith, "The Battle of Gettysburg," *Gettysburg Compiler*, 7 June 1887, and R. Penn Smith, "Inventory of Flags Captured at the Battle of Gettysburg on the 3rd Day of July 1863 by members of the 71st Regt. Penn. Vols.," [July, 1863], and Theodore Hesser to C.H. Banes, July 21, 1863, National Archives. See also [Reynolds], "19th Mass," and Report of Col. R. Penn Smith, July 12, 1863, *OR*, I, 432.

[129] Charles H. Banes, *History of the Philadelphia Brigade* (Philadelphia: J. B. Lippincott & Co., 1876), 194, and [Anonymous], "Re-

port," which identifies this as the flag of the 3rd Virginia. Both the "Letter" and "Record" incorrectly list this as captured on July 2nd.

[130] Testimony of John Buckley, *Supreme Court of Pennsylvania. Middle District. May Term, 1891, Nos. 20 and 30. Appeal of the Gettysburg Battlefield Memorial Association From the Decree of the Court of Common Pleas of Adams County.* [Hereafter cited as *Supreme Court*], 138.

[131] William A. Young, *56th Virginia Infantry* (Lynchburg, Va.: H. E. Howard, 1990), 86.

[132] Testimony of Robert McBride, *Supreme Court*, 127. The Secretary of War's "Letter" lists this flag with an unknown date, but it was numbered among those captured in Gettysburg. See also "Record" #41; Moore, ed., *Rebellion Record*, Vol. 7, 340-341; Report of Col. R. Penn Smith, 71st Pennsylvania, July 12,1863, *OR*, 1, 432; Report of Alexander Webb, 2nd Brigade, 2nd Division, 2nd Corps, July 12, 1863, *OR*, 1, 367 and 374.

[133] James J. Phillips to Gen. F. H. Smith, 18 July 1863, 9th Virginia file, GNMP.

[134] Report of R. Penn Smith, *OR*, I, 432. Clopp was given the Congressional Medal of Honor for the capture. Townsend, *OR*, II, 282. See also "Record" #65, and statements by Clopp, December 6, 1864, and January 4, 1865, RG 94, Box 746, National Archives.

[135] D. B. Easley to Howard Townsend, July 24, 1913, D. B. Easley Papers, Military History Research Collection, USAMHI, Carlisle Barracks, photocopy in 14th Virginia File, GNMP. Easley thought it was the flag of the 13th Virginia, a regiment that was in Winchester acting as provost guard at the moment.

[136] Col. A. F. Devereux to John B. Bachelder, 22 July 1889, John B. Bachelder Correspondence, New Hampshire Historical Society. See also Stewart, *Pickett's Charge*, 236. Report of Col. Charles Candy, 66th Ohio, July 6th, 1863, *OR*, I, 836, erroneously states that the flag of the 14th Virginia was captured on Culp's Hill on July 4th by the 7th Ohio. Waitt, *The History of the Nineteenth Regiment Massachusetts Volunteer Infantry*, 246, incorrectly credits this capture to Pvt. B. Jellison. Report of Brig. Gen. John Geary, July 23, 1863, *OR*, I, 831, erroneously lists the 14th's flag as having been captured by the 7th Ohio on Culp's Hill on the morning of July 3rd. See also A. F. Devereux, "Some Account of Pickett's Charge at Gettysburg," *Magazine of American History*, 1887, 18. Adjutant Townsend mistakenly credits De Castro with the capture of the 19th Virginia's flag, *OR*, II, 282, as does Meade in his statement of Oct. 17, 1864, *OR*, Series III, Vol. 3, 816.

[137] W. A. Hill to Headquarters, July 4, 1869, *Bachelder Papers*, III, 1880.

[138] James F. Crocker, "Gettysburg—Pickett's Charge," *SHSP*, XXXIII(1905), 133-134 [emphasis added].

[139] "The Colonel and Dr. R. W. Martin, of Virginia," *CV*, 70. See

also Carter, "Flag of the Fifty-Third Regiment."

[140] Capt. Benjamin Farinholt, undated, unpublished memoir, quoted in R. Long, "Over The Wall," *GB*, 13(July, 1995), 71.

[141] John Poindexter, "Gen. Lewis Addison Armistead," *CV*, 22(1914), 503.

[142] Poindexter, "Armistead," 503.

[143] Robert Tyler Jones, quoted in *CV*, 3(1895), 271; "Record" #67.

[144] Carter, "Flag of the Fifty-Third," 263.

[145] Quoted in Sublett, *57th Virginia*.

[146] Harrison-Busey, *Glory*, 113-4.

[147] Clement, *History of Pittsylvania County*, 249-250.

[148] "Record" #77 and "Report of William R. Aylett, Colonel, 53rd Virginia Infantry, Commanding Armistead's Brigade," July 12, 1863, *OR*, II, 1000. For Isaac Tibbins as captor see (Anonymous), "Report of Flags Captured in the Battles at Gettysburg, Pa. by the 2nd Army Corps, July 2nd and 3rd, 1863," National Archives, RG 93. See also Hall's and Devereux's Reports, *OR*, 1, 441-444.

[149] J. Francis Amos to the author, November 3, 1994. Mr. Amos is the great-grand-nephew of Sgt. Hutcherson.

[150] "Record" #79 originally listed this as the flag of the 67th Virginia, but the information was corrected; Report of Col. Norman Hall, August 3, 1863, *OR*, I, 441. Adjutant Townsend, *OR*, II, 282, incorrectly credits the 57th's flag to Pvt. John Robinson of the 19th Mass., and credits Jellison with the capture of the flag of the 54th Virginia, a regiment that was not at Gettysburg. Meade, *OR*, Series III, Vol. 3, 816, also misidentified this as the flag of the 54th. Several authors have incorrectly identified this flag as belonging to the 14th Virginia, actually captured by Joseph De Castro of the same regiment. See *19th Mass*, 246, and Stewart, *Pickett's Charge*. Bachelder's notes, *Bachelder Papers*, III, 1991, says that Jellison knocked him down with his fist and fails to identify the flag. One source of the misidentifications of De Castro and Jellison is an anonymous article in the *Adams County Sentinel*, July 25, 1865, naming one Thomas Jellison of the 19th Massachusetts as the captor of an unidentified Virginia flag. See also, about Rice, "Captured Four Regimental Flags," and about Jellison, "Saw the Rebel Flag, Took It," in *Deeds of Valor*, 235, 236.

[151] Report of Maj. Gen. W. S. Hancock, [no date], 1863, *OR*, I, 374.

[152] Harrison and Busey, *Glory*, 379.

[153] Cook, "Wilcox's Brigade," 230.

[154] Wheelock Veazey to G. G. Benedict, 11 July 1864, Vermont Historical Society, photocopy Vermont File, GNMP.

[155] *Deeds of Valor*, 240.

[156] Report of Col. David Lang, 8th Florida, July 29, 1863, *OR*, II, 632. See also David Lang to General E. A. Perry, July 19, 1863, *SHSP*, XXVII(1899), 191, and Thomas Elmore, "The Florida Brigade

at Gettysburg," *GB* 15(July, 1996), 45-59.

[157] Report of Capt. Patrick Hart, August 2, 1863, *OR*, I, 888.

[158] Hart to Bachelder, February 23, 1891, *Bachelder Papers*, III, 1798. In 1891 Hart remembered that the colonel of the "14th Massachusetts" had sent his men out to pick them up. Hart complained to Hancock that these flags should have been given to him, telling him that "those flags were mine by every honorable right." He noted that there was no infantry and no other artillery firing at these men. The 14th Massachusetts was not there. The 15th Massachusetts was nearby, but its colonel was dead. The 19th Massachusetts had already moved north to the Copse of Trees, thus I believe these were the flags claimed by the Vermont Brigade.

[159] Report of Col. David Lang, 8th Florida, July 29, 1863, *OR*, II, 632. See also David Lang to Gen. E. A. Perry, July 19, 1863, *SHSP*, 27(1899), 191. The 2nd Florida's flag was apparently not turned in. There is a 2nd Florida flag in the "Record"[#414], but it is listed with the flags captured in 1865.

[160] *Rebellion Record*, Vol. 7, 341. There is no trace of this flag.

[161] C. C. Benedict, *Vermont at Gettysburgh: A Sketch of the Part Taken by The Vermont Troops in the Battle of Gettysburgh* (Burlington: The Free Press Association, 1870), 19-20.

[162] Quoted in Bellah, *Soldier's Battle: Gettysburg*, 172.

[163] E. D. Townsend to War Department, July 10, 1863, *Rebellion Record* 7(1863), 341. See also Report of Brig. Gen. George Stannard, July 4, 1863, *OR*, I, 349-350, and Report of Col. Wheelock Veazey, July 17, 1863, 1041-42, and "Record" #67.

[164] There is no trace of this flag, but several people apparently witnessed the incident. Benedict, *Vermont at Gettysburgh*, 19-20; Report of Brig. Gen. George Stannard, July 4, 1863, *OR*, I, 350; Report of Col. W. G. Veazey, *OR*, I, 1042, and Veazey to Bachelder (undated), *Bachelder Papers*, I, 62-64. See also *Deeds of Valor*, 239; George H. Scott, "Vermont at Gettysburgh," *Gettysburg Sources* (Baltimore: Butternut and Blue, 1986), Vol. 1, 76-80; Board of State Institutions, *Soldiers of Florida in the Seminole Indian-Civil and Spanish-American Wars*, 1903, 188.

[165] Report of Lt. Col. S. G. Shepard, 7th Tennessee, August 10, 1863, *OR*, II, 647.

[166] Kimble, "Tennesseans at Gettysburg," 461.

[167] Report of Alexander Hays, July 8, 1863, *OR*, I, 455.

[168] Quoted in Fleming, ed., *Hays*, 458.

[169] Kimble, 461.

[170] Mockbee, "Historical Sketch," and Mockbee, quoted in J. C. Cooke, "Gallant Tennesseans in Gettysburg Charge," *Richmond Times Dispatch*, April 3, 1910, Confederate Memorial Literary Society Scrapbook, 1908-1911, 101, Museum of the Confederacy.

[171] C. Wallace Cross, Jr., *Ordeal by Fire: A History of the Four-*

teenth Tennessee Volunteer Infantry Regiment, C.S.A. (Clarksville, TN.: Clarksville Montgomery County Museum, 1990), 72. Rumors have circulated that one of the men who carried the 14th's flag in Pickett's Charge was black. If so, it was probably Boney Smith, who does not appear in the regiment's records in the National Archives and was thus apparently not enlisted. Many of the black Southerners who served and fought for the South did not appear on the muster rolls. See Rollins, ed., *Black Southerners in Gray.*

[172] Shepard's Report, *OR*, II, 647.

[173] Ashe, "The Pettigrew-Pickett Charge," 148.

[174] Fry, "Pickett's Charge," 93.

[175] I. T. Miller, *CV*, 3(1895), 281. See also B. D. Fry to Bachelder, 27 December 1877, *Bachelder Papers*, I, 520, and Shepard's Report, *OR*, II, 647.

[176] Fry, "Pickett's Charge," 93.

[177] Shepard's Report, *OR*, II, 647. See also Report of Col. R. M. Mayo, 14 August 1863, Henry Heth Collection, Eleanor Brockenbrough Library, Museum of the Confederacy; Alfred Scales, undated letter, GNMP File #11; "Record" #43 and Theodore Ellis to Bachelder, 21 January 1864, *Bachelder Papers*, I, 79, and 3 November 1870, 408.

[178] Shepard's Report, 647.

[179] J. H. Moore, "Heroism in the battle of Gettysburg," *CV*, 9(1901), 15.

[180] Quoted in Ashe, "The Pettigrew-Pickett Charge," 150.

[181] Shepard's Report, *OR*, II, 647.

[182] Kimble, 461.

[183] William Frierson Fulton II, *The War Reminiscences of William Frierson Fulton II, Fifth Alabama Battalion, Archer's Brigade, A.P. Hill's Light Division, A. N. V.* (Gaithersburg, Maryland: Butternut Press, 1986), 78. See also Shepard's Report, 646-647.

[184] Charles Page, *History of the Fourteenth Regiment, Connecticut Volunteer Infantry* (Meridian, Connecticut: The Horton Printing Co., 1906), 142-156. See also H. S. Stevens, *Souvenir of the Excursion to the Battlefield by the Society of the Fourteenth Connecticut Regiment* . . . . (Washington: Gibson Bros., 1893), 31. See also Report of Maj. Theodore Ellis, 14th Connecticut, July 6, 1863, *OR*, I, 467, and Adjutant Townsend's Report, *OR*, II, 282.

[185] *Ibid.*

[186] Diary of Captain George Bowen, *The Valley Forge Journal*, Vol. II, No. 1 (June 1884), 135.

[187] J. B. Smith, "The Charge of Pickett, Pettigrew, and Trimble," *Battles and Leaders*, Vol. III, 354. See also Letter of Alfred M. Scales, undated, South Carolina File, GNMP.

[188] Page, *History*; 156. "Record" #85. See also Maj. Gen. George Meade's statement, Oct. 17, 1864, *OR*, Series III, Vol. 3, 815.

[189] J. Rogers Brown, "Additional Sketch Forty-seventh Regi-

ment," in Clark, *Histories,* III, 108.

[190] Report of Col. William Aylett, 53rd Virginia, July 12, 1863, *OR*, II, 1000.

[191] Quoted in Andrew J. Baker, "Tribute to Capt. Magruder and Wife," *CV*, (November, 1898), 507.

[192] T. J. Cureton to Col. J. R. Lane, June 22, 1890, John Randolph Lane Papers, University of North Carolina.

[193] Christopher Mead to Wife, July 6, 1863, USAMHI.

[194] *Ibid.*

[195] T. J. Cureton to John R. Lane, July 22, 1890, John R. Lane Papers, University of North Carolina.

[196] Capt. R. M. Tuttle, "Unparalleled Loss: Company F, 26th N. C. T. at Gettysburg, July 1, 1863," in Clark, *Histories*, V, 601. Tuttle incorrectly spells this name Cozert and fails to give his rank. See the official roster in Moore, *Rosters of North Carolina Troops.*

[197] Quoted in Stewart, *Pickett's Charge*, 226.

[198] Quoted in Ashe, "The Pettigrew-Pickett Charge," 152; Clark, *Histories*, V, 152.

[199] Underwood, "Twenty-Sixth," 366. See also John Hall, untitled essay, *Gettysburg Compiler*, 8 July 1903, GNMP Clipping Book 4, 145.

[200] Edward R. Outlaw in Clark, *Histories*, I, 589-590. See also Lt. W. Stuart Symington's (probably) mistaken recollection that he picked up this flag and carried it back to Longstreet's headquarters, Symington to Charles Pickett, October 17th, 1892, Virginia Historical Society. The letter is published in Michael W. Taylor, "The Unmerited Censure of Two Maryland Officers, Maj. Osmun Latrobe and First Lt. W. Stuart Symington," *GB* 13(July 1995), 75-88.

[201] Diary of Lt. William Peel, in Rollins, ed., *Pickett's Charge*, 253-255; Time-Life, *Echoes of Glory*, 252.

[202] Quoted in Brown, *University Greys*, 45.

[203] William A. Love, "Mississippi at Gettysburg," *Mississippi Historical Society Quarterly*, IX, 45-47.

[204] Baxter McFarland, "The Eleventh Mississippi Regiment at Gettysburg," in Dunbar Rowland, ed., *Publications of the Mississippi Historical Society* Volume 2 (Jackson: Mississippi Historical Society, 1918), 560-561; "Record" #39. The Museum of the Confederacy has identified this as the flag of the 11th Mississippi, and its design characteristics are consistent with others carried by Davis's brigade.

[205] "Record" #78. There was no soldier named Navereck in the 39th New York. The closest name to it is Cpl. Francisco Navarreto. See the roster in *Annual Report of the Adjutant General of the State of New York for the Year 1900* (Albany: James B. Lyon, State Printer, 1901), Serial No. 23. The location of its capture and characteristics of its design indicate that it probably belonged to a regiment in Davis's brigade, probably the 42nd Mississippi. Davis's brigade, previously

Law's brigade, had been issued flags with battle honors during the Antietam campaign. Those of the 2nd and 11th Mississippi captured at Gettysburg are examples. After the Maryland campaign the brigade had been broken up, and the 42nd Mississippi and 55th North Carolina brought up from Richmond to serve with the 2nd and 11th. They had apparently been issued new Third Bunting issue flags. The location of this flag is not currently known.

[206] Terry Winschel, "The Colors Are Shrouded in Mystery," *GB* 6(January 1992), 84, tells the confusing story of three colorbearers at Gettysburg.

[207] "Fifty-Fifth Regiment," Clark, *Histories*, III, 297-301. Sgt. J. W. Whitley says the flag went down about thirty feet short of the wall. J. A. Whitley to the *Galveston News*, June 21, 1896.

[208] For more information on this brigade, see Eric A. Campbell, "'Remember Harper's Ferry!' The Degradation, Humiliation, and Redemption of Col. George L. Willard's Brigade, Part 2" *GB* 8(January 1993), 95-110.

[209] Fleming, ed., *Hays*, 439.

[210] McFarland, "Eleventh Mississippi," 560-61. The lack of primary sources for the men in Scales' and Lane's brigades is striking. I have no idea why there is a lack of information for these men.

[211] Ashe, "The Pettigrew-Pickett Charge," 150.

[212] Trimble, Diary, in Rollins, ed., *Pickett's Charge*, 233. Thomas L. Norwood to Editor, 6 October 1877, *GB*, 8(January 1993), 78. See also "Seventh Regiment," Clark, *Histories*, I, 380.

[213] Kimble, 461.

[214] Whitley in *Galveston News*.

[215] The 55th North Carolina's flag is probably "Record" #75. This is Howard Madaus' tentative conclusion, based on its design and location in the "Record." I agree that this is a reasonable conclusion, and that it will probably never be substantiated.

[216] "Record" #70 and #57. Report of Maj. Theodore Ellis, 14th Connecticut, July 6, 1863, *OR*, 1, 468. See also Maj. Gen. George Meade's statement, Oct. 17, 1864, *OR*, Series III, Vol. 3, 815.

[217] Page, *14th Connecticut*, 156, 166. See also Report of Maj. Theodore Ellis, July 6, 1863, *OR*, I, 467-468; Stevens, *Souvenir of Excursion to Battlefields*, 32, and Townsend's report, *OR*, II, 282; "Record" #70.

[218] Quoted in Stevens, *Souvenir of Excursion to Battlefields*, 32.

[219] John W. Plummer in *The Rebellion Record: A Diary of American Events* ed. Frank Moore Vol. X (New York: D. Van Nostrand, 1873), 177.

[220] Fleming, ed., June 2, 1886, *Hays,* 478-479.

[221] Anthony McDermott to Bachelder, *Bachelder Papers*, III, 1414.

[222] Clark, *Histories*, Vol. II, 108; Replicas of both flag now hang

in the Lee Chapel in Lexington, Virginia. The originals are in storage in Lee Chapel but are owned by the Museum of the Confederacy in Richmond. The 12th New Jersey turned in the flags of the 47th and 26th North Carolina, but at some point the two got mixed up, and currently are not distinguished. "Record" #62 and #68. The 26th's flag was hit many times on July 1st, and there is no account of the 47th's being treated similarly. Thus it seems logical that WD #62, showing far more evidence of combat than #68, would be the flag of the 26th North Carolina, and #68 the flag of the 47th, though again this cannot be verified. Record #62 and #68. Underwood, "Twenty-Sixth," 366. See Report of Maj. John Hall, 12th New Jersey, *OR*, 1, 470 and also John Hall, untitled essay, *Gettysburg Compiler*, 8 July 1903, GNMP Clipping Book 4, 145. As this book was going to press an agreement was reached to return the flags to the Museum of the Confederacy.

[223] See above and "Record" #68.

[224] Adjutant Brown, in Mrs. Arabella M. Willson, *Disaster, Struggle, Triumph. The Adventures of 1000 "Boys in Blue," From August, 1862, to June, 1865* (Albany: The Argus Company, 1870), 186. See also Capt. A. G. Richardson to Bachelder, 8 May 1868, *Bachelder Papers*, I, 341; "Record" #66. The Museum of the Confederacy has identified this as the flag of the 28th; several sources called this the flag of the 14th North Carolina, a regiment not in the charge.

[225] Eliakim Sherrill, *Dedication of the Monument to the 126th Regiment New York Infantry on the Battlefield of Gettysburg, October 3, 1888* (Canandaigua, N.Y.: W. G. Lightfoote, 1888), 40. See also Meade's statement, *OR*, Series III, Vol. 3, 815.

[226] Statement by Maj. Gen. George G. Meade, October 17, 1863, *OR*, Series III, Vol. 3, 815. See also Sherrill, *Dedication of the Monument to the 126th Regiment*, 40. Townsend's report, *OR*, II, 282; "Record" #63. Since all flags in Pettigrew's division, and those of the 28th and 7th North Carolina in Lane's brigade on the left flank of Trimble's division have been accounted for, this flag almost certainly belonged to the 18th or 33rd North Carolina. Neither of those two has been accounted for.

[227] Galway, *The Valiant Hours*, 118. See also Sawyer, *Eighth Regiment Ohio Vols.*, 131.

[228] "Record" #64. Adjutant Townsend lists the captor as John Miller; Meade calls this man John Miller, *OR*, Series III, Vol. 3, 816; the Secretary of War's "Letter" calls him David Miller. The 8th Ohio had a Sgt. Daniel Miller and a Sgt. John Miller. *Official Roster of the Soldiers of the State of Ohio in the War of the Rebellion, 1861-1865* (Cincinnati: Vilstach, Baldwin & Co., 1886), Vol. 2, 253. Report of Lt. Col. Franklin Sawyer, 8th Ohio, July 5, 1863, *OR*, 1, 462.

[229] *Ibid.*

[230] Report of Col. Robert Mayo, 47th Va. Regt., August 14, 1863, Henry Heth Collection, Eleanor S. Brockenbrough Library, Museum of

the Confederacy.

[231] Quoted in Bellah, *Soldier's Battle: Gettysburg*, 171.

[232] Report of Franklin Sawyer, 8th Ohio, July 5, 1863, *OR,* I, 462; Gregory, *38th Virginia*, 42; "Record" #45. See also Pvt. Horace Judson to Bachelder, October 17, 1887, *Bachelder Papers*, III, 1514.

[233] G. H. Daggett, "Glimpses of the Nation's Struggle," photocopy, 8th Ohio file, GNMP, 362. See also C. H. Stewart, *Pioneer Life as It Was and Is: An Address Delivered Before the 28th Annual Meeting of the Firelands Historical Society, July 16, 1884*, 8th Ohio File, GNMP, and G. H. Daggett, "An Address By G. H. Daggett," *MOLLUS*, 8th Ohio File, GNMP; Townsend's Report, *OR*, II, 282, and Meade's statement, Oct. 17, 1864, *OR*, Series III, Vol. 3, 816.

[234] Quoted in Adams, *Nineteenth Massachusetts*, 70. This was probably the flag of the 19th Virginia, accounted for earlier.

[235] Devereux's Report, *OR,* I, 444. The Robinson/Rice capture was accounted for earlier.

[236] *Supreme Court*, 186. McDermott's claim that no flags were captured is of course not correct and probably attributable to his limited perspective and rancor at others being given kudos when he failed to recognize that the symbolic power of captured flags far outweighed the significance of prisoners.

[237] Anthony McDermott to Bachelder, October 21, 1889, *Bachelder Papers*, III, 1656.

[238] Report of Col. Norman Hall, August 3, 1863, *OR,* I, 441. See also *Rebellion Record*, Vol. 7, 340-341.

[239] Haskell.

[240] Quoted in *Ibid.*, 424. For other accounts see Willson, *Disaster, Struggle, Triumph*, 186; Statement of Benjamin W. Thompson, October 13, 1910, 126th New York File, GNMP, and John Egan to Bachelder, *Bachelder Papers*, I, 389.

[241] Capt. G. A. Richardson to Bachelder, August 18, 1867, *Bachelder Papers,* I, 316-7.

[242] Willson, *Disaster, Struggle, Triumph*, 186, 341.

[243] Fleming, ed., *Hays*, 464-65, emphasis added.

[244] Capt. F. M. Colston, "Gettysburg As I Saw It," *CV*, 5(1897), 551-553.

[245] Lt. John L. Brady to Bachelder, May 24th, 1886, *Bachelder Papers*, III, 1399-1400. Brady says Smith's body was not found until July 5th and had been cut in two and robbed of everything, including the flag. The 1st Delaware's regimental history, William Seville, *History of the First Regiment, Delaware Volunteers* Reprint (Hightstown, MD: Longstreet House, 1986), 117, tells a slightly different story, saying that Smith had delivered the captured flag to headquarters and was returning to his regiment when he was killed. See also Lt. John T. Dent, 1st Delaware, n.d. in Fleming, ed., *Hays*, 464-466. See also Shepard, "Seventh Tennessee," *OR*, II, 646-7. I find the 1st Delaware cred-

ited with four captures, not five.

[246] Fleming, ed., *Hays* , 466. Fulton, *War Reminiscences*, 78. Dent's Report, 469; Report of Col. Thomas Smyth, 1st Delaware, July 17, 1863, *OR*, 1, 465. I have concluded that Smith got the 5th's flag because all accounts agree that the Delaware regiment did not get credit for the flag he found, and McCarren's Company C did receive credit for the 13th's flag. Smith was captain of Company A. Also, the condition of WD #60 is consistent with the colorbearer having had a lance or spear on the flagstaff, the 5th's is not. Furthermore, the 5th's flag has tears and stains consistent with being torn while being removed from under a body. The 5th Alabama flag eventually ended up in the hands of Joshua Chamberlain, who donated it to the Alabama Archives, where it now rests. I thank David Neel for his help and research into the Alabama flags.

[247] J. S. Harris, *Seventh Regiment North Carolina*, 37; "Record" #44. See also Maj. Gen. George Meade's statement, Oct. 17, 1864, *OR*, Series III, Vol. 3, 815.

[248] Fulton, *War Reminiscences*, 78, and Fry, "Pickett's Charge," 93. Dent, in *Hays*, 464. Townsend's Report, *OR*, II, 282, credits McCarren's capture but not Williams'; the same is true for Meade's statement, *OR*, Series III, Vol. 3, 815.

[249] Quoted in Fleming, ed., *Hays*, 431. Verified by courier, 461.

[250] Bell, *11th Virginia*, 42.

[251] *Ibid.*

[252] Report of Col. D. M. DuBose, 15th Georgia, July 27, 1863, *SHSP*, X, 179-183.

[253] W. A. Flanagan, "Account of How Some Flags Were Captured," *CV* 18(1910), 250.

[254] H. N. Minnigh, *History of Company K. First (Inft,) Penn's Reserves* (Duncansville: "Home Print" Publisher, 1891), 26-27; Report of Brig. Gen. Samuel Crawford, July 10, 1863, *OR*, I, 652-655, stated that this incident took place on July 2nd, as did Flanagan, 250. See also Huntington W. Jackson, "The Battle of Gettysburg," in *Military Essays and Records* (Chicago: A. C. McClurg, 1891), Vol. I, 182. "Record" #47. See also Maj. Gen. George Meade's statement, Oct. 17, 1864, *OR*, Series III, Vol. 3, 817.

[255] Diary of E. M. Woodward, Adjt., 2nd Regt. P. R. V. C., Henry E. Huntington Library, San Marino, California.

[256] Statement of Benjamin W. Thompson, 13 October 1910, GNMP.

[257] Bellah, *Soldiers' Battle: Gettysburg*, 170. Report of Brig. Gen. William Hays, July 17, 1863, *OR,* I, 378 reported finding "one female (private), in rebel uniform."

[258] *Ibid.*, 170.

[259] Loehr, "The Old First," 37-8.

Chapter Eight

Epilogue: Monterey Pass and Falling Waters

The retreat from Gettysburg was perhaps the most miserable period in the life of the Army of Northern Virginia, certainly the worst before the winter of 1864-1865. The train of wounded 17 miles long rolled slowly south toward the Potomac River and Virginia. Men lay in excruciating pain as the springless wagons bumped along rutted roads, through rain and wind, for several days. At times the rain came down so hard it turned the dirt into sticky, thick mud. The cries of the wounded resounded off the hills, day and night. At one point local citizens came out and hacked away at the wagons' wheels, and Federal cavalry sporadically struck the lines in attack.

On the morning of July 4th, the Federal cavalry received orders to begin following the Confederate wagon trains, and to harass them whenever possible. The division led by Brig. Gen. Judson Kilpatrick headed through the rain toward Emmitsburg, Maryland, with the intention of cutting off the Confederate retreat. Southwest of Emmitsburg it climbed to the top of a mountain, but there ran headlong into Rebel infantry and artillery in Monterey Pass.

Kilpatrick's men found themselves on a narrow mountain road, with a steep ravine on one side and a cliff on the other. Then suddenly Jeb Stuart's cavalry appeared in their rear. Kilpatrick recalled what happened next:

> Never under such perilous circumstances did a command behave better; not a word was spoken; there was no confusion. From a farmer's boy I learned the nature of the road and country on the mountain, made my disposition, and ordered a charge. In a moment the heights were gained and many prisoners taken. Now the rumble of the enemy's train could be heard rolling down the mountain.

The charge was made by only one regiment, the 1st West Virginia Cavalry, and about 40 men from other scattered units. These were the remnants of Brig. Gen. Elon Farnsworth's brigade which he had led to disaster and his own death on the afternoon of July 3rd, near Big Round Top. They were now commanded by Col. Nathaniel Richmond of the 1st West Virginia. One trooper remembered that it was an "inky darkness," and that "nothing was discernible a half dozen paces ahead." They got very close to the Confederate wagon train when they were met with a heavy volley of small arms fire that lit up the

Edwin Forbes, "Gallant Charge....of the 6th Michigan...near Falling Waters"
(Courtesy of the Library of Congress)

night. They continued the charge and got in among the wagons, where hand to hand fighting ensued. "The scene was wild and desolating. The road lay down a mountain growth of underbrush," recalled Maj. Charles Capehart, in command of the 1st West Virginia.[1] The Confederates were the 6th Virginia Cavalry from Brig. Gen. W. E. Jones' brigade, the 4th North Carolina Cavalry from Brig. Gen. Beverly Robertson's brigade, and Capt. R. P. Chew's Virginia Battery. The chase went on down the mountain trail, a distance of more than eight miles, until the Rebels made a brief stand at the foot of the mountain, where they were overrun. Gen. Jones fled through the fields and was the first Confederate officer to reach the Potomac River at Williamsport.[2] Eventually the Federals captured 300 wagons, 15 ambulances, and 1,300 prisoners.[3] Kilpatrick reported the capture of "one entire regiment, colonel and lieutenant-colonel, most of the officers, and one battle-flag."[4] This flag was not identified and apparently not turned in to the War Department. It was most likely the flag of the 4th North Carolina Cavalry.[5]

General Lee reached Williamsport on the Potomac River on July 7th, and the men continued to trickle in for several days. They threw up breastworks on a ridgeline about one mile from the Potomac, and waited for the swollen river to recede.

The night of July 13th was especially miserable for the Confederates. Brig. Gen. James Lane reported that "my whole command was so exhausted that they all fell asleep as soon as they were halted—about a mile from the pontoon bridge at Falling Waters."[6] Gen. Henry Heth described the night as "entirely dark and the roads in a dreadful condition, being ankle-deep in mud."[7] They were drawn up facing north, with Heth's division on the right and Pender's behind them, about one and a half miles north of the village of Falling Waters. The Federals managed to destroy one pontoon bridge, but the Confederates constructed two more, using canal boats, boards and planks taken from surrounding houses and farms.[8]

On the morning of July 14th most of the Army of Northern Virginia crossed the river. Four brigades were left behind as a rear guard, one of which was Brockenbrough's ill-fated Virginians. They had been severely mangled in the fighting along Seminary Ridge on July 1st, and had broken and retreated during the early stages of Pickett's Charge. Only a few hundred men remained in the entire brigade.

The rear-guard was entrenched and supported by at least one battery. It was approached by a small detachment of Brig. Gen. Judson Kilpatrick's cavalry, led by Brig. Gen. George Custer's Michigan Brigade, formed in column of fours. As the Yankee skirmishers rode up to the Rebel earthworks, their commander ordered a charge. One battalion of 70 men charged up a lane toward the Confederate right, dashing through a line of artillery emplacements and into the rear. They met a hail of bullets from some Confederate reserves, yet kept

Alfred Waud, "Charge of the 6th Michigan Over the Rebel Earthworks"
(Courtesy of the Library of Congress)

up their charge already through the line. Sgt. Charles M. Holton of the 7th Michigan Cavalry remembered that:

> Seeing the color-bearer of the 55th Virginia fall wounded, I sprang from my horse and seized the colors. As I remounted, I heard the wounded color-bearer say: 'You yanks have been after that old flag for a long time, but you never got it before.' While we were forming up to charge them again from their rear, the Confederates threw down their arms, and we marched 400 prisoners from the field.[9]

Somewhere in this small chaotic scene one of the Confederacy's best officers, Gen. J. J. Pettigrew, already wounded in the hand at Gettysburg, was hit by a pistol bullet and mortally wounded. Heth brought one or two of his brigades back across the river to stem the tide. Col. L. J. Lowrance commanded one, and he "found the men quite exhausted from pressure of heat, want of sleep, want of food, and the fatigue of marching. . . ."[10] Yet they managed to turn back the Federal cavalry.

The flag of the 55th Virginia was handed to Kilpatrick, and on it were found the names of all the great battles of the Army of Northern Virginia. Sgt. Holton was later awarded the Congressional Medal of Honor for his deed. Also in this engagement the 1st Michigan Cavalry captured the flags of the 40th and 47th Virginia infantry. All three had been lost by Col. John Brockenbrough's unfortunate brigade.[11]

After the repulse of the Federal cavalry, the rear guard of the Army of Northern Virginia crossed the Potomac River, into the familiar countryside of Loudon County, Virginia. As they reentered the Confederacy, a private in the Lamar Rifles of the 11th Mississippi yelled out to their band leader: "Stewart, by blood, play Dixie!" The band responded, and as the strains of "Look Away, Look Away, Dixie Land" were heard, the old Rebel Yell went up again from the stumbling column. The Gettysburg Campaign was over. The Wilderness, Petersburg and Appomattox, and Reconstruction lay ahead.

Notes

[1] Report of Maj. Charles Capehart, 1st West Virginia Cavalry, August 17, 1863, *OR*, I, 1019.

[2] Report of Brig. Gen. W. E. Jones, July 30, 1863, *OR*, I, 753.

[3] Capehart's report.

[4] Reports of Brig. Gen. J. Kilpatrick, July 5, 1863, and August 10, 1863, *OR*, I, 988 and 994.

[5] Based on location and a conversation with Howard Madaus.

[6] Report of Gen. James Lane, August 13, 1863, *OR*, II, 667.

[7] Report of Maj. Gen. Henry Heth, October 3, 1863, *Ibid.*, 640.

[8] J. Watts De Peyster, *The Decisive Conflicts of the Late Civil War. . . .* (New York: MacDonald and Co., 1867), 102, 103.

[9] *Deeds of Valor*, 255.

[10] Report of Col. L. J. Lowrance, August 12, 1863, *OR*, II, 672.

[11] Report of Brig. Gen. George A. Custer, September 9, 1863, *OR*, I, 998. See also "Letter," 21; "Record" #69 is the 47th Virginia and #100 is the 40th Virginia's flag. Wayland Fuller Dunaway, *Reminiscences of a Rebel* (New York: Neale, 1913), 96. The 55th's flag was carried home to Michigan by Col. W. D. Mann of the 7th Michigan Cavalry, and is now in the Museum of the Confederacy. See also Report of Major General Judson Kilpatrick, August 7, 1863, *OR*, I, 990, and Report of Major General George Gordon Meade, July 16, 1863, *OR*, I, 95.

Chapter Nine

"Such a Capture of Flags Was Never Known Before":
Counting The Colors

On the evening of July 3rd, while lying in a hospital bed and in the midst of being treated for a serious wound, Maj. Gen. Winfield Scott Hancock penned a note to his commander, Maj. Gen. George Gordon Meade:

> General: A great many colors were taken by our troops to-day—one brigade took ten. In order to collect them, it would be well to send a circular for each regimental commander to report the number taken. I have seen several on the road to-day.[1]

This is a significant note, for it underscores several important points. First, no formal order existed in the Army of the Potomac governing the treatment of captured Confederate battle flags. If Hancock had no system set up for processing them for his II Corps, it is almost certain that no other unit in the army had one. Thus neither the men who captured the flags nor their officers at the regimental, brigade, division or corps level had clear directions about what should be done with captured flags. Second, the army's best field commander thought the issue of the number of Confederate battle flags captured and who took them important enough to take time and effort at a busy, stressful and painful moment to urge his superior to action. Third, rumor and gossip were already spreading concerning the number captured and by whom they were taken. Fourth, several flags had already been carried away and would soon disappear into private homes, never to be officially counted.

Finally, no one in the entire Army of the Potomac knew how many Confederate battle flags had been captured in the fighting on July 3rd, or at the battle of Gettysburg, or in the Gettysburg campaign. What were the totals, and how many reached the wall during Pickett's charge? How many had been carried inside the Angle? The record is unclear, and no modern historian has hazarded an informed guess.

Brig. Gen. Alexander Hays recorded the sense of astonishment and awe he shared with his men at the incredible number of Confederate battle flags they now proudly displayed. "Such a capture of flags was never known before," he wrote, and he was correct.[2] The Army of the Potomac had never seen anything like the collection of Confederate battle flags now paraded in their midst. They simply had no frame of reference for what had occurred on July 3rd or in the entire battle of Gettysburg. Very few had been captured in previous battles, and in most, none at all. The capture of even a single flag had been an occasion for wild celebration, as we have seen in the case of the Texas flag captured at Antietam, described in the Introduction to this book.

The Army of Northern Virginia was not accustomed to leaving its banners in the hands of the enemy, especially when victory was theirs, as it had normally been. Nothing like this loss of battle flags would happen again during the remainder of the war.[3] This was the highest number ever captured in combat in a single battle or campaign, excluding major surrenders. The second highest number was at Nashville, where the Army of Tennessee lost 22 flags during its collapse and dissolution in December of 1864.[4]

Some northerners were amazed by the events and confused by the various and contradictory claims and rumors. Just after Pickett's repulse, Haskell counted "these defiant banners, some inscribed with '1st Manassas,' 'South Mountain,' 'Sharpsburg,' . . . 'Fredericksburg,' 'Chancellorsville,' and many more names, our men have, and are showing about, *over thirty of them*."[5] Yet later in the same essay Haskell stated that 40 or more were taken.[6] The commander of the 111th New York said his men captured "a number" of flags, but that "it was impossible to state the number."[7] Col. Norman Hall, commanding a brigade in the Second Corps, reported that "twenty battle-flags were captured in a space of 100 yards square."[8] Yet later he would claim only six were captured by men of his brigade.[9] At one point Gen. Alexander Hays reported that 23 were captured by his division, but that six were handed over to Gen. Alexander Webb when Webb claimed that they had been captured by his men but given to Hays for safekeeping. Hays added that at least two captured flags had been secreted away by the men who took them and were never turned in.[10] To one correspondent, Hays reported just 15 captured,[11] but to another he counted 17 plus an unidentified number not turned in.[12] Hancock reported 27 captured by his men,[13] yet on July 5, Hancock had his Aide, Capt. E. F. Brownson, send to Meade just "twenty-two flags captured by the corps in the last battle at Gettysburg."[14] Alexander Webb reported that his brigade captured six, but then turned in only four.[15] Meade sent 31 captured flags to the adjutant-general on July 8, five on July 10, three (from Falling Waters) on July 16 and two on July 28th.[16] In his final report on the Gettysburg campaign he counted 41 captured, a number equaling the sum of the previous returns.[17] It is unclear if Meade was writing about all flags captured in the campaign, from the middle of June through July 15, or just those taken during the main battle; it appears that in his last report he meant during the entire campaign.

* * *

At times it seems as though every officer at Gettysburg in 1863 made a statement about how many Confederate battle flags had been captured. Each and every one of them was either partially or completely incorrect, and misleading. In fact, no one then had any clear conception of how many Confederate battle flags were captured at Gettysburg, nor has anyone since 1863.

What procedure for handling captured flags was generally followed at Gettysburg? From the record it is clear that some officers told their men to hand over the flags, marked with strips of paper or cloth on which the information concerning who had taken them was written. Brigade commanders gave them to division commanders, division to corps commanders, and corps commanders to Meade's adjutant, who in turn saw to it that they were sent to the War Department in Washington. But since no formal directions had been issued, several were not turned in.

If we study the post-battle reports and claims sent up the chain of command, and later included in the *Official Records*, we find contradictory and confusing information. A systematic analysis of the reports by regiment, brigade, division or corps is no less confusing. If we look at just the reports of the Corps commanders, we find that a total of 38 flags were reported captured: 5 by the I Corps, 23 by the II Corps, 1 by the V Corps, 1 by the XI Corps and 3 by the XII Corps. Five more were claimed by the Cavalry Corps.

Yet if we read the reports by division commanders, only 26 flags were claimed. The II Corps division commanders alone reported 24 captured, one more than their commander recorded. Thirty-seven were counted at the brigade level, 38 at the regimental level. It should also be noted that some regimental and brigade commanders did not file reports, and therefore the total number is short of the true number for those command levels.

Several other problems mar the count. Some of the men who captured flags kept them for themselves, as trophies of war to be taken home and paraded around. Col. Francis Heath of the 19th Maine reported that "two battle-flags of the enemy were taken by men of my regiment, but were torn from the lances by men of other regiments."[18] While claiming 15 for his division, Brig. Gen. Alexander Hays added that "a number of other flags were captured, but had been surreptitiously disposed of, in the subsequent excitement of battle, before they could be collected."[19]

Also, officers sometimes demanded flags be given to them, and they took them home as war trophies. Lt. Col. Frank Sawyer of the 8th Ohio reported that the flag captured by Pvt. James Richmond of his regiment was "taken from him on the field by a staff officer of our army, but whose name is unknown."[20] As a Federal brigade commander reported,

> Several colors were stolen or taken with violence by
> officers of high rank from brave soldiers who had rushed

forward and honestly captured them from the enemy, and were probably turned in as taken by commands which were not within 100 yards of the point of attack. Death was too light a punishment for such a dastardly offense.[21]

Further complicating the matter, as the incidents surrounding Pvt. Jacob Polack of the 1st Virginia on the evening of July 3rd reveal, Confederate quartermaster wagons at some level carried extra flags with them, and replacement flags were handed out during the battle. These extra flags were not officially issued through normal channels. (For that to happen, a requisition had to be made at the brigade or division level, sent to Richmond through correct channels, the proper paperwork completed, and the new flags sent back down the chain of command.) The flags handed out on the field of battle were instead flags that had been obtained through various means by brigade or division-level quartermasters, and handed out as necessary. In this way a new flag was given to the 2nd Mississippi, and carried on July 3rd. The 13th Virginia Cavalry lost their flag at Hanover on June 30th, but carried a new one in the battle on July 3rd.[22] It will not be surprising to find that other regiments obtained new flags during the battle, and it is possible that a single regiment lost more than one flag during the campaign, or even during the three days at Gettysburg. The fact that new flags were given out in non-divisional issues may explain at least some of those captured with no regimental designation. By 1863 flags were issued with designation and honors, except those given to Pickett's division in June. The latter had a designation but no honors on them.[23] Some regiments, such as the 8th, 14th and 38th Virginia, were issued new flags in the Spring, but chose to carry their old ones at Gettysburg.

In some cases multiple accounts of the same capture of a single flag were recorded, and those must be sorted out on an individual basis.

Another potentially complicating fact is that many of the flags were not actually *captured* in the sense of being taken from the hands of the enemy colorbearer, but instead were picked up on the field after the action had ceased. The flag of the 8th Florida, picked up by Sgt. Horan of the 72nd New York on July 2nd after the 19th Maine had run over it, is a case in point. Col. Theodore B. Gates, 20th N. Y. S. M., reported that "two colors were left upon the ground by the enemy, and were picked up by some troops who came upon the field from our right after the fighting was over."[24] Pvt. Anthony McDermott, who had fought desperately with the 69th Pennsylvania at the Angle, seemed unimpressed by stories of capturing flags:

I would not like to say that as far as the capturing of

the colors was concerned . . . they were not captured in the same than any honor would attach to it. It was just like picking up muskets that had been thrown down. I saw, myself, in the space near the wall, two stand's of Pickett's colors, but I was in no hurry to take them and while I was there I saw men from the Forty-second New York grab a flag and rush back, but I made a remark then that I did not see anything very brave in that but they went with the colors.[25] [Pvt. Michael McDonough, 42nd New York, is credited with capturing the flag of the 22nd North Carolina.]

The number of flags captured by a particular unit sometimes became important in discussions that took place after the war centering on the question of who fought valiantly and who did not. McDermott scoffed at this idea and recalled what happened after Pickett's repulse. Writing in 1889, he rejected the claim by others that reinforcements came to their aid at the stone wall, insisting instead (and incorrectly) that they had fought alone. Others may have picked up flags in their front after the fight was over, but that did not mean that they had helped the 69th Pennsylvania at the wall:

> when the fighting ceased, these troops [Hall's brigade and the 72nd Pennsylvania] came to the wall, gathered up flags and other trophies and returned back to their positions. The men of the Sixty-ninth were busily engaged in sending the rebel soldiers to the rear to be gathered in by the troops posted there, and also in looking up their dead and wounded; had they known, however, that a reward would be given to those who turned in the flags picked up off the field of battle, it was more than likely they also would have gathered up flags.[26]

Hays' men noted that in their front over 20 flags had been taken, and that they had come from six different brigades and three different divisions. They concluded that,

> from the fact that these standards were taken in Hays' front the assertion was indisputable that the men were there with their colors, and in greater force than on Hays' left. The contention was that Pickett's Brigades(sic) on the right of the moving columns, harassed by the enfilading artillery fire that came from Round Top and our batteries on that flank, and the incessant and deadly musketry fire in front and on his

right flank, in desperation rushed forward to break the line and save themselves if they could. . . .[27]

* * *

It is not possible to be completely sure how many Confederate battle flags were captured during the Gettysburg campaign. We are dealing with documentation left behind by men who did not carefully compile records for us to read 130 years later. The stories are sometimes contradictory, and in some cases important information simply no longer exists. In others, no doubt, memory played its tricks.

In this chapter and the accompanying charts I have placed an asterisk * in front of the number of a flag that has not been previously attributed to a specific regiment. These are the conclusions of various scholars and myself, based on the evidence available, and are subject to further clarification.

Appendix A contains a table of all flags referred to in this chapter, in alphabetical order by state, numerical order by unit.

* * *

On June 30th and July 1st, nine and one half Confederate battle flags were claimed captured by Federal troops. I believe the final tally should be seven and one-half. The flag of the 13th Virginia Cavalry was taken on June 30th at Hanover by the 5th New York Cavalry. Reasonably reliable documentation exists on six and one-half flags taken on July 1st, all by the I Corps: the capture of the 2nd Mississippi by the 6th Wisconsin; the *26th Alabama and 23rd North Carolina by the 88th Pennsylvania; the half of the flag of the 20th North Carolina captured by the 97th New York; the 5th North Carolina by the 12th Massachusetts; the *12th North Carolina flag by the 76th New York; and the unidentified flag captured by the 27th Pennsylvania.

Two claims can be safely counted out. Maj. Gen. Abner Doubleday reported the capture of a second flag (in addition to the 2nd Mississippi) from Davis' brigade.[28] No corroborating evidence has been found, so this claim is dismissed. However, the possibility remains that the report is true, and if so it was probably the flag of the 55th North Carolina. A severe struggle over that flag occurred, with several colorbearers shot down, but there is no record of its loss or claim of its capture. The second claim rejected is one of the seven flags reported by Doubleday's successor, Maj. Gen. John Newton. Among Newton's seven he counted one recaptured by the Confederates (20th N.C.) and one flag "taken from the private who captured it by some unknown colonel."[29] The flag and the mysterious colonel disappeared, and no other account of this incident has been found, so it is also dismissed.

Table 1: Flags Captured on June 30th and July 1st							
No	Carried By	Unit Captor	Date	Place	Individual Captor	Location Now	WD #	Type
1	13th Virginia Cavalry	5th New York Cavalry	6.30	Hanover	Sgt. Thomas Burke	MOC	WD 17	ANV
2	2nd Mississippi	6th Wisconsin	7.01	Rail Road Cut	Cpl. Francis Wallar	Miss. Archives	WD 40	ANV
3	*26th Alabama	88th Pennsylvania	7.01	Oak Ridge	Unknown	Unknown	None	ANV
3.5	20th North Carolina	97th New York	7.01	Oak Ridge	Sgt. Sylvester Riley	Unknown	None	?
4	23rd North Carolina	88th Pennsylvania	7.01	Oak Ridge	Sgt. Edward Gilligan	N.C. Archives	WD 46	ANV
5	5th North Carolina	12th Massachusetts	7.01	Oak Ridge	Capt. Erastus Clark	Kept by Clark	None	?
6	*12th North Carolina	76th New York	7.01	Oak Ridge	Unknown	Unknown	None	?
7	Unidentified	27th Pennsylvania	7.01	Brickyard	Capt. Hugo Siedlitz	Unknown	None	?
* = Author's conclusion					ANV = Army of Northern Virginia			
MOC = Museum of Confederacy					WD = War Dept. Inventory # in "Record"			

* * *

Reports exist of 13 Confederate flags possibly being captured on July 2nd (and early on the 3rd and 4th on East Cemetery and Culp's Hill). I conclude that insufficient evidence exists for two, and two others are accounts of the same flag at different moments, so the final count should be nine. The least convincing citation is by Col. Norman Hall, in his report on the 3rd Brigade, 2nd Division, II Corps: "two colors were left on the ground within 20 yards of the 7th Michigan Volunteers."[30] He did not claim their capture, either in his narrative of the regiment's action or in his summary of his brigade's achievements in the battle. I therefore conclude that these were flags claimed by other regiments. The "best guess" is that they were the flag of the 8th Florida, credited to the 72nd New York, and the second banner seen and passed over by the 19th Maine, for which no supporting evidence could be found. The latter might have been the flag of the *2nd Georgia Battalion.

Sgt. George Roosevelt of the 26th Pennsylvania captured a color-bearer and his flag during the fighting along the Emmitsburg Road, then retreated toward Cemetery Ridge. Before he could get there, he was hit in the leg and knocked down. He was severely wounded and his leg amputated. After the war Roosevelt conducted extensive correspondence in an effort to win a Congressional Medal of Honor for his deed, and was successful. However, at no point in his letters did he state that he kept control of the flag after being hit, or that he managed to carry it to safety. He gave no information about the identification or even the design of the flag. Furthermore, none of the many people who wrote letters in support of his application ever described the flag, stated that they actually saw it in the possession of Federal troops, or that they saw it being turned in. I believe it is logical to conclude that he dropped the flag when he was hit. A few minutes later the 19th Maine passed over the same territory. I believe it is safe to conclude that the flag dropped by Roosevelt is most likely the 8th Florida flag or the second flag described by members of the 19th Maine. Since Roosevelt's possession of the flag was at best temporary, and also disputable with no reliable second account, I do not count this as a *bona fide* capture.

Reliable documentation exists on the capture of nine flags: the 8th Florida(twice, but for the purposes of this chapter counted only as one flag); 48th Georgia; the two taken on Culp's Hill, the *25th Virginia and a regimental color; the *1st or 3rd North Carolina flag captured by the 78th New York; the 4th Virginia(on July 4th); the 8th Louisiana, and 21st North Carolina. The flag known as WD# 59, not credited to any Confederate unit or Federal captor, and now in the Museum of the Confederacy, is most likely, though not certainly, the flag of the *2nd Georgia Battalion. Thus the number of flags captured on July 2nd and early on July 3rd and 4th on Culp's Hill stands at nine, and the total up to this point at 16 1/2.

No.	Carried By	Unit Captor	Date	Place	Individual Captor	Location Now	WD#	Type
8	*2nd Georgia Btn	Unidentified	7.02	Near Emmitsburg Rd	Unknown	MOC	WD 59	1st Nat.
9	8th Florida	72nd New York	7.02	Plum Run	Fla. Mus. History	WD 73	ANV
	Note: 8th Florida probably also captured, then lost by Sgt. George Roosevelt, 26th Pennsylvania							
10	48th Georgia	59th New York	7.02	Cemetery Ridge	Sgt. James Wiley	Georgia Capitol	WD 38	ANV
11	*25th Virginia (Jones)	60th New York	7.02	Culp's Hill	Unknown	MOC	WD 30	ANV
12	Unidentified (Regtl. Flag)	60th New York	7.02	Culp's Hill	Unknown	MOC	WD 22	1st Nat
13	8th Louisiana	107th Ohio	7.02	E. Cemetery Hill	Lt. Peter Young	Unknown	None	?
14	21st No. Carolina	14th Indiana	7.03	E. Cemetery Hill	Capt. Oliver Rood	Unknown	None	?
15	4th Virginia	7th Ohio	7.04	Culp's Hill	Capt. J. Pollock	Unknown	None	?
16	*1st or 3rd No. Carolina	78th New York	7.04	Culp's Hill	Unknown	Smithsonian MAH	None	ANV

Table 2: Flags Captured on July 2nd and Early July 3rd or 4th (excluding Pickett's Charge & 15th Ga)

* * *

The mass of documentation concerning flags captured during and after Pickett's Charge is similarly marked by inaccurate, conflicting and confusing data. The first step in sorting it out is to identify the total number of flags carried by Confederate units during the Charge.

Fifty units (48 regiments and 2 battalions) participated in all or part of Pickett's Charge.[31] I have found no documentation that any of the four flags in the Brockenbrough/Mayo brigade were carried as far as the Emmitsburg Road. Five units managed to carry their flag back to Seminary Ridge: the 24th Virginia(Kemper), 7th Tennessee(Fry), 11th North Carolina(Marshall), 5th Florida(Lang) and 2nd Mississippi(Davis).[32] Thus 41 Confederate battle flags were apparently "at risk" to be lost during Pickett's Charge.

Federal soldiers and officers, in official reports and in other writings, laid claim to captures of 44 flags. While that is theoretically possible it is highly unlikely since we know that five of the 50 possible were reported as being saved and Brockenbrough's four were essentially not engaged.

Of the 44 claims, six can be dismissed. The two flags described by Capt. Andrew Cowan in Chapter Seven, page 165, cannot be identified or substantiated. Lt. John Dent of the 1st Delaware reported that his regiment captured five flags, but I have found accounts or claims of only four.[33] The claim of Pvt. William Williams of the same regiment cannot be substantiated. The flag described by Col. Arthur

Devereux as turned over to Brig. Gen. Webb is counted as one of the Philadelphia Brigade's total. The 14th North Carolina, claimed by the 126th New York as captured by Capt. Morris Brown, was not in the charge. It was not turned in, and Brown actually captured the flag of the 28th North Carolina as listed as "Record" #66, and that is the correct flag.

That leaves 38 claims worthy of consideration. Of those, 29 were turned in to the various authorities including the War Department and appear in government documentation. I classify these as certain captures. They are the 1st, 3rd, 7th, 8th, 9th, 14th, 18th, 19th, 28th, 38th, 53rd, 56th and 57th Virginia; 13th Alabama and 5th Alabama Battalion; 1st and 14th Tennessee; 11th Mississippi; and 7th, 16th, 22nd, 26th, 28th 34th, 47th, 52nd North Carolina, and the unidentified flag taken by Dore (WD #63). Two flags, WD #78 and WD #75 are tentatively identified by Howard Madaus as belonging to the 55th North Carolina or 42nd Mississippi of Davis' brigade, and I think this is probably true based on the position of the troops involved. For the purposes of this chapter, I count WD #78 as the flag captured by Cpl. Navaretto of the 39th New York, and believe it is the flag of the *42nd Mississippi. Therefore WD #75 is probably the flag of the *55th North Carolina, although the reverse is possible. It is certainly possible that these flags were among those counted in the next paragraph as probable captures, but there is no evidence that so suggests.

I classify nine flags as probably captured because they were reported by two or more reasonably reliable sources, but then disappeared. In some cases reports exist of their theft by officers or the Provost Guard. The nine include the flag captured by Pvt. John Robinson and absconded with by Major Edmund Rice; the flag captured by Pvt. William Deming and stolen by an unidentified colonel; the 2nd Florida reported by both Col. Lang and Brig. Gen. Stannard; an unidentified flag taken by the 16th Vermont; the flag taken by Pvt. George Moore of the 71st Pennsylvania; the flag taken by Pvt. Jerry Wall of the 126th New York; the one captured by Pvt. James Richmond of the 8th Ohio; the silk flag captured by the 14th Connecticut and kept by its captor, and the "4th Virginia" flag taken by the 14th Connecticut and apparently kept by the Provost Guard. Of the above, the 2nd Florida was turned in but given to the 16th Vermont, taken home, and has since vanished. The others may well be among the many listed in the "Record" as having been turned in with no identifying information, or turned in and the accompanying identification lost sometime after 1863.

Thus 38 Confederate battle flags were either certainly or probably captured during or shortly after Pickett's Charge. With the five that were saved, the total accounted for is 43.

Of the 50 regiments and battalions participating in Pickett's Charge, the flags of eleven are apparently unaccounted for: the 11th Virginia(Kemper) in Pickett's division, the 13th and 38th North

Carolina(Scales) and 18th, 33rd and 37th North Carolina (Lane), all in Trimble's demi-division; the 8th, 9th, 10th, 11th and 14th Alabama, all of Wilcox's brigade. Given their location at the far right of the Confederate line, and their lack of serious casualties, I think it is probable that none of the flags of Wilcox's brigade were taken.

That would leave just six flags unaccounted for. Since eight of the captured flags are unidentified, including WD #63 that was turned in and is now at the Museum of the Confederacy, it seems likely that the six unaccounted for were among those unidentified. That is not certain, however, and probably never will be.

There are alternative possible explanations for the origins of the unidentified flags. It is possible, though I think not likely, that they came from regiments in the four brigades that occupied Long Lane, just west of the Bliss farm, during the Charge. Numerous Federal

Table 3: Flags Captured During & After Pickett's Charge

No.	Carried By	Unit Captor	Date	Place	Individual Captor	Location Now	WD#	Type
17	1st Virginia	82nd New York	7.03	West of the wall	Sgt. Martin McHugh	MOC	WD37	ANV
18	7th Virginia	82nd New York	7.03	On the wall	Pvt. Hugh Carey	MOC	WD 36	ANV
19	19th Virginia	19th Massachusetts	7.03	West of the wall	Pvt. Benjamin Falls	MOC	WD 71	ANV
20	Unidentified	19th Massachusetts	7.03	West of the wall	J. Robinson/ E. Rice	Unknown	None	?
21	Unidentified	7th Michigan	7.03	At the wall	Wm. Deming/Colonel ?	Unknown	None	?
22	18th Virginia	59th New York	7.03	In front of wall	Lt. Charles F. Hunt	MOC	WD 56	ANV
23	28th Virginia	1st Minnesota	7.03	At Cushing's guns	Pvt. M. Sherman	Minn. Hst. Societ	WD 58	ANV
24	Unidentified	71st Pennsylvania	7.03	East of the Wall	Pvt. George Moore	Unknown	None	?
25	3rd Virginia	71st Pennsylvania	7.03	East of the wall	Capt. Alex McCuen	Unknown	WD 35	?
26	56th Virginia	71st Pennsylvania	7.03	East of the wall	Capt. Robert McBride	MOC	WD 41	ANV
27	9th Virginia	71st Pennsylvania	7.03	East of the wall	Pvt. John Clopp	MOC	WD 65	ANV
28	14th Virginia	19th Massachusetts	7.03	At Cushing's guns	Cpl. J. De Castro	Private Owner	None	ANV
29	53rd Virginia	71st Pennsylvania	7.03	At Cushing's guns	Pvt. Isaac Tibbins	MOC	WD 77	ANV
30	57th Virginia	19th Massachusetts	7.03	At Cushing's guns	Sgt. Ben Jellison	MOC	WD 79	ANV
31	2nd Florida	16th Vermont	7.03	SW of the wall	Capt. Charles Brink	Unknown	None	?
32	8th Virginia	16th Vermont	7.03	SW of the wall	Pvt. Piam Harris	MOC	WD 67	ANV
33	Unidentified	16th Vermont	7.03	SW of the wall	Unknown	Unknown	None	?
34	1st Tennessee	14th Connnecticut	7.03	On the works	Unknown	Tenn. St. Archives	WD 43	ANV
35	14th Tennessee	14th Connecticut	7.03	West of the wall	Sgt. Maj. William Hincks	Tenn. St. Archives	WD 85	ANV
36	11th Mississippi	39th New York	7.03	On the wall	Sgt. Maggi	MOC	WD 39	ANV
37	*42nd Mississippi	39th New York	7.03	West of the wall	Cpl. Navaretto	MOC	WD 78	ANV
38	*55th North Carolina	Unknown	7.03	Unknown	Unknown	MOC	WD 75	ANV
39	52nd North Carolina	14th Connecticut	7.03	West of the wall	Cpl. Christopher Flynn	N.C. Archives	WD 70	ANV
40	16th North Carolina	14th Connecticut	7.03	West of the wall	Cpl. Elijah Bacon	N.C. Archives	WD 57	ANV
41	Unidentified (silk)	14th Connecticut	7.03	West of the wall	Unknown	Unknown	None	?
42	"4th Va"\Provost Guard	14th Connecticut	7.03	West of the Wall	Unknown	Unknown	None	?
43	13th Alabama	1st Delaware	7.03	West of the wall	Pvt. Bernard McCarren	Alabama Archives	WD 60	ANV
44	7th North Carolina	1st Delaware	7.03	West of the wall	Pvt. John Mayberry	N.C. Archives	WD 44	ANV
45	5th Alabama Btn	1st Delaware	7.03	West of the wall	Capt. William Smith	Alabama Archives	None	ANV
46	22nd North Carolina	42nd New York	7.03	West of the wall	Pvt. Michael McDonough	Unknown	WD 76	ANV
47	*47th North Carolina	12th New Jersey	7.03	10' W. of the wall	Unknown	Lee Chapel\MOC	WD 68/62	ANV
48	*26th North Carolina	12th New Jersey	7.03	At the wall	Unknown	Lee Chapel\MOC	WD 62/68	ANV
49	28th North Carolina	126th New York	7.03	Near Emmitsburg Rd	Capt. Morris Brown	MOC	WD 66	ANV
50	Unidentified	126th New York	7.03	West of the wall	Pvt. Jerry Wall	Unknown	None	?
51	*38th North Carolina	126th New York	7.03	West of the wall	Pvt. George Dore	MOC	WD 63	ANV
52	34th North Carolina	8th Ohio	7.03	Near Emmitsburg Rd	Sgt. Daniel Miller	N.C. Archives	WD 64	ANV
53	38th Virginia	8th Ohio	7.03	Near Emmitsburg Rd	Sgt. Daniel Miller	MOC	WD 45	ANV
54	Unidentified	8th Ohio	7.03	Near Emmitsburg Rd	Pvt. James Richmond	Unknown	None	?
55	15th Georgia	1st Penn. Rifles	7.03	Houck's Ridge	Sgt. James Thompson	Georgia Capitol	WD 47	ANV

regiments sortied out on the field past the Emmitsburg Road directly after the repulse, and some of the captures in this area could possibly be from those regiments. Combat had taken place on the slope west of Cemetery Ridge on July 2nd, thus another possibility is that flags had been dropped on the 2nd and were picked up after Pickett's Charge. And of course it is also possible that one, or more, of the claims were false.

How many Confederate battle flags were carried over the stone wall during Pickett's Charge? One Federal eyewitness, a man in the 106th Pennsylvania who testified in court, said he saw six Confederate battle flags inside the angle.[34] Lt. Haskell described "those red flags . . . accumulating at the wall" as numbering "a dozen" but did not specify their exact location on the wall or east or west of it. Yet at another point he mentioned 12 Federal flags at the wall and "nearly double this number of the battle flags of the enemy."[35]

At least nine Confederate battle flags crossed the wall and/or were in the Angle at one time or another, though perhaps not all at exactly the same time. Those were the flags of the 1st, 3rd, 9th, 14th, 28th, 53rd, 56th and 57th Virginia regiments, and the unidentified flag captured by Pvt. George Moore of the 71st Pennsylvania. All were seized in the Angle. Two more, the unknown flag captured by Col. Devereux and the unknown flag captured by Pvt. Robinson and then given to an Colonel Rice, crossed the wall south of the Copse of Trees. That brings the total of flags crossing the wall to eleven.

How many reached the wall? Documentation exists to count eight flags, those of the 7th, 11th and 19th Virginia, 26th North Carolina, 1st and 7th Tennessee, 13th Alabama and 11th Mississippi, as having reached the wall. In sum, the battle flags of at least 19 Confederate regiments were carried to or over the Federal line.

This is as far as the existing documentation can take us. Federal troops probably captured 38 flags during and shortly after Pickett's Charge.

Add to this the flag of the 15th Georgia, captured in the evening, and the total comes to 39 flags taken on July 3rd(excluding Culp's Hill). The total for the three days (and Hanover) comes to 55 1/2.

* * *

No.	Carried By	Unit Captor	Date	Place	Individual Captor	Location Now	WD#	Type
	Table 4: Flags Captured During The Retreat, July 4th to 15th.							
56	*4th N.C. Cavalry	Unknown	7.04	Monterey Hills	Gen. J. Kilpatrick (?)	Unknown	None	?
57	55th Virginia	7th Michigan Cav.	7.14	Falling Waters	Sgt. Charles M. Holton	MOC	None	ANV
58	40th Virginia	1st Michigan Cav.	7.14	Falling Waters	Unknown	MOC	WD 100	ANV
59	47th Virginia	1st Michigan Cav.	7.14	Falling Waters	Unknown	MOC	WD 69	ANV

Add one at Monterey Pass on July 4th and three at Falling Waters and the total number of Confederate flags captured during the Gettysburg Campaign is probably 59 1/2. The total was probably no lower, but could be higher.

Notes

[1] Hancock to Meade, XII Corps hospital, July 3, 1863, *OR*, I, 367.

[2] Hays to John McFadden, July 13, 1863, in Fleming, ed., *Hays*, 409.

[3] I have combat situations in mind, not major surrenders such as occurred at Vicksburg, Ft. Donelson, Saylor's Creek and Appomattox, etc.

[4] Madaus and Needham, *Army of Tennessee*, 133-137.

[5] Frank Haskell, "Gettysburg."

[6] *Ibid.*

[7] Report of Capt. A. P. Seeley, n.d., 1863, *OR*, I, 476.

[8] Report of Col. Norman Hall, July 17, 1863, *OR*, I, 440.

[9] *Ibid.*, 441.

[10] Fleming, ed., *Hays*, 463.

[11] Hays to Capt. E. F. Brownson, July 22, 1863, National Archives, RG 93.

[12] Hays to John B. McFadden, July 13, 1863, in Fleming, ed., *Hays*, 409, 413.

[13] Report of Major General Winfield Scott Hancock, n.d., 1863, *OR*, I, 377.

[14] Brownson to Meade, July 5, 1863, *OR*, I, 367.

[15] Webb, *Bachelder Papers,* III, 428.

[16] Dent's report, *OR*, I, 469-470.

[17] Report of Major General George G. Meade, August 4, 1863, *OR*, I, 118; Meade's Reports, July 10, *OR*, I 89, July 16, I, 95, and July 28, I, 998-1000.

[18] Report of Col. Francis E. Heath, July 4, 1863, *OR*, I, 422.

[19] Report of Brig. Gen. Alexander Hays, July 8, 1863, *OR,* I, 454.

[20] Sawyer's Report, *OR*, I, 462.

[21] Hall's report, *OR*, I, 440.

[22] Ed Longacre, *The Cavalry At Gettysburg: A Tactical Study of Mounted Operations During the Civil War's Pivotal Campaign* (Rutherford, N.J.: Associated University Press, 1986).

[23] Note from Howard Madaus, February, 1996.

[24] Gates' report, *OR*, I, 318-9.

[25] *Supreme Court,* 235.

[26] A. W. McDermott, *A Brief History of the 69th Reg. Pa. Vet. Volunteers* (Philadelphia: n.p., 1889), 33.

[27] Lt. David Shields, quoted in Fleming, ed., *Hays*, 459.

[28] Report of Maj. Gen. Abner Doubleday, December 14, 1863, *OR*, I, 246, 249.

[29] Report of Maj. Gen. John Newton, September 30, 1863, *OR*, I, 263-4. Brig. Gen. John Robinson, commander of the 2nd Division of which Baxter's brigade was a part, reported three flags captured; see his Report, July 5, 1863, *OR*, I, 292.

[30] Hall's Report, *OR*, I, 436.

[31] Pickett, 15 regiments; Pettigrew, 12 regiments, 1 battalion; Trimble, 13 regiments, 1 battalion; Wilcox and Lang, 8 regiments.

[32] Harrison and Busey, *Glory*, 221; Shepard's report, *OR*, II, 647; Winschel, "The Colors Are Shrouded In Mystery," 86; Clark, *Histories*, V, 131.

[33] Report of Lt. John Dent, First Delaware Infantry, n.d. [1863], *OR*, I, 469.

[34] Lynch, *Supreme Court*, 305.

[35] Haskell.

Acknowledgments

My thanks to the following people who read all or part of the manuscript and offered helpful suggestions for improvement: Harold Bernstein, Greg Biggs, John Coski, Charles Fennell, Ed Franks, Scott Hartwig, John Jackson, Gary Kross, Ken Legendre, James McPherson, Howard Madaus, Wayne Motts, Tim Smith, Jim Stanbery and Harry Thaete. Special thanks to George Otott, who read the entire manuscript several times, offered lots of significant comments of a factual nature and improved the writing. Any errors of fact or interpretation are the responsibility of the author.

Dave Shultz did an outstanding job on the maps. Ken Hammond's talent as a graphic designer is clearly visible in the jacket. Wayne Motts helped with the research. Scott Hartwig, in charge of the archives in the Gettysburg National Military Park, was always helpful in locating items I needed and could not find myself.

Howard Michael Madaus is deservedly acknowledged as the leading expert on Civil War flags. His knowledge of the subject, based on more than 20 years of work, is encyclopedic. His curatorial research on the materials, design, and making of the flags has been extremely valuable to all the archivists who have flags in their possession and to the scholarly community. He has been very kind in providing information that I could not have developed on my own.

We are fortunate to live during a renaissance in historical and representational art. Many excellent artists are currently producing outstanding visual depictions of the Civil War. Don Troiani's research and attention to detail, combined with the vibrancy of the figures in his work, result in a level of historical accuracy unsurpassed by any other modern artist. I owe a special thanks to him for allowing me to include several of his prints. I only wish that I could have printed them all in color.

Many thanks to Cliff and Peggy Bream for their warm hospitality during many research trips.

The staff of the Palos Verdes Public Library diligently obtained an amazing number of items through interlibrary loan. The staffs of the following libraries assisted in providing documentation: Perkins Library of Duke University, Woodruff Library at Emory University, Florida State University Special Collections, Henry E. Huntington Library, San Marino; Library of Congress, Los Angeles Public Library, Minnesota Historical Society, Mississippi State Archives, Eleanor S. Brockenbrough Library, Museum of the Confederacy; National Archives, National Museum of American History, Smithsonian Institute; New Hampshire Historical Society, Southern Historical Collection at the University of North Carolina, Chapel Hill; North Carolina Department of Archives and History, Pennsylvania Historical Society, Tennessee

State Library, United States Army Military History Institute, University of Virginia, Virginia Historical Society, Virginia State Library, Wisconsin Historical Society Archives, Yale University.

The surviving battle flags are in the hands of some professionally skilled and helpful people, and without them this project would have been less successful and a lot less enjoyable. Rebecca Rose, Curator of the Flag Collection at the Museum of the Confederacy, provided much information and helped in many ways. Corrine Hudgins, Curator of the Photographic Collection at the Museum of the Confederacy, helped obtain photographs of 24 flags, all but a couple of which had not been previously photographed. Tom Belton of the North Carolina Museum of History helped obtain photographs of six flags from storage at the North Carolina Museum of History. Bob Bradley helped obtain information about and photographs of the flags in the collection of the Alabama Department of Archives and History.

Appendix A

Confederate Battle Flags Captured During the Gettysburg Campaign In Alphabetical and Numerical Order

Carried By	No.	Captured By	Date	Place	Individual Captor	Location Now	WD #	Type
5th Alabama Btn	45	1st Delaware	7.03	West of the wall	Capt. William Smith	Alabama Archives	None	ANV
13th Alabama	43	1st Delaware	7.03	West of the wall	Pvt. Bernard McCarren	Alabama Archives	WD 60	ANV
*26th Alabama	3	88th Pennsylvania	7.01	Oak Ridge	Unknown	Unknown	None	ANV
2nd Florida	31	16th Vermont	7.03	SW of the wall	Capt. Charles Brink	Unknown	None	?
8th Florida	9	72nd New York	7.02	Plum Run	Sgt. Thomas Horan	Fla. Mus. History	WD 73	ANV
Note: 8th Florida probably also captured, then lost by Sgt. George Roosevelt, 26th Pennsylvania								
*2nd Georgia Btn	8	Unidentified	7.02	Near Emmitsburg Rd	Unknown	MOC	WD 59	1st Nat
15th Georgia	55	1st Penn. Rifles	7.03	Houck's Ridge	Sgt. James Thompson	Georgia Capitol	WD 47	ANV
48th Georgia	10	59th New York	7.02	Cemetery Ridge	Sgt. James Wiley	Georgia Capitol	WD 38	ANV
8th Louisiana	13	107th Ohio	7.02	E. Cemetery Hill	Lt. Peter Young	Unknown	None	?
2nd Mississippi	2	6th Wisconsin	7.01	Rail Road Cut	Cpl. Francis Wallar	Miss. Archives	WD 40	ANV
11th Mississippi	36	39th New York	7.03	On the wall	Sgt. Maggi	MOC	WD 39	ANV
*42nd Mississippi	37	39th New York	7.03	West of the wall	Cpl. Navaretto	MOC	WD 78	ANV
*1st or 3rd No. Carolina	16	78th New York	7.04	Culp's Hill	Unknown	Smithsonian MAH	None	ANV
5th North Carolina	5	12th Massachusetts	7.01	Oak Ridge	Capt. Erastus Clark	Kept by Clark	None	?
*12th North Carolina	6	76th New York	7.01	Oak Ridge	Unknown	Unknown	None	?
7th North Carolina	44	1st Delaware	7.03	West of the wall	Pvt. John Mayberry	N.C. Archives	WD 44	ANV
16th North Carolina	40	14th Connecticut	7.03	West of the wall	Cpl. Elijah Bacon	N.C. Archives	WD 57	ANV
21st North Carolina	14	14th Indiana	7.03	E. Cemetery Hill	Capt. Oliver Rood	Unknown	None	?
22nd North Carolina	46	42nd New York	7.03	West of the wall	Pvt. Michael McDonough	Unknown	WD 76	ANV
23rd North Carolina	4	88th Pennsylvania	7.01	Oak Ridge	Sgt. Edward Gilligan	N.C. Archives	WD 46	ANV
*26th North Carolina	48	12th New Jersey	7.03	At the wall	Unknown	Lee Chapel\MOC	WD 62	ANV
28th North Carolina	49	126th New York	7.03	Near Emmitsburg Rd	Capt. Morris Brown	MOC	WD 66	ANV
34th North Carolina	52	8th Ohio	7.03	Near Emmitsburg Rd	Sgt. Daniel Miller	N.C. Archives	WD 64	ANV
*38th North Carolina	51	126th New York	7.03	West of the wall	Pvt. George Dore	MOC	WD 63	ANV
*47th North Carolina	47	12th New Jersey	7.03	10' W. of the wall	Unknown	Lee Chapel\MOC	WD 68	ANV
52nd North Carolina	39	14th Connecticut	7.03	West of the wall	Cpl. Christopher Flynn	N.C. Archives	WD 70	ANV
*55th North Carolina	38	Unidentified	7.03	Unknown	Unknown	MOC	WD 75	ANV
*4th N.C. Cavalry	56	Unidentified	7.04	Monterey Hills	Gen. J. Kilpatrick (?)	Unknown	None	?
1st Tennessee	34	14th Connnecticut	7.03	On the works	Unknown	Tenn. St. Archives	WD 43	ANV
14th Tennessee	35	14th Connecticut	7.03	West of the wall	Sgt. Maj. William Hincks	Tenn. St. Archives	WD 85	ANV
1st Virginia	17	82nd New York	7.03	West of the wall	Sgt. Martin McHugh	MOC	WD37	ANV
3rd Virginia	25	71st Pennsylvania	7.03	East of the wall	Capt. Alex McCuen	Unknown	WD 35	?
4th Virginia	15	7th Ohio	7.04	Culp's Hill	Capt. J. Pollock	Unknown	None	?
7th Virginia	18	82nd New York	7.03	On the wall	Pvt. Hugh Carey	MOC	WD 36	ANV
8th Virginia	32	16th Vermont	7.03	SW of the wall	Pvt. Piam Harris	MOC	WD 67	ANV
9th Virginia	27	71st Pennsylvania	7.03	East of the wall	Pvt. John Clopp	MOC	WD 65	ANV
14th Virginia	28	19th Massachusetts	7.03	At Cushing's guns	Cpl. J. De Castro	Private Owner	None	ANV
18th Virginia	22	59th New York	7.03	In front of wall	Lt. Charles F. Hunt	MOC	WD 56	ANV
19th Virginia	19	19th Massachusetts	7.03	West of the wall	Pvt. Ben Falls	MOC	WD 71	ANV
*25th Virginia (Jones)	11	60th New York	7.02	Culp's Hill	Unknown	MOC	WD 30	ANV
28th Virginia	23	1st Minnesota	7.03	At Cushing's guns	Pvt. M. Sherman	Minn. Hst. Society	WD 58	ANV
38th Virginia	53	8th Ohio	7.03	Near Emmitsburg Rd	Sgt. Daniel Miller	MOC	WD 45	ANV
40th Virginia	58	1st Michigan Cav.	7.14	Falling Waters	Unknown	MOC	WD 100	ANV
47th Virginia	59	1st Michigan Cav.	7.14	Falling Waters	Unknown	MOC	WD 69	ANV
53rd Virginia	29	71st Pennsylvania	7.03	At Cushing's guns	Pvt. Isaac Tibbins	MOC	WD 77	ANV
55th Virginia	57	7th Michigan Cav.	7.14	Falling Waters	Sgt. Charles M. Holton	MOC	None	ANV
56th Virginia	26	71st Pennsylvania	7.03	East of the wall	Capt. Robert McBride	MOC	WD 41	ANV
57th Virginia	30	19th Massachusetts	7.03	At Cushing's guns	Sgt. Ben Jellison	MOC	WD 79	ANV
13th Virginia Cavalry	1	5th New York Cavalry	6.30	Hanover	Sgt. Thomas Burke	MOC	WD 17	ANV
Unidentified	7	27th Pennsylvania	7.01	Brickyard	Capt. Hugo Siedlitz	Unknown	None	?
Unidentified (Regtl. Flag)	12	60th New York	7.02	Culp's Hill	Unknown	MOC	WD 22	1st Nat
Unidentified	20	19th Massachusetts	7.03	West of the wall	J. Robinson/ E. Rice	Unknown	None	?
Unidentified	21	7th Michigan	7.03	At the wall	Wm. Deming/Colonel ?	Unknown	None	?
Unidentified	24	71st Pennsylvania	7.03	East of the Wall	Pvt. George Moore	Unknown	None	?
Unidentified	33	16th Vermont	7.03	SW of the wall	Unknown	Unknown	None	?
Unidentified (silk)	41	14th Connecticut	7.03	West of the wall	Unknown	Unknown	None	?
"4th Va"\Provost Guard	42	14th Connecticut	7.03	West of the Wall	Unknown	Unknown	None	?
Unidentified	50	126th New York	7.03	West of the wall	Pvt. Jerry Wall	Unknown	None	?
Unidentified	54	8th Ohio	7.03	Near Emmitsburg Rd	Pvt. James Richmond	Unknown	None	?
* = Author's conclusion					ANV = Army of Northern Virginia pattern			
MOC = Museum of Confederacy					WD = War Dept. Inventory # in "Record"			

Stars: 13, 3 1/2" - 3 3/4" wide, 6" apart.
Borders: Orange, 1 1/2" wide.

Examples captured at Gettysburg: 14th Virginia.

5. Third Wool Issue. July, 1862 through May, 1864.
Issued to Maj. Gen. D. H. Hill's division (commanded at Gettysburg by Maj. Gen. Robert Rodes) in April, 1863; to Maj. Gen. A. P. Hill's division (commanded at Gettysburg by Maj. Gen. William Pender) in May, 1863, and to Maj. Gen. George Pickett's division in June, 1863.
Field: Wool bunting, red.
Size: 46 - 48" square including borders.
Cross: 5" wide, 1/2" white fimbration.
Stars: 13, 3 1/2" wide, 6" apart.
Borders: 1 1/2" - 2" wide, white.

Examples captured at Gettysburg (36): 5th Battalion and 13th Alabama; 8th Florida; 15th Georgia; 13th Virginia Cavalry and 1st, 3rd, 7th, 8th, 9th, 18th, 19th, 28th, 38th, 40th, 47th, 53rd, 55th, 56th and 57th Virginia; 2nd, 11th and *42nd Mississippi; 7th, 16th, 22nd, 23rd, *26th, 28th, 34th, *47th, 52nd and *55th North Carolina; 1st and 14th Tennessee and the unidentified flag marked as WD #63.

[1] Much of this information was supplied by Howard Madaus. Madaus to Author, April 1, 1996. Note: two First National pattern flags were also captured.
* Designates flags tentatively identified.

Appendix B
Variations of the
Army of Northern Virginia Battle Flag
1861 to 1863[1]

Prototype.

Created by Ms. Constance, Hetty and Jenny Cary in Richmond, in September, 1861. One each given to Generals P.G.T. Beauregard, Joseph Johnston and Earl Van Dorn. None appeared at Gettysburg.

1. First Issue, Silk. November, 1861.
Field: Silk, pink or rose in color.
Size: About 48" square, including borders.
Cross: 8 - 9" wide, blue, 1/2" white fimbration
Stars: 12. 4 1/2 - 5" wide, gold (painted), 6 - 8" apart.
Border: 3 yellow silk, leading edge blue silk, 2 1/2" wide, o f t e n folded to 1 1/4".

Examples captured at Gettysburg: *1st or 3rd North Carolina.

2. Cotton Issue. Probably in May, 1862.
Issued only to Elzey's, Steuart's and Hood's brigades.
Field: Cotton, light red.
Size: About 48" square, including borders.
Cross: 7", blue, no fimbration(outline).
Stars: 12, 5 1/2" wide, 7 1/2" apart, white.
Borders: Orange tape, about 3/4" wide.

Examples captured at Gettysburg: *25th Virginia.

3. First Wool Issue. May and/or June, 1862.
Field: Wool bunting, red.
Size: 48" square including borders.
Cross: 8" wide with 1/2" white fimbration.
Stars: 13, 3" wide, 6" apart, white.
Borders: Orange, 1 1/2" wide.

Examples captured at Gettysburg: 48th Georgia.

4. Second Wool Issue. June, 1862.
Field: wool bunting, red.
Size: 48" square including borders.
Cross: 5" wide, with 1/2" white fimbration.

Appendix C:
Materials and Measurements of
Confederate Battle Flags
Captured at Gettysburg

Flag No. 01   **WD#** 17   **Regt:** 13th Virginia Cavalry

Staff: 41.4"   **Fly:** 41.5"   **Type:** 3rd wool

Field: Red bunting

Cross: 5" dark blue bunting

Fimbration: White cotton twill, .75" wide

Border: White bunting, 1.75" wide

Stars: 13 White, 3.5 to 3.875" diameter

Unit Designation: None

Battle Honors: None

Method of Attachment: 3 whipped eyelets pierce 1.75" white canvas heading

---

Flag No. 02   **WD#** 40   **Regt:** 2nd Mississippi

Staff: 47"   **Fly:** 49"   **Type:** 3rd wool

Field: Red bunting

Cross: 5" dark blue bunting

Fimbration: White cotton cambric, .5" wide

Border: White bunting, 2" wide

Stars: 13 White cotton cambric, 3.25" diameter

Unit Designation: None

Battle Honors: Manassas(19" long), Seven Pines(21.75"), Gaines Farm(21"), Malvern Hill(23"), painted yellow-gold in Gothic script. Letters 2.75" high, obverse only

Method of Attachment: 3 whipped eyelets pierce 2" white twill weave cotton heading

Flag No. 04   **WD#** 46   **Regt:**   23rd North Carolina

Staff: 44.5"   **Fly:**   45"   **Type:**   3rd wool

Field: Red bunting

Cross: 5.5" dark blue bunting

Fimbration: White cotton twill
.5" wide

Border: White bunting
2" wide

Stars: 13 white cotton, 3.5" diameter

Unit Designation: Painted yellow block letters 1.25" high

Battle Honors: Williamsburg, Seven Pines, Mechanicsburg, Cold Harbor, Malvern Hill, South Mountain, Sharpsburg, Fredericksburg. Painted dark blue, block letters, 1.5" high, obverse only.

Method of Attachment: 3 whipped eyelets pierce 2" wide white canvas heading

---

Flag No. 09   **WD#** 73   **Regt:**   8th Florida

Staff: 49.5"   **Fly:**   47.5"   **Type:**   3rd wool

Field: Red bunting

Cross: 4.875" dark blue bunting

Fimbration: .5" white cotton

Border: Orange bunting, 1.5" wide

Stars: 13 White, each 3.875" diameter

Unit Designation: Painted in black figures and Roman uncials and miniscules, 2.5" and 1.5" high, on a 3.5" cotton strip

Battle Honors: None

Method of Attachment: 3 whipped eyelets pierce 2" white canvas heading

Flag No. 10 **WD#** 38 **Regt:** 48th Georgia

Staff: 47" **Fly:** 49" **Type:** 1st wool

Field: Red bunting

Cross: 5.5" dark blue bunting

Fimbration: White cotton 1/2" wide

Border: White bunting 2" wide

Stars: 13 White cotton, 3.5" diameter

Unit Designation: None

Battle Honors: Cedar Run, Manassas, Ox Hill, Mechanicsville, Cold Harbor, Frazier's Farm, Harpers Ferry, Shepardstown, Chancellorsville

Method of Attachment: 3 whipped eyelets pierce 2" wide canvas heading

Flag No. 11 **WD#** 30 **Regt:** *25th Virginia

Staff: 42" **Fly:** 42" **Type:** Cotton issue

Field: Red cotton

Cross: Medium blue cotton 6.75-7" wide

Fimbration: None

Border: Orange cotton, 6" wide

Stars: 12 White cotton

Unit Designation: None

Battle Honors: None

Method of Attachment: Not apparent, probably nailed to staff

Flag No. 12   **WD#** 22   **Regt:**   Unknown

Staff: 55"   **Fly:**   65.5"   **Type:**   1st National

Field: 3 horizontal bars, red, white, red.   **Fimbration:** None

Cross: None

Border: .375" White cotton border 3 sides

Stars: 11 Gold 4.5-4.75" diameter, set in an arc, 29" across its base around motto, obverse only

Unit Designation: None

Battle Honors: None. Motto: Dulce Et Decorum\Est Pro\Patria Mori, gold sans serif Roman uncial letters

Method of Attachment: A single cord, looped into eyelets at each end, runs the full length of a sleeve, 3/4" wide

Flag No. 16   **WD#** None   **Regt:**   *1st or 3rd North Carolina

Staff: 51"   **Fly:**   49.75"   **Type:**   1st issue, silk

Field: Pink/rose silk   **Fimbration:** White silk, 4" wide

Cross: 8.5" dark blue silk

Border: Yellow silk, 2.375" wide

Stars: 12. White silk, 4.975 to 5" diameter

Unit Designation: None

Battle Honors: None

Method of Attachment: Dark blue silk sleeve heading, torn out holes

Flag No. 17   **WD#** 37   **Regt:**   1st Virginia

Staff: 45.5"   **Fly:**   45"   **Type:**   3rd wool

Field: Red bunting

Cross: 4.75" dark blue cotton

Fimbration: White cotton, . 5" wide

Border: White bunting, 2 - 2.125" wide

Stars: 13 white cotton, 3.5" diameter

Unit Designation: Painted 1" and 1.375" white figures and Roman uncial letters

Battle Honors: None

Method of Attachment: 3 whipped eyelets pierce 2" wide bunting

Flag No. 18   **WD#** 36   **Regt:**   7th Virginia

Staff: 50"   **Fly:**   43"   **Type:**   3rd wool

Field: Red bunting

Cross: 4.5" dark blue bunting

Fimbration: White cotton twill, .375" wide

Border: White bunting 1.75" wide

Stars: 13 White cotton, 3.5" diameter

Unit Designation: Painted in white Roman uncial characters, 1.375" and 1"

Battle Honors: None

Method of Attachment: 3 eyelets pierce white cotton heading 1.875" wide

Flag No. 19   **WD#** 71   **Regt:**   19th Virginia

Staff: 45"   **Fly:**   46.5"   **Type:**   3rd wool

Field: Red bunting   **Fimbration:** White cotton twill
                                       .5" wide
Cross: 4.785" dark blue bunting

                           Border: White bunting
                                       2" wide

Stars: 13 White cotton, 3.25 - 3.5" diameter

Unit
Designation: Painted white Roman uncial letters, 1.75" and 1" Note:

Battle
Honors: None

Method of
Attachment: 3 whipped eyelets pierce white canvas bunting

Flag No. 22   **WD#** 56   **Regt:**   18th Virginia

Staff: 44.5"   **Fly:**   47"   **Type:**   3rd wool

Field: Red bunting   **Fimbration:** White cotton twill
                                       .5" wide
Cross: 4.75" dark blue bunting

                           Border: White bunting
                                       2" wide

Stars: 13 White cotton 3.25-3.5" diameter

Unit   White Roman uncial figures 1.375 and 1" high
Designation: obverse only

Battle
Honors: None

Method of
Attachment: 3 whipped eyelets pierce 2" white canvas headings

Flag No. 23   **WD#** 58   **Regt:** 28th Virginia

Staff: 44.5" **Fly:** 48"   **Type:** 3rd wool

Field: Red bunting

Cross: 4.5" dark blue bunting

Fimbration: White cotton cambric .75" wide

Border: White bunting, 2" wide

Stars: 13 white, 3.25" diameter

Unit Designation: Painted white Roman uncial figures 1.5" and 1" obverse only

Battle Honors: None

Method of Attachment: 3 whipped eyelets pierce white canvas heading, 2.125" wide

Flag No. 25   **WD#** 35   **Regt:** 3rd Virginia

Staff: 45" **Fly:** 45"   **Type:** 3rd wool

Field: Red bunting

Cross: 5" dark blue bunting

Fimbration: White cotton .5" wide

Border: White bunting 1.875" wide

Stars: 13 White, 3.25" diameter

Unit Designation: Painted white Roman uncial figures, 1.375 & 1" diameter

Battle Honors: None

Method of Attachment: 3 whipped eyelets pierce 2" wide canvas

Flag No. 26   **WD#** 41   **Regt:**   56th Virginia

Staff: 43"   **Fly:**   45"   **Type:**   3rd wool

Field: Red bunting   **Fimbration:** White cotton
Cross: 4.5" dark blue bunting   .875" wide

                               Border: White cotton,
                                       1.75 - 1.875" wide

Stars: 13 white, 3.125 - 3.25" diameter

Unit
Designation: Painted white Roman uncial figures 1.375" & 1"

Battle
Honors: None

Method of
Attachment: 2 whipped eyelets pierce 2" white canvas heading

Flag No. 27   **WD#** 65   **Regt:**   9th Virginia

Staff: 45"   **Fly:**   46.5"   **Type:**   3rd wool

Field: Red bunting   **Fimbration:** White cotton
Cross: 5.25" dark blue bunting   .75" - .875" wide

                               Border: White bunting
                                       1.875" wide

Stars: 13 White cotton, 3.5" diameter

Unit
Designation: Painted white Roman uncial figures, 1.375" & 1"

Battle
Honors: None

Method of
Attachment: 3 whipped eyelets pierce 2" white canvas heading

Flag No. 28   **WD#** 82   **Regt:**   14th Virginia

Staff: 45"   **Fly:**   48"   **Type:**   3rd wool

Field: Red bunting   **Fimbration:** White, 1/2" wide

Cross: 5.5" dark blue bunting

                       Border: Orange, 1.25" wide

Stars: 13 White, each 3.5" diameter

**Unit
Designation:**   None

**Battle
Honors:**   Seven Pines on separate cloth strip

**Method of
Attachment:**   3 Whipped eyelets in 1.75" wide white canvas heading

---

Flag No. 29   **WD#** 77   **Regt:**   53rd Virginia

Staff: 45"   **Fly:**   45"   **Type:**   3rd wool

Field: Red bunting   **Fimbration:** White cotton, .5" wide

Cross: 5" dark blue bunting

                       Border: White bunting 2" wide

Stars: 13 white 5 ptd., 3.5" - 3.75" diameter

**Unit
Designation:**   Painted white Roman uncial figures 1" to 1.375" high, obverse only

**Battle
Honors:**   None

**Method of
Attachment:**   3 whipped eyelets pierce 2" white canvas heading

"The Damned Red Flags of the Rebellion"

Flag No. 30   **WD#** 79   **Regt:**   57th Virginia

Staff: 45"   **Fly:** 48.5"   **Type:** 3rd wool

Field: Red bunting

Cross: 4.75-5" dark blue bunting

Fimbration: White cotton, .5" wide

Border: White bunting, 2" wide

Stars: 13 White cotton 3.25" diameter

Unit Designation: Painted white Roman uncial figures 1.375" - 1" high,

Battle Honors: None

Method of Attachment: 3 whipped eyelets pierce 2" white canvas heading

Flag No. 32   **WD#** 67   **Regt:**   8th Virginia

Staff: 47"   **Fly:** 46.5"   **Type:** 3rd wool

Field: Red bunting

Cross: 5" Dark blue bunting

Fimbration: White cotton cambric .5" wide

Border: White bunting 2" wide

Stars: 13 white cotton cambric, 3.75" diameter

Unit Designation: Painted in black block letters 3.125" high on 4" high white linen

Battle Honors: None

Method of Attachment: 3 whipped eyelets pierce 2" wide white cotton twill heading

Appendix C

Flag No. 34 **WD#** 43 **Regt:** 1st Tennessee

Staff: 44.5" **Fly:** 45.5" **Type:** 3rd wool

Field: Red bunting **Fimbration:** White cotton, .5" wide

Cross: 4.75" Dark blue bunting

Border: White bunting, 2" wide

Stars: 13 white cotton, 3.5" diameter

Unit Designation: Painted in 1" and 1.25" high yellow figures and Roman uncial on obverse

Battle Honors: Seven Pines, Mechanicsville, Cold Harbor,Ox Hill, Harpers Ferry, Sharpsburg, Shepherdstown, Fredericksburg, Chancellorsville, Frazier's Farm, Cedar Run, Manassas. Painted in dark blue block letters 1.375" high on obverse.

Method of Attachment: 3 Whipped eyelets pierce 2" white canvas heading

Flag No. 35 **WD#** 85 **Regt:** 14th Tennessee

Staff: 43.75" **Fly:** 46" **Type:** 3rd wool

Field: Red bunting **Fimbration:** White cotton, .5" wide

Cross: 5" dark blue bunting

Border: White bunting 1.75" wide

Stars: 13 white cotton, 3.5" diameter

Unit Designation: Painted in yellow figures and Roman uncial letters 1.25" & .75" high on obverse

Battle Honors: Seven Pines, Mechanicsville, Cold Harbor, Ox Hill, Harpers Ferry, Sharpsburg, Shepherdstown, Fredericksburg, Chancellorsville, Frazier's Farm, Cedar Run, Manassas. Painted in dark blue block letters 1.375" high on obverse

Method of Attachment: 3 whipped eyelets pierce 2" wide canvas heading

Flag No. 51   **WD#** 63   **Regt:** Unknown

Staff: 48"   **Fly:** 47.5"   **Type:** 3rd wool

Field: Red bunting

Cross: 4.5" dark blue bunting

Fimbration: White cotton twill
.5" wide

Border: White bunting
1.75" wide

Stars: 13 white cotton cambric, 3.5" wide

Unit Designation: None

Battle Honors: None

Method of Attachment: 3 whipped eyelets pierce 1.75" wide white canvas heading

Index

Adams, Sgt. Silas, 19th ME, 125-126
Alabama Troops, 100-106, 118-119
  2nd, 31
  3rd, 78, 101-102
  5th, 101-102
  5th Btn., 148, 179-181, 194, 227
  6th, 101-102
  8th, 120, 147, 150, 227
  9th, 147, 156, 227
  10th, 147, 227
  11th, 124, 147, 155, 227
  13th, 92-93, 148-149, 179, 181, 227, 229
  14th, 147, 227
  15th, 118
  26th, xxiv, 34, 101-102, 224
  44th, 118
  47th, 118
  48th, 118
Alexander, Col. E. P., 150
Allen, Col. Robert, 28th VA, 170
Ames, Brig. Gen. Adelbert, 133
Anderson, Brig. Gen. George "Tige", 118
Anderson, Maj. Gen. Richard, 147
"Any Fate But Submission", 58
Archer, Brig. Gen., James, 92
Archibald, Ens. John, 15th AL, 118
Armistead, Brig. Gen. Lewis, 146, 175
Articles of Confederation, 24
Ashe, Capt. S. A., Pettigrew's division, 18, 157
Avery, Col. Isaac, 130-135

Bacon, Cpl. Elijah, 14th CT, 251
Baker, Lt. A. J., 11th MS, 184
Ballenger, Pvt. David, 26th AL, 34
Barclay, Pvt. Alexander "Ted", 4th VA, 33, 43-44
Barksdale, Brig. Gen. William, 119
Batchelor, Pvt. Albert, 2nd LA, 16
Battleflags captured
  *1st\3rd NC, 135
  1st TN, 181
  1st VA, 159
  2nd FL, 179
  *2nd GA Btn., 127
  2nd MS, 98
  3rd VA, 173
  *4th NC Cav., 186
  4th VA, 186
  5th AL Btn., 195

Polak, Pvt. J. R., 1st VA, 159, 197, 222
Pollock, Capt. John, 7th OH, 135
Pollock, Capt. Theodore, 7th VA, 153
Powell, Cpl. George, 14th TN, 180

Ramseur, Brig. Gen. Stephen D., 87, 100
Rice, Maj. Edward, 19th MA, 164, 168, 176, 227
Richard, Capt. Joseph, 88th PA, 104, 106
Richmond, Pvt. James, 8th OH, 189, 227
Richmond, Col. Nathaniel, 1st WV Cav., 213
Riley, Sgt. Sylvester, 97th NY, 104
Rimington, Lt. William, 6th WI, 95
Robertson, Brig. Gen. Beverly, 215
Robinson, Pvt. John, 19th MA, 164, 227, 229
Rodes, Maj Gen. Robert, 86, 99
Rogers, Maj. J. C., 5th TX, 118
Rogers, Capt. R. Lewis, 57th VA, 44-45
Rogers, Lt. Robert, Batt. B, 1st NY Arty., 162
Rood, Capt. Oliver, 14th IN, 135
Roosevelt, Sgt. George, 26th PA, 122, 225

Satterfield, Capt. E. Fletcher, 55th NC, 186
Sawyer, Lt. Col. Frank, 8th OH, 221
Scales, Brig. Gen., Alfred, 106-109
Scott, Cpl. John, 53rd VA, 175
Sellars, Maj. A. J., 90th PA, 103
Shaner, Pvt. Joe, Rockbridge Art., 30
Shepard, Lt. Col. Sam, 14th TN, 181
Sherman, Pvt. Marshall, 1st MN, 170-172
Sherrill, Col. Eliakim, 14th CT, 185
Shields, Lt. David, 193
Shotwell, Sgt. Randolph, 39
Sic Semper Tyrannis, 22
Siedlitz, Capt. Hugo, 27th PA, 108
Simpson, Cpl. Charles, 11th VA, 61
Singleton, Cpl. Joseph, 38th VA, 177
Slavery, xvii-xviii, xi, 17-19, 40-43
Smith, Boney, 14th TN, 180
Smith, Capt. John Holmes, 11th VA, 163
Smith, Lt. William, 1st DE, 194-195
Smith, Sgt. W. H., 26th NC, 183
South Carolina Troops, 9-10, 36, 106-109, 120-122
    1st, xxii, 121
    3rd, 120
    8th, xxii, 121
    13th, 106-107
    14th, 106-109
Spessard, Capt. Michael, 39, 170
"Southern Chivalry", 26
Spalding, Maj. Israel, 141st PA, 119
Stannard, Brig. Gen. George, 160